A Cornish Revival

*The Life and Times of
Samuel Walker of Truro*

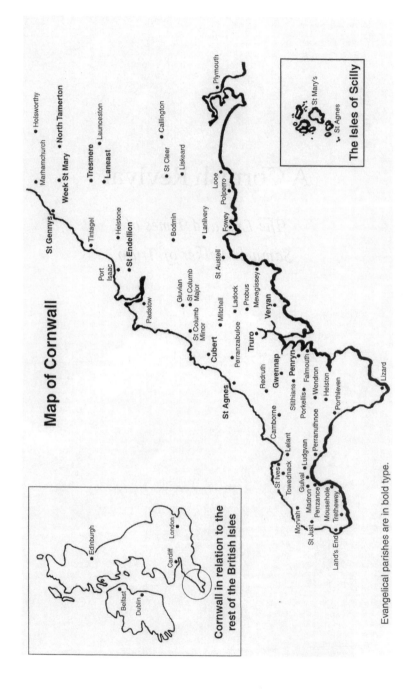

Map of Cornwall

Holsworthy

Marhamchurch

Week St Mary • North Tamerton

Tresmere • Launceston

Laneast

St Cleer • Callington

Liskeard

St Gennys

Tintagel

Helstone

Bodmin

St Endellion

Lanlivery

Port Isaac

Fowey

Loe

Polperro

Padstow

St Austell

Mevagissey

Gluvian

St Columb Major

Probus

St Columb Minor

Ladock

Veryan

Mitchell

Cubert

Perranzabuloe

Truro

St Agnes

Gwennap

Penryn

Redruth

Stithians

Falmouth

Camborne

Porkellis

Wendron

Lelant

Perranuthnoe

Helston

St Ives

Ludgvan

Porthleven

Towednack

Gulval

Lizard

Morvah

Madron

St Just

Penzance

Mousehole

Land's End

Trethewey

Plymouth

The Isles of Scilly

St Mary's

St Agnes

Cornwall in relation to the rest of the British Isles

Edinburgh

London

Cardiff

Belfast

Dublin

Evangelical parishes are in bold type.

A Cornish Revival

The Life and Times
of Samuel Walker of Truro

Tim Shenton

  EVANGELICAL PRESS

EVANGELICAL PRESS
Faverdale North Industrial Estate, Darlington, DL3 0PH,
England

Evangelical Press USA
P. O. Box 825, Webster, New York 14580, USA

e-mail: sales@evangelicalpress.org

web: www.evangelicalpress.org

First published 2003

British Library Cataloguing in Publication Data available

ISBN 0 85234 5224

Map by kind permission of Stuart Mantell

Printed and bound in Great Britain by Creative Print & Design
Wales, Ebbw Vale

Contents

To Pa,
whose never-ceasing help and encouragement
have been so very much appreciated.
You're the best.

Acknowledgements

I express my sincere thanks to S. J. Taylor of the Evangelical Library, London, for his prompt and efficient service; to my friend Stuart Mantell, for research done in the Evangelical Library of Wales and for drawing a map of Cornwall; to Robert Oliver, for writing the foreword; to Christina Mackwell of the Lambeth Palace Library; to Peter Isaac, for searching out Cornish books for me; to Barrie S. May of the Cornish Methodist Historical Association; to Jenny Cook of the Cornish Studies Library, Redruth; to the staff at the British Library; to Stephen Coombes, for his computer help; and to my father Townley, for his companionship on my research travels and for his careful correcting of the MS. It is to him I dedicate this book.

Tim Shenton

Foreword

In the first half of the eighteenth century the county of Cornwall was one of the most lawless parts of the kingdom. Its long coastline was the scene of smuggling and wrecking. Its tin miners were notorious for violent and drunken behaviour. Spiritually the people were neglected and the area was noted for depravity at a time when in the nation spirituality was weak. Yet into this area God intervened in a most glorious and gracious way making Cornwall the scene of powerful revival blessings.

Focussing on Samuel Walker, Tim Shenton has provided a fascinating account of this great change. Samuel Walker has been one of the lesser-known figures in the eighteenth century revival. In part this may be because his ministry was fairly short and was concentrated in a remote town in the west of Cornwall. Another reason is that John Wesley's visits to Cornwall are well known and seem to have overshadowed Walker's work.

Tim Shenton has helped to rectify this. We are given a detailed account of Walker's conversion after he entered the ministry and the way in which he was used of God in Truro and further afield. In these pages he is allowed to speak for himself in his letters and writings. We are also shown how he co-operated with other ministers and provided societies for the converts of the revival. There were important differences between his work and that of Wesley, and these are explained. There is a fascinating account of the relationship between these two remarkable men. All of this helps to provide an important perspective on the work of the revival in Cornwall as a whole.

This is an important study for all who are concerned for revival and especially for those interested in that most fascinating movement of God in the eighteenth century. I am delighted that Mr Shenton has provided us with this work.

Robert W. Oliver
Bradford on Avon
January 2003

Preface

In recent years historians have overlooked the early Evangelical movement in the Established Church in Cornwall. At the time of writing there are only two in-print books that deal with that period in the eighteenth century. The first, *Cornwall in the Age of the Industrial Revolution* by John Rowe,[1] mentions the religious scene in an unsympathetic and brief manner. The second, *A History of Evangelical Christianity in Cornwall* by Peter Isaac, published privately, gives a general view of Christianity in Cornwall from the coming of the gospel to the present day, but does not cover the eighteenth century in any depth. In 1984 Paul Cook delivered a paper *The Forgotten Revival*, which examined the move of God in the county in the early nineteenth century, and in 1996 a memoir of William Carvosso, a Cornish lay evangelist, was republished. Apart from the above there is little material.[2]

In the following work I have tried to give an account of the Evangelical revival in Cornwall, and to examine it in the light of its central figure, Samuel Walker, who, as J. C. Ryle rightly said, 'lived in a day when the very existence of Christianity in England was at stake, and when the main business of true-hearted Christians was to preserve the very foundations of revealed religion from being swept away'.[3]

I have also attempted to rescue Walker from a fourfold injustice:

1. From those authors who pay him scant regard. John Overton is one example. In his book *The Evangelical Revival in the Eighteenth Century* he relegated Walker to 'the second rank' of clergymen, below men such as Isaac Milner and Richard Cecil, and was content to take 'some slight notice' of him. In his short sketch of Walker he managed to get both his birth and death dates wrong, and blamed his 'inadequate influence throughout the country' on the remoteness of Cornwall and on his being born too early! At least he admitted that Walker was 'an Evangelical before Evangelicalism' and 'the central figure of that remarkable revival in West Cornwall'.[4]

2. From the unfair criticism he has received, especially to do with his efforts to prevent Methodism separating from the Church of England. Luke Tyerman called Walker, Charles Wesley's 'unwise adviser';[5] while others, in reference to Walker's disagreement with John Wesley, claimed he had 'little understanding of Methodist problems'. These are just two of many negative comments.

3. From the over-shadowing effect of John Wesley. Many know of Walker only as a man who corresponded with Wesley and allow him to be buried under the vast amount of literature available on that champion of the faith. It is hardly surprising that someone of the stature of Wesley should have so much written about him, but when Walker is mentioned in his connection, Wesley is pictured as the great oak and Walker as the tiny sapling. Gordon Rupp is a prime example. In his 'Introductory Essay' to *A History of the Methodist Church in Great Britain*, he said that 'The story of the Evangelical Revival without Samuel Walker and William Grimshaw would be Hamlet without Rosencrantz and Guildenstern,' whereas 'without John and Charles Wesley it would be Hamlet without the Prince of Denmark and Horatio'.[6]

Perhaps there is no better illustration of this differential than in the present cathedral at Truro, the town where Walker was so mightily used of God. In a stained glass window near the south porch John Wesley is depicted preaching at Gwennap Pit, while Walker, along with Charles Wesley, is sitting humbly at his feet! R. J. E. Boggis, in his work *A History of the Diocese of Exeter*, compared Wesley and Walker, and rightly allowed 'that the former was the more remarkable and his influence vastly more extensive, yet Walker's principles were the sounder and his influence more intensive'.[7] One of the purposes of this biography is not to put Walker on the same footing as Wesley, that of course would be historically naive, but to redress the balance, and to give Walker a much fairer hearing so that his role and influence in the Evangelical awakening can be more fully appreciated.

4. From historical inaccuracies that tend to lessen the impact he had on the Evangelical scene of the eighteenth century. Arnold Dallimore, for instance, in his rightly acclaimed work on George Whitefield, said that Thomas Haweis, rector of Aldwincle, Northampton (1764-1820), was 'converted under the ministry of George Thompson',[8] when clearly Haweis was one of Walker's converts.

It is comments and inaccuracies such as the above that have demoted Samuel Walker unfairly.

I am indebted to Edwin Sidney's excellent biography (1838). He has reproduced in full many of Walker's letters, opinions and writings, and if the reader can ignore his insistence on promoting Walker's churchmanship above his Christianity, he will enjoy a thorough account of the Truro curate's ministry. Throughout my work I have tried to examine and unveil the man himself – his walk with God, the difficulties he encountered on a private as well as a public level, the characteristics of his life and faith, the reasons behind his actions, and so on – and to allow Walker to speak for himself, all in the hope that, in these days of doctrinal liberalism, the reader will be challenged and strengthened by the beliefs and conduct of a true Evangelical and so turn to God with renewed devotion.

Turning over local records [of mid-eighteenth century Cornwall], one may see how petty malefactors were still flogged through the streets of Cornish towns; how public hangings were regarded as a fashionable entertainment for rich and poor; how lunatics were displayed in cages for the amusements of passers-by; whilst honest paupers were sentenced to conditions which now seem scarcely credible in a country paying even lip-service to the principles of Christianity. Whilst the poor were subjected to such treatment as this, it was a time amongst the well-to-do of duelling and hard hitting, of drunkenness and debauchery – an age in which the expression 'as drunk as a lord' was still significant of the manner of living in the houses of the great.

A. K. Hamilton Jenkin.[1]

1
'A County of Lawless Barbarians'?

Aaron Seymour in his work *The Life and Times of Selina, Countess of Huntingdon* summed up the religious state of England at the beginning of the eighteenth century by calling the guardians of the Church

> ... unworthy ... cold formalists, husky verbalists, who gave the chaff to the flock, denying the grain; human learning was exalted at the expense of deep conviction of the Gospel scheme of salvation... The parson sat in the kitchen of the village inn smoking tobacco and drinking ale with his parishioners, or he played the fiddle and attended the merry-making of the neighbourhood... But ... the earnest, eloquent, persuasive, energetic, urgent messenger of the Gospel was almost unknown...
>
> Lambeth Palace had its balls and routs; music parties for Sunday evenings even the Bishops countenanced, and card parties were not unfrequent on the Sabbath evening. The humbler classes imitated *their betters*, a sneer at religion was wit; the parson was the standing joke, and the Church was used chiefly to rail at... millions had never heard a sermon![2]

Thomas Haweis observed that the 'nation was sunk down into corruption, and the Church erected a feeble barrier against the fashionable pursuits. The life and power of godliness fell to a very low standard, and only here and there an individual cleaved to the faith once delivered to the saints, and dared to be singular.'[3]

The Church in Cornwall was an example of the gross darkness that had invaded the Church throughout the land, and while it is true that it was not as ineffective as some have indicated, and there were conscientious clergymen working hard for the benefit of their parishioners, the overall impact of their efforts on society and the prevailing vices was minimal. Even after the establishment of Methodism in the county, vast numbers of tinners were 'living in the most deplorable state of ignorance and barbarism'. On 23 September, 1775, the Countess of Huntingdon, then in Cornwall, wrote to one of her students, John Hawkesworth, whom she invited to join her, saying, 'My call here is to the tinners, thousands and tens of thousands of poor perishing creatures whom all seem to neglect their souls.'[4] Trades such as smuggling were still rife. In fact, 'some of the most notorious of Cornish smugglers were also staunch supporters of the dissenting cause', and many were called 'honest men' by their natural enemies, the officers of the excise.[5]

> The Cornish smugglers, led by 'King Nick' in the mid-century, acquired national renown. This Nicholas Buzza owned a fleet of armed smugglers, cheated the revenue out of thousands a year, fooled the riding-officers times out of number, beat off the militia and fought big privateers. And this romantic idol of the West Country, the hero of song and story, was said to have been 'a powerful local preacher'.[6]

But smuggling was not confined to Cornwall. It was widespread throughout the British Isles. As early as 1733 it was estimated that

> ... the loss to the revenue by smuggling on tobacco alone amounted to a third of the whole duty; that less than a third of the tea imported passed through the Customs; that quite half the brandy and much of the silk imported, contrived to evade duty. On moonless nights long lines of mounted

smugglers, each with his horse laden with tubs, filed silently along; they showed their familiarity with squire and parson so far as to use the church itself as depot for contraband goods.[7]

Because of the encouragement and protection the smugglers received on land, and because naval vessels were deployed elsewhere during the European wars, the latter half of the eighteenth century has been called 'The Golden Age of Smuggling'.

In 1783 a government committee, set up to investigate the illegal trade, found that vessels as large as 300 tons and manned by 100 men were used to bring contraband across the Channel. Some of these vessels were able to make seven or eight voyages a year. 'The largest of them,' they reported, 'can bring, in one freight, the enormous quantity of three thousand half-ankers [tubs] of spirits, and ten or twelve tons of tea, whilst their strength is such as to enable them to bid defiance to the revenue cruisers.'[8] The vessels used in Cornish ports ranged in size from 30-250 tons and were often heavily armed. Some of these vessels, with their huge sails, could cross the Channel in eight hours and consequently were in great demand from Land's End to Dover. It was the practice of these large armed vessels to protect smaller craft employed in the same trade, while on the coast batteries were built to protect the landing of the illicit cargo. Once safely on land the commodities, continued the report, 'are distributed on the coast at little more than half the usual price, or brought to the metropolis under insurance, and delivered to retail traders or private housekeepers at about two-thirds of their proper price'.[9]

In Cornwall there was not a poor family in any parish without 'its tea, its snuff and tobacco, and (when they have money or credit) brandy'. John Rowe commented that 'Smuggling was almost a regular occupation enabling many to earn, if not their daily bread, at least something to spread on that bread.'[10] In 1753 George Borlase wrote: 'The coasts here swarm with smugglers from the Land's End to the Lizard, so that I wonder the soldiers (which were late quartered here) should have been ordered off without being replaced by others.'[11] In 1759 the local controller of the Isles of Scilly, in a plea against seized goods being sold on the islands, said that there was nobody but smugglers to whom the goods could be sold. Four years later, the new controller of Scilly, because smuggling had reached such proportions, asked for 'six blunderbusses, six fusils, twenty pairs of pistols of different sizes, twenty hangers, two dozen tucks, two dozen long tucks and two dozen laterns'[12] in order to tackle the problem. By 1770 some '470,000 gallons of brandy and 350,000 pounds of tea were being smuggled into Cornwall every year at a cost of about £150,000 to the Exchequer'.[13] This deficit amounted to 'a twentieth of the whole smuggling carried on in the Kingdom, to a fifth of the amount of "free trade" in the Home Counties, and the brandy run into Cornwall alone represented a yearly loss of revenue equivalent to the estimated yield of the notorious Stamp Duties from all the American Colonies'.[14]

Smuggling in Mousehole had reached such a height by the middle of the century that the goods were often carried openly in the middle of the day, with the local excise man on one occasion excusing himself from his duty by saying that he was confined to his bed, having been pelted with stones a few days before. In 1778 Edward Giddy of Tredrea wrote to the chief custom officer, complaining that 'In the western part of this county smuggling, since the soldiers have been drawn off, has been carried on almost without control.'[15] Two years after this letter the customs officers seized 636lb of tea in one day in the parishes of Sithney and Breage, and in 1786, 9981 pounds weight of wool, about to be smuggled out of Cornwall, was confiscated. On top of this a considerable amount of tin was smuggled to the Mediterranean markets by those employed in the pilchard trade.

All classes of society were involved in the illegal trade and regarded the offence lightly. Many of the clergy appreciated being supplied with everyday luxuries free of duty, and at St Ives in 1753 John Wesley complained that nearly the whole society 'bought or sold uncustomed goods'.[16] The local gentry argued that the government only had itself to blame for placing a high duty on foreign liquors in order to increase the revenue to the Treasury, for its inefficiency in dealing with the problem and for that of its agents; customs officers turned a blind eye to the loss of revenue, excise men were offered tubs of brandy in return for their cooperation, and even members of Parliament connived at the activities of smugglers; magistrates and juries, not generally recognising defrauding the revenues of the realm as a crime, refused to convict those brought to the courts; and the law itself punished thieves more severely than smugglers.

In such a lax climate the daring of the smugglers, who were often in alliance with persons of local standing, was sometimes outrageous.

In 1772, a Penzance custom boat was plundered and sunk by a smuggler, and on 29th November of the same year, another sailed into Penzance harbour and carried off the revenue cutter *Brilliant*, which was lying there with captured cargo in her hold. In 1775, two vessels lay off Penzance for three days discharging cargo, the custom collector looking on helplessly meanwhile, since everyone ashore was either actively interested in the success of the 'run', or a passive sympathizer. About the same time an excise ship off Padstow, instead of chasing, was chased into the port by a large Irish vessel which by way of bravado fired seven guns at the mouth of the harbour and hung out a flag in triumph, afterwards sailing away to discharge her cargo at Newquay, in which place the smugglers and excise officers were stated to be on excellent terms. It was not uncommon, indeed, for a hundred horses to be awaiting the arrival of such cargoes here nearly every day of the week.[17]

The violence of the smugglers was well known and it was not uncommon for conflicts with government officials to end in bloodshed or even loss of life. On many occasions excise men were in danger of losing their lives as they attempted to seize contraband goods. In 1748 the collector of customs at Penzance complained that the crew of a boat that had anchored off the pier with illegal goods swore bitterly at the officers as they approached and tried 'to knock out their brains with a boat-hook, besides throwing large stones at them'.[18] In 1768 William Odgers, an excise officer stationed at Porthleven, 'was murdered by a party of smugglers in a most barbarous manner'.[19]

The people of Cornwall in the eighteenth century were also notorious for looting vessels that had foundered on the rocks and reefs, although there is no reliable evidence that they deliberately lured ships into these dangerous areas. The law defined 'a wreck of the sea' as anything from which no living creature reached the shore. If a man or animal survived, the vessel was not legally a wreck. If all perished, it became the property of the lord of the coastal manor, or in reality, the property of whoever reached it first. This meant that by ignoring the cries of a drowning man or by pushing survivors back into the raging sea, the wreck became 'legal' and its cargo 'legally' plundered. If custom officials intervened and tried to enforce the Crown's right to wreckage, they were either threatened or ignored by the common folk, who 'believed that if any man ran the hazard of saving something from the sea and succeeded, to him it belonged'.[20]

It is said that when the first steamship appeared off the Lizard, huge crowds of hungry wreckers followed her along the cliff tops, believing she was on fire and waiting eagerly for her to be swept onto the rocks. When news of a wreck reached the towns and villages, there was a stampede to the scene, with every family hoping to salvage something of value from the doomed vessel. Violence frequently erupted as men and women fought over the prized spoils. To the poorer classes, a wreck was viewed as a 'gift from God', and even men of the church were tempted to 'pray for wrecks of providence'. Parson Troutbeck's epilogue to the Litany sounds like the words of a wolf in sheep's clothing: 'We pray thee, O Lord, not that wrecks should happen, but that if any wrecks do happen, thou wilt guide them into the Scilly Isles, for the benefit of the poor inhabitants.'[21]

For the people of Scilly wrecking was 'almost a major occupation... For days after heavy gales they would be found wandering about the shores looking for any chance wreckage that might have been cast up, neglecting their farms and fishing nets.'[22] In October, 1707, three men-of-war went down off St Mary's with the loss of nearly two thousand men, thus benefiting 'the poor inhabitants'. It was reported that the Admiral, Sir Cloudesley Shovell, 'was cast up alive on Porth Hellick beach, where he was murdered by a woman for the sake of an emerald ring'.[23]

Those who attended the wrecks were usually tinners, who hurriedly left their mines to pillage whatever the sea gave up. George Borlase, writing on 1 February, 1753, noted the reputation of the tinners of Breage and Germoe, the most barbarous of all Cornish wreckers:

The late storms have brought several vessels ashore and some dead wrecks, and in the former case great barbarities have been committed. My situation in life has obliged me sometimes to be a spectator of things which shock humanity. The people who make it their business to attend these wrecks are generally tinners, and, as soon as they observe a ship on the coast, they first arm themselves with sharp axes and hatchets, and leave their tin works to follow those ships... They'll cut a large trading vessel to pieces in one tide, and cut down everybody that offers to oppose them. Two or three years ago, a Dutchman was stranded near Helston, every man saved, and the ship whole, burthen 250 tons, laden with claret. In twenty-four hour's time the tinners cleared all. A few months before this, they murdered a poor man just by Helston who came in aid of a custom-house officer to seize some brandy... I have seen many a poor man, half dead, cast ashore and crawling out of the reach of the waves, fallen upon and in a manner stripped naked by those villains, and if afterwards he has saved his chest or any more clothes, they have been taken from him.[24]

The men of Breage and Germoe did not always wait for a wreck, but plundered damaged ships as they lay in the harbour waiting to be repaired. For instance, in 1750 troops were summoned to arrest the Breage and Germoe men who had stripped a damaged vessel lying at anchor near the Mount. In the words of Walter Borlase, it was an 'act of inhumanity and rapine', which 'surpassed all former acts of that kind in barbarity and violence'.[25]

Other examples of wrecked vessels include the *Alcida* of Bordeaux. She was wrecked at Porthleven in December, 1748, with a cargo of 160 tons of wine. The violence and brutality of the country people were such that the excise men could not save a single cask and were fearful of being murdered. In 1764 a French ship was wrecked at Perranzabuloe. Not only was the whole cargo carried away by the zealous wreckers, but the crew were stripped to their shirts.

With the huge inflow of cheap spirits entering Cornwall through the smuggling trade, many eighteenth century households, in all classes of society, were characterised by heavy drinking. The working classes were particularly vulnerable. It has been estimated that a sum of over £30,000 was spent annually on drink by the working classes in a typical Cornish parish such as Redruth, leaving many heavily in debt and pursued by bailiffs. Tonkin, commenting on this vice, said, that in the mining districts, 'If there were but three houses together, two of them shall be ale-houses.'[26] When a ship carrying a cargo of wines or spirits was wrecked, the plunderers sometimes became so inebriated that they fell into the sea and drowned.

As can be imagined violence erupted when the miners were drunk or, because of their excesses, they were left without money to buy food.[27] In April, 1707, thousands of tinners invaded Truro to force the Stannary Parliament to submit to their demands. There were food riots in 1727, and two years later there was a more serious uprising of the tinners, 'who ravaged up and down the country in a very insolent manner and in great numbers'.[28] On this occasion three or four of their leaders were hanged. In 1737 there was so much trouble at Falmouth that the alarmed Treasury consulted the Secretary at War. Further outbreaks of violence occurred after this 'at least once every decade [throughout the century], and in times of scarcity the gentry and middle classes lived in fear of a general insurrection'.[29]

Sometimes the violence of the miners was more organized. Early in the century a mob from Redruth set out to attack the men of Gwennap. They dyed a handkerchief in the blood of a dog they had slaughtered and used it as a flag as they marched against their enemies. In the ensuing battle the Redruthers were routed and at least one of their 'army' was killed. It was gratuitous violence such as this that caused the English to regard Cornishmen as 'lawless barbarians', and the tinners as little more than savages, whom no one would or could control. The miners of the 1730s in the St Just district were once described as 'ferocious in manners, obtuse in intellect, alternatively servile and riotous, their more serious employment, when disengaged from the mines, was smuggling and wrecking, while their amusements partook of the same savage and brutal character'.[30]

Among the eighteenth century 'amusements' were such cruel sports as cock fighting and bull baiting. The birds had small steel or silver spurs attached to their legs and their beaks were sharpened to transform them into deadly weapons. Their owners, who often gambled large sums of money on their birds, trained them to fight fiercely to the death. Bull baiting was just as vicious. The poor animal was chained to a post or an anchor, pepper was blown into its nose to madden it, and then dogs were set loose to tear it to pieces.[31] Then there were the traditional sports of hurling and wrestling, the latter 'often accompanied by excessive drinking, the brutality common to past ages, unfair play and rioting'.[32] John Rowe called them 'violent recreations in which serious and even fatal injuries some-times occurred. Hurling matches between adjoining villages provided opportunities to pay off old scores and to gratify long-rankling feuds and hatreds.'[33] Daniel Defoe, during his tour of Great Britain, could see nothing in hurling, except 'It is a rude violent play among the boors, or country people; brutish and furious, and a sort of evidence, that they were, once, a kind of barbarians.'[34]

Folklore and superstition were also rife during the century. Stories of 'human monsters who lured ships to their doom with bobbing lanterns, who knocked sailors on the head with hatchets, or cut off their hands as they clung to ledges of rock', before they themselves were carried off by fiends in circumstances of the utmost horror,[35] were perhaps nearer to the truth than most. Other tales spoke of giants living on the moors – 'The flat boul-ders [were] their "bob-buttons"; the logan rocks their quoits; the water-worn hollows in the stones their bowls and cups; the long, flat rocks their beds and tables; and the massive lumps of granite that strew the hillsides bore witness to their ferocious battles.'[36] Tales of underground spirits of the mines, which were said to be haunted by 'knackers', mischievous elves that were the spirits of the Jews who had crucified Christ, and apparitions were commonplace. A belief in fairies prevailed, especially among the miners, who talked of how these small magical beings discovered mines, played music very sweetly and danced in circles and rings. Most people out at night were afraid of 'the spirits'.

Many Cornishmen had a superstitious veneration of holy wells and their ability to heal or protect. It was thought that each well had its own peculiar virtue. For instance, St Nun's Well cured insanity, the waters of St Uny's Well at Redruth were believed to protect all those baptised in them from being hanged, and the Wells of St Keyne and St Martin's were best known for their reputed influence on married life. Along with these super-natural notions came the study and practice of magic arts, part of everyday life for some: 'In many instances the more studious members of the old West Country families who dwelt in the isolated mansions of West Penwith were wont to pass much of their time in drawing horoscopes, concocting drugs and distilling strange compounds and cordials, by the aid of which they predicted remarkable events.'[37] In addition, it was said that

> ... Cornish witches rode through the air on stalks of ragwort ... thoroughly malicious and ill-wishing both men and cattle. They also stirred up tempests, usually from their stone chairs on the cliff edge, but occasionally by riding the sea in a stone boat and beating the waves with a ladle. There were a few white witches, but the evil ones predominated.
>
> Then there were the mermaids, those hauntingly beautiful inhuman creatures who seemed to have no hearts, yet fell in love with the sons of men. Both their weeping and their singing were ravishing to hear; but woe to the handsome young man who gave ear to them. For the mermaid's way with her beloved was like the spider's; and he who followed her down to the sea never came back.
>
> Then came the saints, men mighty in spirit, though some-times of pigmy size. They wrestled with and overcame the powers of darkness. They had at their command those spir-itual resources that attend the Lord's anointed; the winds and waves fell calm before them; millstones floated them across the sea; the sun stayed his setting to light them home; when they were hungry, animals ministered to them; when

they suffered, the very rocks wept. Powerful in blessing, powerful in cursing, they were yet human beings, with human failings. Sometimes they quarrelled, and threw huge rocks at each other after the manner of the giants; they were even known to steal, but only from their brother saints.[38]

It was into this wild, ignorant and unrestrained county that Samuel Walker stepped in 1746. While it would be an over-statement to say that he transformed the spiritual and moral condition of Cornwall, it is nevertheless true that he made a significant impact for good not only on the religious scene in and about Truro, but on other clergymen in the county, and on Evangelicalism generally throughout Great Britain. In the words of Balleine, the 'work that he accomplished was extraordinary'.[39]

The record of Evangelicalism in Cornwall makes rather distressing reading. In the early days there were two strong groups, that in the north-east of the county, and that round Walker at Truro; and at this period Evangelicalism was probably more flourishing in Cornwall than in any part of England. Then it suddenly collapsed. The reasons for this are various. There was episcopal and clerical disapproval, and changes of incumbencies, for, when the Evangelicals died off, they were followed by clerics of a different colour; but most potent of all was the stronger appeal made by the emotional preaching of the Methodists to the temperament of the people, and the aggressive tactics which they adopted...

The Methodists regarded even men like Walker as 'well-meaning legalists' and had no scruples about attracting their followers. Nonetheless, Wesley had spoken very highly of the work being done by the Evangelical clergy, writing on September 8, 1760: 'By these and the Methodists together, the line is now laid, with no considerable intervals, all along the north sea from the eastern point of Cornwall to the Land's End.'

L. E. Elliot-Binns.[1]

2
The Church in Eighteenth Century Cornwall

In the eighteenth century the Church in Cornwall was imbibed with the spirit of the age to an alarming extent. A common synopsis of the religious state of the time reads: 'The bishops were godless men, seeking only to advance their own standing in society; an arid formalism pervaded the activities of the clergy, and their parishioners looked on the church as merely a building to which men, women and children were taken to be baptised, married or buried; the services of the church were cold, lacking authority and fervour, and a slothfulness hung over the small Sabbath congregations.' Lach-Szyrma commented that 'The four "D's" – dreariness, dolefulness, deadness, and dullness – reigned supreme in the Cornish churches;'[2] Miles Brown noted that the Church in the county, along with the rest of England, had 'settled down into a deep slumber';[3] and Hamilton Jenkin stated that 'The latent spiritual fervour of the Cornish people ... lay ... not dead, but asleep. During this time the Church itself was sinking into a slow spiritual decay, sufficiently alert, it is true, to claim its dues and privileges, but giving little or nothing in return to the "hungry sheep" who still looked up but were not fed.'[4]

John S. Simon, in reviewing the 'spiritual gloom' of Cornwall, classed many of the clergy with the 'old school of drunken, hunting, rough-tongued parsons', who 'share the characteristic vices of the county, and their lives travesty the truths which they drearily read to their scanty congregations out of their

prayer-books and Bibles on Sunday'. [5] Certainly, there were
men like 'Cardinal' Pole, so nicknamed by his friends because
of his love for hunting pink; later in the century there was Thomas
Wills, vicar of Wendron, who was 'known to have two illegitimate children at least', and whose 'main interests, outside the
bottle and lechery, were hunting and farming'; [6] and Parson
Kemp, another 'assiduous follower of hounds'. [7] There is a story
told, which, though somewhat amusing, is sadly indicative of
the attitude in the church at this time. A parson was just about to
go hunting when he was told that the bishop was in the village.

> Hastily sending away his horse, he ran upstairs and jumped
> into bed, still clothed in his riding-boots, spurs and red coat.
> A minute later the bishop's carriage drew up at the door. 'Tell
> his lordship I'm ill,' called out the parson to his housekeeper
> as he snuggled down under the bedclothes.
>
> A few moments afterwards the woman tapped at the
> vicar's door, 'Please, your honour, the bishop says he's brave
> and sorry, and can he come up and sit with you?'
>
> 'What!' cried the vicar, 'come up and sit with me? Good
> heavens, no! Tell his lordship I'm took cruel bad with the
> scarlet fever. Say it's an aggravated case and very catching!' [8]

A man who was converted through the ministry of Samuel
Walker complained that before Walker was raised up by God
'Almost all this country [i.e. Cornwall] was involved in gross
darkness; the cry of salvation was scarce heard amongst us;
almost every one ignorant of the first principles of Christianity;
a lifeless ministry, and a debauched or a formal people.' [9] This
'ignorance' is confirmed by Risdon Darracott, whose first regular
charge was at the Market Jew Street Chapel in Penzance. He
was stationed there in the autumn of 1738. The following year
he wrote to a friend and told him that he had requested George
Whitefield 'to come down into Cornwall... This country is sadly
ignorant, and does deserve as much compassion as Wales can
do.' [10] Whitefield himself, in May, 1743, spoke of a contemplated

visit to Exeter and Cornwall, adding, 'That is dry ground. I love to range such places.'[11]

Francis Truscott said that when the Wesleys first visited Cornwall, there was a village, some five miles from Helston, that did not have even one copy of the Bible. The only religious book the villagers possessed between them was a single copy of The Book of Common Prayer, kept at a public house.

> On one occasion, during a terrific storm, when the people feared that the world was ending, they fled in consternation to the tavern that Tom, the tapster, might secure them protection by reading them a prayer. Having fallen upon their knees, Tom hastily snatched a well thumbed book, and began, with great pomposity, to read about storms, wrecks and rafts, until his mistress, finding that some mistake was made, cried out, 'Tom, that is Robinson Crusoe!'
>
> 'No,' said Tom, 'it is the Prayer Book,' and on he went until he came to a description of man Friday, when his mistress again vociferated that she was certain Tom was reading Robinson Crusoe. 'Well, well,' said Tom, 'suppose I am; there are as good prayers in Robinson Crusoe as in any other book.' So Tom proceeded till the storm abated, when the company dispersed with great composure of mind, believing they had done their duty.[12]

Coupled with such ignorance was a growing restlessness among the clergy, many of whom were indifferent to the needs of their parishioners and neglectful of their religious duties. In one parish, John Hingston of Towednack, near St Ives, complained that his child, along with many other children, had died without being baptised by the vicar. By the middle of the century the majority of clergymen cared more about pleasure-seeking 'than looking after the poor and attending to the services of the church'.[13] 'Even an amiable apologist,' wrote another author, referring to the same period, 'must admit that among them were men whose character and conduct it is useless to defend.'[14]

The attitudes and conduct of the clergy are partly explained by the fact that many of the livings in the mining districts, particularly of west Cornwall, were held not by men of deep conviction, but by the sons and relations of the mine-owning gentry. Before the eighteenth century the clergy had been drawn from all classes of society, but by 1700 the majority of beneficed clergymen were the younger sons or relatives of the landowning classes, whose importance was declining with economic change. John Rowe stated:

> Four of the great mining parishes by 1740 were in the rather indifferent hands of two of the sons of John Borlase; Walter held Madron and Kenwyn, William Ludgvan and St Just in Penwith. The Pendarves and Bassets were using livings in the Redruth and Camborne district to provide for younger sons or other family connections; St Aubyns and Godolphins along with the Duchy interests held most of the remaining livings in the western mining region.[15]

In 1776, when Walter Borlase died, the Madron living was 'inherited' by his son William, and Kenwyn passed to John Trist, who was already benefiting from the livings of Veryan and of Kea. When Walter's younger brother William died in 1772 St Just passed to G. P. Scobell of Sancreed, who carried on Borlase's system of employing curates to attend to the spiritual needs of the far western mining parish. Ludgvan went under the oversight of the curate John Penneck, the son of the then vicar of Gulval. With these successors narrow class loyalties were served and religion became a means to support that class of society from which the clergymen were drawn. It would not be an exaggeration to say that men took orders, not because of their love for Christ and the souls of men, but out of convenience, for the benefit of their families, and in the hope of securing a better standard of living.

A further reason for what has been called 'a century of somnolence' in the Anglican Church was the dry and academic teaching of many clergy that appealed to intellectuals and controversialists but left the unlettered miners and labourers unmoved. Sermons were made up of philosophical and rational arguments, religious essays were presented to congregations without emotion, and moralising exhortations were the norm. 'Dignity, reason, the seemliness of worship left a great gap in the souls of the humble,' said Miles Brown. Instead of preaching the simple gospel in a passionate and relevant way that reached every tier of society, men spoke to impress the great minds of the day and the leading families, and the lower classes, who looked up to the clergy more as squires and magistrates than shepherds, were left to fend for themselves.[16]

The two principal evils in the church at this time were pluralism and absenteeism. At the beginning of the century residence was insisted upon and an incumbent who was absent from his parish for more than three months was admonished, but by 1744 non-residence was on the increase, and the dispensations that permitted plurality were easy to obtain, mainly because the dispensing authorities were just as guilty. The available returns for that year's visitation 'show that there were 110 clergy who resided, with eight curates resident in parishes where the incumbent was an absentee. Thirty-six did not reside, and nine resided outside the parish, but so near as to be able to serve it.'[17]

[By] 1768, statistics show only eighty-two resident incumbents in Cornwall, at least seventy-one being non-resident... The worst deaneries were Trigg Major and Trigg Minor, stretching from Kilkhampton in the north of the county along the coast to Tintagel, and inland to Launceston, also covering a large part of Bodmin moor. The former deanery had fourteen non-residents out of twenty-six, and the other [had] thirteen out of nineteen.[18]

By 1779 the number of non-residents had fallen to 57, with 89 living in their parishes.

One of the problems was that Cornwall was an archdeaconry in the diocese of Exeter, which embraced two counties. The bishops rarely visited the county – partly because of the distance and travel difficulties in Cornwall, and partly because of a lack of concern – and when they did their time was crowded with business affairs. (There was no bishop residing in Cornwall until 1877.) To ordinary folk they were 'misty and semi-legendary' people. 'Perhaps once in every three years or so an Episcopal Visitation and Confirmation might be held in a handful of the larger county towns, and crowds of imperfectly prepared ordinates received the laying on of hands, but that was about all the Cornish ever saw of their bishops.'[19]

The archdeacons also lived outside the county and only visited when legally bound to do so, in theory once a year on behalf of the bishop. Some held the office with other preferment, which prevented them from discharging their duties in Cornwall. John Sleech, archdeacon from 1741-1788, seldom travelled within a hundred miles of Truro, except for annual visitations, occasions which presented the local clergy with a rare opportunity to meet together for discussion. All this meant that there was no one on hand to ensure that the clergy fulfilled their obligations. The clergy themselves, not averse to the freedom from authority they enjoyed, took full advantage. In order 'to live in greater state and worldly comfort', they often held more than one living and on occasions pursued separate careers, and sometimes employed curates, who were mostly poorly paid and not infrequently half starved, to watch over their flocks.

For example, the vicar of Tintagel had been living for nearly thirty years at Penryn, where he had acted as lecturer and schoolmaster. The vicar of St Cleer, who was also rector of St Mary Tavy near Tavistock, had for thirty years resided at East Looe, whose church he served. The rector of Creed and the vicar of St Austell had both spent the last five years in Bath; and the rector of Stokeclimsland, resident at St Austell, had for twenty years past left his parish to a curate, non-resident in 1765, and his other cure of St Germans to an unlicensed curate, his house at Stokeclimsland being uninhabitable and the chancel in ruinous condition.

In what is now Stratton deanery, out of eleven parishes, the rector of Kilkhampton lived in London, putting in as curate only a deacon, unlicensed. The vicar of Stratton also held Luffincott, twelve miles distant in Devon, where he resided, and served it with Werrington; Stratton being left to an unlicensed curate, too infirm to reside. Marhamchurch's rector was an absentee 'by reason of his necessary attendance on his affairs in Berkshire'. The rector of Jacobstow permanently resided at St Veep; and the vicar of Poundstock served Modbury, South Devon. A curate, whom they supported between them, conducted one service at either church.[20]

Many other examples could be cited.[21] William Borlase, in a letter to Sir John St Aubyn, dated 31 December, 1736, tried to defend the system when he claimed that 'Conferring two livings on one person is neither contrary to Scripture nor reason ... that it is no more than enlarging the trust... Abolishing pluralities,' he said, would be 'a dangerous amputation' and parochial clergy particularly would be 'deprived of the only method of advancing themselves into leisure and a capacity of studying without falling into any inferior occupation to maintain themselves or educate their families'.[22] It is obvious where Borlase's priorities lay. Richard Polwhele also defended pluralities and the employment of curates on the basis that it enabled the clergy to concentrate on their studies and literary careers.

When these non-resident clergymen visited their flocks, it was often to suit their own convenience. The vicar of Towednack, already mentioned for his neglect at the end of the previous century, also lived outside his parish, and turned up to take services at unpredictable times. Sometimes he arrived at seven in the morning, sometimes at eleven or one, and sometimes at sunset. Instead of gathering his parishioners, he went immediately into the church and began prayers, although there were only a few in the congregation. Some of the clergy were careful in the choice and supervision of their curates, but their main purpose was to maintain an outward appearance of conformity and decency, rather than to win their parishioners for Christ. William Borlase rebuked Tregarthen, the curate of St Just, for

> ... neglecting services in St Just in order to officiate for other clergymen; for holding services at times inconvenient to the folk living in the outlying hamlets of the parish; for absenting himself from a populous parish in which burials were frequent and not even putting in appearances at times he had arranged with bereaved parishioners to bury their dead; for failing to insist that godparents at baptisms were confirmed communicants; for failing to keep the registers of baptisms, marriages and burials regularly; for undertaking to perform fortnightly afternoon services at Paul to the neglect of the people of St Just, without first asking Borlase's permission.[23]

Some curates, in order to boost their incomes, would sell their services and in doing so neglect their own charge. The more affluent would not inconvenience themselves by conducting services or burials in bad weather.

One of the reasons why pluralities were necessary was because of the very low stipends of most benefices. At the beginning of the century the usual annual stipend was £30, although a few favoured clergy received £50. It simply was not possible to survive on a single income, especially as in several cases no house was provided. Robert Blachford, for instance, earned eleven pounds per annum as vicar of Tywardreath and eight pounds as vicar of St Samson. At neither place was there a vicarage. Samuel Gurney, pluralist and non-resident, put a curate in charge of Warleggan and another to serve Colan; 'but Gurney was paid only ten pounds from one and twenty pounds from the other. Having seven children to support, he made his home at Tregony, where he was master of the grammar school, and served the churches of Merther and Cornelly for thirty-eight pounds per year.'[24]

Whatever legitimate reasons there were for pluralities and absenteeism, it is true to say that they 'not only reduced preferment in the church [which was based on patronage of the great and not on ministerial gifts and qualifications] to a stock-jobbing business, but also left vicars and curates evading and shuffling the responsibilities of the care of souls'.[25] In many parts of the county the sheep were left without a shepherd, and by the middle of the century the authority of the church had reached its lowest ebb.

Although the church had little effect on the surrounding vices, it was not completely 'dead', as some have suggested. The efforts of the more conscientious clergy did produce some results and compare favourably with conditions in other parts of the country. Frederick Hockin went as far as to say that no part of England produced such a roll of clerical worthies as Cornwall possessed during the early and middle part of the eighteenth century. Along with Samuel Walker he lists Vowler; Collins of Redruth, whose preaching Wesley applauded; Thomson, Michell, and Charles Peters of St Mabyn, one of the first Hebrew scholars of his day, and 'a friend to the poor, a father of the fatherless, a Christian indeed in whom was no guile'; Bedford, vicar of Philleigh, 'a truly godly man, attentive to all his parochial duties'; John Whitaker, a historian of some note, whose 'dauntless rebuke of profanity in exalted stations is on record [he openly reproved the Bishop of Derry for irreverent conversation] as well as his zeal as a Christian minister'; Stackhouse, rector of St Erme, described as manifesting in his life the beauty of holiness; Thomas Wills, the curate of St Agnes, whose church was so full that often it was 'with difficulty he could get to the reading desk'; Penrose and others – all of whom are named to support Hockin's argument.[26] To this list could be added John Bennet and Henry Phillips, and later in the century Thomas Biddulp, vicar of Padstow (1770-1790). Many of these men were connected with the Evangelical movement that gathered momentum in the middle of the century, and their influence spread far beyond their parish boundaries.

At St Just, William Borlase commonly had a congregation of 1000 in the morning and 500 in the afternoon. An aged parishioner of Tintagel testified that before Wesley came the church had been 'always crowded ... the monthly celebration of the sacrament was most largely attended, and the children catechized every Sunday afternoon'. Another parishioner of Dr Martin's at St Breward 'remembered her father's expression that "when he was young you might have walked a mile to church on the heads of the people in the lanes"'.[27] After the spread of Methodism several parish churches were rebuilt, Helston in 1761 and Redruth seven years later, for instance, and in others galleries were erected to accommodate the growing congregations.

G. C. B. Davies has reproduced some of the answers to queries sent out to the clergy of the diocese by the Bishop of Exeter, Nicholas Claggett, in 1744, in order to elicit information concerning the various parishes in preparation for Episcopal visitation. They show that the life of the church was not entirely stagnant:

> At the parish church of Truro, Joseph Jane reports in 1744 that, out of 340 families, there were 500 eligible communicants, with an average of fifty at the monthly celebration of the Sacrament, and 120 at the two Easter celebrations... At Veryan, with 126 families, Thomas Michell declared the same year that he held two services a Sunday, with a sermon in the mornings and on Saints' days. He read prayers daily throughout the year. There were 150 eligible communicants, of whom eighty came regularly, and 130 at Easter. He held eight Sacraments a year... At Fowey, which held a monthly

celebration, with 180 eligible communicants, the monthly average was sixty to seventy, and 126 at Easter. St Just in Penwith, with three celebrations a year, had an average of 120 communicants; while out of 300 eligible at St Ives, 160 attended at Easter. Neighbouring Towednack, with forty families, reported forty eligible communicants; Lelant, 180 families, with sixty communicants at Easter out of one hundred eligible.[28]

And so the report goes on.

In 1745 Bishop Lavington confirmed 14,000 candidates at Truro and Penzance, most of whom had been carefully prepared, although at the services themselves all was 'confusion and haste'.[29] Bishop Keppel's candidates twenty years later numbered over 40,000 in Devon and Cornwall, with a ratio of four to three in each county respectively. John Rowe, on the other hand, uses a table to show the decline in the number of communicants in the Established Church in proportion to the population as revealed by the returns of the clergy to Bishop Claggett in 1745 and to Bishop Ross in 1779 from sixteen parishes in eastern Cornwall. In 1745 the estimated population in those parishes was 7,910 and the number of communicants was between 716 and 1048, whereas in 1779 the estimated population had risen by 3000 and the number of communicants fallen to between 591 and 641.[30] While it is always difficult to gauge the effectiveness of the Church purely from numbers, at least the figures reveal that as far as the Establishment was concerned there was an outward show of religion in the lives of many Cornish people in the eighteenth century.

Daniel Defoe, writing from Liskeard in the second decade of the eighteenth century, noted 'a large new built meeting house for the Dissenters, which I name, because they assured me there was but three more, and those very inconsiderable in all the county of Cornwall; whereas in Devonshire ... there are reckoned about seventy, some of which are exceedingly large and fine'.[31]

By the middle of the century the number of Dissenters in Cornwall, sometimes labelled Methodists as early as 1745, was still relatively small. For instance, at Kilkhampton, out of 150 families in the parish, only sixteen were Dissenters (i.e. Methodists). They were taught by George Thomson, vicar of St Gennys, and had no licensed meeting house. There were no other denominations represented. In the parish of Marhamchurch there were fifty-eight families and only one of these was classed with the Dissenters. According to the vicar, John Cory, who resided in North Tamerton parish, this family 'frequent Mr Thomson's irregular meetings and accompany him at his circumforaneous vociferations'.[32] There was no licensed meeting house in the parish.

At St Hilary there was only one Methodist, 'an infamous woman of Marazion, fit only to associate with so infamous a sect', according to the vicar. At St Ives there were twenty families of Dissenters (Presbyterians), who had their own meeting house, as well as many Methodists. The Presbyterians also had meeting houses at Liskeard and Bodmin, and the two Presbyterian families at Marazion attended the Church instead of their own meeting in Penzance. At Fowey there were five Presbyterian families who had a meeting house but no minister. Thomas Serle at Treneglos had a few Methodists in his parish, 'a set of people who are chiefly encouraged and abetted ... by a neighbouring clergyman', George Thomson; while at Truro Joseph Jane reported that there were six or seven families of Presbyterians or Independents, but no meeting house.[33]

At Gwennap, out of about a hundred families in the parish, there were some forty to fifty Methodists, who had an unlicensed meeting house. At St Martin near Looe, there were a few Anabaptists, a few Presbyterians and a few Quakers. The rector of Creed, John Hughes, who reported that there were five or six Anabaptists meeting in a poor dwelling house, showed his contempt for them when he said, 'Their teacher is one

Buffet of Penryn who now seldom visits them, to so low a condition, by the blessing of God, are they reduced.'[34] The Baptist decline, which had begun in 1741, continued until 1764, when, with the opening of a meeting at Chacewater, new life appeared in the denomination. The Quakers, who could boast of 27 societies in the county with about 400 adherents in 1700, had also declined by the middle of the century, with several meeting houses 'seldom frequented'. All these figures mean that if the number of Methodists is excluded, the Dissenting cause in Cornwall was small and reduced to a low condition by the time Samuel Walker started his Truro ministry.

Two men who deserve a special mention in connection with the Evangelical cause in Cornwall, the 'cradle of Anglican Evangelicalism',[35] are George Thomson, the first Evangelical cleric, and John Bennet. Thomson was a brilliant scholar, who was presented to the benefice of St Gennys near Bude on 10 September, 1732, when he was about thirty-five years old. Within a year or two, through a recurring dream of his imminent death and appearance 'before the judgement of Christ, to give an account of the dreadful abuse of all your talents and the injuries done to the souls committed to your care',[36] and from reading Romans chapter three, he was converted. He immediately set about proclaiming the gospel with boldness and zeal, the forgiveness of sins becoming a central theme, and soon he was established as one of the leading Evangelicals of the Establishment. His church was crowded with earnest worshippers and several less prominent Evangelical clergy benefited from his encouragement and leadership.

Thomson was not content with urging his own people to turn to Christ, but preached around the district to the disgust of his clerical neighbours, many of whom closed their pulpits to him. On one occasion, when Bishop Lavington threatened him to his face that if he continued his irregularities he would be defrocked, Thomson took off his gown, threw it down at the

bishop's feet, and said, 'I can preach the gospel without a gown.'
It is not surprising that Balleine called him 'a firebrand of the
Berridge type'.[37] On account of his zeal and for acting in an
'unorthodox' manner, when Thomson was called before
Lavington, he was charged 'with having preached in parishes
not belonging to him, and at unlicensed places', and admonished 'to confine his preaching to his own church only, under
pain of ecclesiastical censure'. Bennet shared in these charges,
which referred to their private itineraries in North Cornwall.[38]

Thomson was a friend of Whitefield, who described a
Sunday service in Thomson's church as 'a glorious day of the
Son of Man';[39] and in correspondence with Lady Huntingdon,
he detailed how the worthy vicar of St Gennys accompanied
him on his tour through the county: 'Mr Thomson is mighty
hearty and is gone to his parish in a gospel flame.'[40] Thomson
also welcomed both the Wesleys into his pulpit and in the early
years was a strong supporter of Methodism. When Howel Harris
visited St Gennys in 1747, the Welshman 'sat up from eleven
to past three with the dearest and most affectionate Mr
Thomson'.[41] Doddridge alluded to him as 'one of the most
useful members which [the Established Church], or perhaps any
Christian communion, can boast'.[42] And James Hervey, a close
friend, described him

> ... as unfurling the gospel standard with a tongue touched
> from the heavenly altar, pleading with his people not to
> follow the wiles of Satan and lean on his broken reeds, but
> to build their faith on the Rock of Ages. He preached to his
> flock as the ruined and undone sinners they were, showing
> how God's mighty arm was still strong to save them from
> their plight. His message was always that 'They who know
> Christ's free goodness, will put their whole trust in him, and
> seek no other way to the Father of mercy, but through his
> merit.'[43]

Thomson died on 12 November, 1782.

John Bennet, a neighbouring curate in charge of three isolated parishes of North Tamerton (about twelve miles from St Gennys), Laneast and Tresmere, and who in his earlier years had known the Wesleys' father, was converted through Thomson's ministry about the autumn of 1742. He was then over seventy years old. Charles Wesley recorded, 'I met an aged clergyman... Upon Mr Thomson's preaching salvation by faith, he had received the kingdom as a little child, and has ever since owned the truth and its followers.'[44] On another occasion Charles Wesley was at Laneast preaching 'against harmless diversions'. Three clergymen, John Meriton, Thomson and Bennet were present.

> 'By harmless diversions,' exclaimed the preacher, 'I was kept asleep in the devil's arms, secure in a state of damnation, for eighteen years.'
>
> No sooner were the words uttered than Meriton added aloud, 'And I for twenty-five!'
>
> 'And I,' cried Thomson, 'for thirty-five!'
>
> 'And I,' said Bennet, the venerable minister of the church, 'and I for above seventy.'[45]

Bennet too supported the Methodists, welcomed them into his pulpit and practised an itinerant ministry. In a letter written by Whitefield, dated 11 November, 1743, the great evangelist spoke of the aged Bennet's zeal: 'He lately preached three times and rode forty miles the same day.'[46] Balleine rightly said that he 'crowded into his last ten years more aggressive Christian work than most men accomplish in a lifetime'.[47]

Thomson and Bennet, along with John Turner, rector of Week St Mary, were the pioneers of Cornish Evangelicalism and the men who prepared the way for Walker and the Wesleys. They overcame the hostility of their brother clergy, the spiritual indifference of the times, and deplorable moral standards to exercise a ministry that was owned by God to the praise of his glory and the extension of his kingdom.

There are many names more conspicuous in the religious history of the [eighteenth] century than that of Samuel Walker of Truro, because their exertions extended over a wider surface; but no minister has left for the imitation of posterity, a more distinguished pattern of parochial administration. While others, engaged in a laborious itinerancy, were endeavouring to break the spell of that lethargy which had spread its fatal charm over the land, this exemplary pastor was constructing from limited and unpromising materials, a model of the private duty of such as are appointed to spiritual cures among settled portions of the people.

Edwin Sidney.[1]

3
Walker's Early Years

There are many great names connected with the eighteenth century Evangelical awakening. Across the Atlantic Jonathan Edwards, that noble prince, stands foremost in the mind. Samuel Davies regarded him as 'the profoundest reasoner, and the greatest divine, that America ever produced'.[2] His sermon *Sinners in the Hands of an Angry God*, preached at the church in Enfield, Connecticut, on 8 July, 1741, is, according to John D. Currid, 'the most famous sermon ever delivered in the history of America'. In England the name of George Whitefield is pre-eminent. At sixteen he was a tapster, at twenty-six 'the most brilliant and popular preacher the modern world has ever known'.[3] Also John Wesley, whose tireless itinerancy, outstanding preaching powers and organizational skills, have meant that succeeding generations have risen to call him 'blessed of God'. His brother Charles is remembered for the ageless hymns he wrote, many of which are still sung today, but he was also a fearless evangelist, whose preaching was 'so tender, so pathetic, so full of convincing power'.[4] Lady Huntingdon deserves a place high on the list. Her 'soul glowed with a fervent faith' and her 'princely mansions were open with a tireless hospitality to everyone who loved her Lord'.[5]

There are others: William Grimshaw, a man who, in the words of Wesley, 'carries fire wherever he goes'; William Romaine, 'a great man, and a mighty instrument in God's hands for good', wrote J. C. Ryle;[6] John Berridge of Everton, whose 'life is a pattern to us all', remarked Henry Venn, 'and an incitement to love and serve the Lord with all our strength'.[7] Venn himself was described by his intimate friend Charles Simeon as having a character 'above all praise'. John Fletcher of Madeley was a man of 'rare grace and a minister of rare usefulness'.[8] John Wesley, not a man to exaggerate his praise, said of him: 'So unblameable a man, in every respect, I have not found, either in Europe or America, nor do I expect to find another such on this side of eternity.'[9] Then there is John Newton of Olney, deemed by William Jay as the 'most perfect instance of the spirit and temper of Christianity I ever knew ... with the addition of Cornelius Winter'.[10] James Hervey of Weston Favell 'used to speak of the love of the adorable Redeemer like one who had seen him face to face in the fulness of his glory', wrote Romaine in his tribute.[11] And Martin Madan, chaplain to the Lock Hospital in London, was a man distinguished by 'activity, zeal, gentleness of temper, love of study'.[12]

Among the English Dissenters the two leaders were Isaac Watts in London and Philip Doddridge at Northampton. William Cowper, writing to his wife on 18 April, 1766, said, 'I know no greater names in divinity than Watts and Doddridge.'[13] In Wales the two pioneers of the eighteenth century Christian Church were Howel Harris and Daniel Rowland. Of the former Martyn Lloyd-Jones wrote, he was 'a great man and a genius in a natural sense, a brilliant organiser and improviser ... but what amazes us and humbles us and condemns us is his humility and his utter submission to our Lord at all costs. This is why God used him in such a mighty manner.'[14] One of his biographers Hugh Hughes commented that he possessed 'qualities that entitle him to rank with the most heroic and saintly Reformers'.[15] According to Romaine, Rowland was 'the greatest minister in the whole world', and for Christmas Evans he was 'a star of the greatest magnitude ... and perhaps there has not been his like in Wales since the days of the apostles'.[16]

Geoffrey Nuttall made the point that 'Whether beneficed, itinerant or chaplains to Lady Huntingdon, whether Arminian or Calvinistic in doctrine, whether Dissenters or clergy of the Establishment, all these men and many others were working together – in no all-embracing organization, but in close bonds of friendship, correspondence and inter-visitation.'[17] Their love for Christ and for the souls of men, along with the gifts God had given them, united and empowered them to preach Christ and him crucified.

If the great Christians of Cornish origin are the topic of conversation, then two names immediately spring to mind. The first is Henry Martyn, born in Truro in 1781, whose father was a follower of Samuel Walker. Because of his translation of the Bible and Liturgy into Hindustani and the sufferings he endured, he is rightly remembered as one who 'forsook all for Christ'. 'His fear of God,' said John Sargent, 'and tenderness of conscience, and watchfulness over his own heart, could scarcely be surpassed in this state of sinful infirmity. But it was his humility that was most remarkable ... the warp of which the entire texture of his piety was composed.'[18] The second name is William Bray, whose motto was: 'Souls I must have, and souls I will have.' According to his biographer, 'No person in Cornwall, in the humbler ranks of life at least, was better known or more respected than Billy Bray.'[19]

One of the names that should be near the top of these lists is Samuel Walker, a man who is often undervalued in the history of the eighteenth century Evangelical awakening. The reasons are several: he never courted attention or sought preferment, happy as he was to remain as curate-in-charge; he seldom left his parish or preached abroad, as many clergymen did; he lived in an isolated and inaccessible part of the country, where, before the advent of the railway, travel was difficult and communications poor; he died at an early age; and his full biography was not written until some seventy years after his death.

The neglect of Walker is surprising when his life, the testimony of others, and the impact he had on many of the more prominent men of the revival, are examined. Skevington Wood, in reference to Walker's early ministry, regarded him as 'the real prophet of Evangelicalism in the West'. He went on: 'If any single figure in those pioneering days could be regarded as the chief, it would surely be Walker.' After admitting that his 'importance has all too often been overlooked by historians', he said that in this 'early period Evangelical clergymen everywhere looked to Walker for a lead'.[20] Elliot-Binns is of the same opinion. He stressed that the significance of Walker in the early days of Evangelicalism 'can scarcely be exaggerated'. Had the movement not been robbed of his services by his untimely death, it 'might have found unity and coherence much sooner than it did',[21] and Walker might have risen to become its leader, to whom all could look for guidance and inspiration.

In his biography of Walker, G. C. B. Davies commented: 'Few men exercised a greater or more lasting spiritual influence in a sphere limited to his own parish and immediate neighbourhood. As a pastor, teacher, and faithful servant of Christ, and the leader of the "awakened" clergy in that part of the country, his life and work can bear comparison with that of any incumbent of his day.'[22]

> He was one [wrote J. C. Ryle] who, in his day, was most highly esteemed by such men as Wesley, Whitefield, Romaine and Venn, for his eminent spirituality and soundness of judgement. Above all, he was one who cultivated his own corner of the Lord's vineyard with such singular success, that there were few places in England where such striking results could be shown from preaching the gospel as at Truro.[23]

Again, Bishop Ryle said, 'When the secrets of all ministries shall be disclosed, few will be found to have done better work for

Christ in their day and generation than Walker of Truro.'[24] His deliberate impression was that if Walker had been an itinerant he would probably have been 'reckoned one of the best preachers of his day',[25] while Charles Simeon regarded Walker's printed sermons as 'the best in the English language'.[26] In the eyes of the world his attainments may have been small, yet, said James Stillingfleet, he possessed 'in an eminent degree ... the knowledge, spirit, and zeal of a primitive Christian teacher'; a life that was 'rich in faith and good works', and that had 'learned to esteem the reproach of Christ greater riches than the treasures of Egypt'.[27]

In his preface to *The Star of the West*, James Bennett classed Walker with those who are 'dear to the memory of Christians in Britain'.[28] Thomas Wills called him 'that zealous and successful champion in the public cause of God ... whose name is had in remembrance, and his praise in all the churches, to this day; and will probably be until "time shall be no longer"'.[29] As if to reinforce Will's hope, Davies, in an article on Walker for the *Evangelical Magazine of Wales* (1961), after stating that his death was 'a severe loss to the Evangelical movement', urged the Anglican Church and Evangelicals in particular to remember 'with gratitude one whose devoted witness and service represent the finest example of parochial ministry'.[30] We shall now endeavour to do just that.

Samuel Walker was born at Exeter on 16 December, 1714, the same year as Howel Harris, William Romaine and James Hervey, and on the same day as George Whitefield. He was the fourth son and the seventh and youngest child of Robert and Margaret Walker. Robert Walker, of Withycombe Raleigh in Devon, 'a gentleman of some fortune in Exeter', was the only son of Sir Thomas Walker, who, with several generations of his family, represented Exeter in Parliament during the reigns of Charles I and II. Sir Thomas's wife Mary was the only daughter of Samuel Hall, the youngest son of Joseph Hall, who became

Bishop of Exeter on 23 December, 1627. He was later translated to the see of Norwich (15 November, 1641), where he
was 'at first received with considerable respect, and his
sermons attentively listened to'. But after the passing of the act
for sequestration of the property of malignants (April, 1643), in
which Hall was mentioned by name, he suffered financial straits
and other hardships before being ejected from his palace.[31] Hall,
a God-fearing man, was called by James Hervey 'the devout
and sprightly orator of his age',[32] and George Whitefield said
he 'would earnestly recommend [his works] to everyone'.[33]
Margaret Walker was the only daughter of Richard Hall, the
minister of St Edmund and All Hallows, Exeter.

Samuel's elder brother, Robert, is best remembered for his
manuscript collections about the history of Cornwall and Devon,
which at one time belonged to the baronet, antiquary and
bibliophile Sir Thomas Phillipps. Thomas Walker, another of
Samuel's brothers, was vicar of Lanlivery and a man of happy
temperament. R. Polwhele, in *Biographical Sketches in Cornwall*, said of him:

> He delighted in the feeling that he was at peace with himself
> and all around him. Uncommonly deformed as he was – his
> breadth equal to his length, like half a giant if a giant were
> cut in two with eyebrows black and bushy; – who, convers-
> ing with Mr W., could have thought of his uncomeliness –
> could not (I had almost said) have imagined him handsome?
> His habitual good humour, his facetiousness, his kind hearted-
> ness have seldom been equalled.[34]

The ecclesiastical historian John Walker, rector of St Mary
Major, Exeter, was also a relative of our subject. In 1714, the
year of Samuel's birth, he published a work entitled *An
Account of the Numbers and Sufferings of the Clergy*, which
was hailed by Thomas Bisse as 'a record which ought to be
kept in every sanctuary'.[35] In a letter to Thomas Adam, dated

9 February, 1758, Samuel Walker confirmed that his family was 'nearly related to that Dr Walker who wrote the *Sufferings of the Clergy*, so we stand up for the highest edition of the Church of England'.[36]

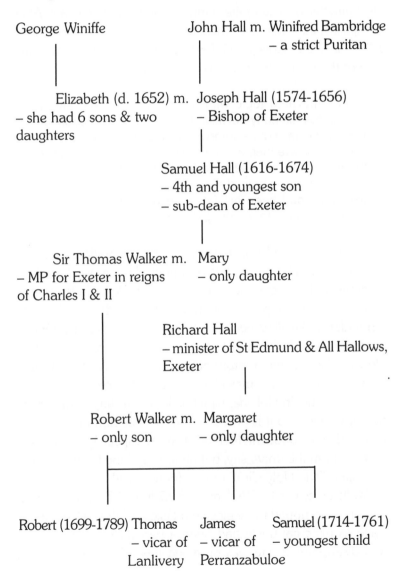

George Winiffe

John Hall m. Winifred Bambridge
– a strict Puritan

Elizabeth (d. 1652) m. Joseph Hall (1574-1656)
– she had 6 sons & two   – Bishop of Exeter
daughters

Samuel Hall (1616-1674)
– 4th and youngest son
– sub-dean of Exeter

Sir Thomas Walker m. Mary
– MP for Exeter in reigns   – only daughter
of Charles I & II

Richard Hall
– minister of St Edmund & All Hallows,
Exeter

Robert Walker m. Margaret
– only son   – only daughter

Robert (1699-1789) Thomas   James   Samuel (1714-1761)
– vicar of   – vicar of   – youngest child
Lanlivery   Perranzabuloe

For eight years Samuel Walker received parental tuition at home before going to Exeter Grammar School, where he was a contemporary of John Penrose, later his neighbour at St Gluvias, Penryn. There is no account of the education he received, of his character or way of life during these formative years. After ten years at the Grammar School he was enrolled on 4 November, 1732, at Exeter College, Oxford, where he was put under the care of the rector Dr Francis Webber. There

> ... he cultivated logic with much success, and always considered his early devotion to that study, as the foundation of the facility he afterwards attained in a clear and methodical arrangement of his ideas. When complimented by his friends, who admired the lucid and argumentative mode in which he treated every subject, he always observed that logic had been his favourite pursuit in youth, and recommended it to all young divines.[37]

At university he did not succumb to the temptations that surrounded him. He tried to live an upright life among his fellow students and concentrated on acquiring the knowledge necessary for his chosen profession in the Church. He soon became a popular and well respected member of the university. One of his friends was William Talbot, who became vicar of Kineton. He was also a contemporary at Oxford of the Wesleys, Whitefield, Romaine and James Hervey. John Wesley was Resident Fellow of Lincoln College, which is less than fifty metres from Exeter College, so it is probable that he saw him from time to time and heard about his Methodist group, especially as it caused quite a stir in the university, but there is nothing to suggest that he visited 'The Holy Club' or was friendly with its members.

Walker received his BA degree on 25 June, 1736. After graduating he had hoped to be elected a Fellow of the college, especially as his great-uncle had been a benefactor there, but he was disappointed. He was ordained towards the end of that year. At the time of his ordination he had no idea of the responsibilities and high-calling of such a sacred office, as he later admitted in a letter of advice to a young man, Mr Harris, about to take orders. The letter is dated 6 March, 1756:

> I remember the week before my ordination I spent with the other candidates, as dissolute I fear as myself, in a very light, indecent manner; dining, supping, drinking and laughing together, when God knows we should all have been on our knees, and warning each other to fear for our souls in the view of what we were about to put our hands to. I cannot but attribute the many careless, ungodly years I spent in pleasure after that time to this profane introduction; and, believe me, dear Sir, the review shocks me. While I write, I tremble in the recollection of the wounds I then gave Jesus.[38]

In the same letter he went on to explain that if he were to 'pass that awful transaction' again, it would be in a very different manner:

> I would be, as much as possible, alone in prayer and humiliation. If I could find none deeply impressed with the ordination, I would have nothing to do with them; or if I could find any, I should still take care to be mostly alone. I would, again and again, pray over many passages of Scripture relating to the ministerial office, particularly the epistles to Timothy and Titus, and also the ordination offices, both of them; I would pass two days of the week fasting; I would commit to paper all my present views, that I might have recourse to them. I would seek to obtain the most distinct and lively impressions of the importance of the ministerial office to God, myself and others; in short, I would do nothing the whole week, but what would dispose me, with all seriousness, sincerity and heartiness, so to undertake the office, as I should wish I had done when standing before the judgement.[39]

His first curacy, at the age of twenty-three, was Doddiscombsleigh, near Exeter, which he held until August

1738. He worked diligently to perform the duties of a pastor and his private character was said to be blameless, but there was no spiritual life in his own soul which he could pass on to others. He left Doddiscombsleigh after being invited by Lord Rolle to accompany his youngest brother through France as his companion and private tutor. During this year and a half on the Continent he enjoyed all the frivolous activities of an unregenerate socialite, in particular satisfying his love of music and dancing. About the time of his return from France he was invited by Lord Cathcart to accompany him and his son into Italy, but he refused 'on a piece of honour'.

On his return home he went to Lanlivery, near Lostwithiel, in Cornwall, as curate to his friend Nicholas Kendall, canon of Exeter and archdeacon of Totnes. When Kendall died on 3 March, 1740, Walker became vicar of the parish, to hold that position during the minority of a nephew of Walter Kendall, patron of the living. Upon Kendall's nephew coming of age, he resigned, and in midsummer 1746 he entered the curacy of Truro, where he was to remain until his death in 1761.

During the six years he spent at Lanlivery he was a diligent and conscientious pastor. He reproved, exhorted, catechized, visited and watched over his flock with the utmost care. He was regarded as a good preacher, whom the parishioners esteemed as a man of God and for the regularity and decency of his conduct, and he grieved over the fruitlessness of his spiritual vineyard. By affability and a readiness to communicate and listen he rendered himself approachable and popular. In appearance he was tall, with a commanding presence, handsome expressive features, and an air of authority that demanded respect. 'His countenance,' remarked one writer, 'indicated the possession of a calm but exalted understanding, and his conversation was replete with the piety of a saint, the information of a scholar, the judgement of a sage, and the courtesy of a gentleman.'[40] In a letter to Thomas Adam, dated 7 October,

1756, he mentioned that while at Lanlivery he 'narrowly escaped going to sea as a ship's chaplain with Captain Edgecumbe, at the insistence of Lord Edgecumbe, and had a greater escape from a very unpromising attempt for matrimony'.[41] There are no further details.

Although he received some glowing accounts of his ministerial labours, he knew that all was not as it seemed. In a letter written in November, 1754, to his friend Dr Guise in London, he looked back over the beginning of his ministerial career, with some reference to the wasted years he had spent before he moved to Truro:

> In the year 1746 I undertook (as Curate) the charge of this populous and large town [Truro], in many respects the principal town in the county. God knows upon what unworthy views I did it, and how utterly disqualified my heart and head were for my ministerial trust. I had been then some years vicar of a neighbouring parish. But, dear Sir, how must I have suffered the poor souls there to starve and perish, while I was only possessed of historical notions of all the vitals of Christianity; *the corruption of man's nature, his misery and helplessness, the satisfaction and sufficiency of CHRIST; the necessity of a renewed mind, the need of the work of the Spirit.* These I knew notionally, but neither felt nor taught them practically. You must own I ought to go sorrowing to the grave upon a review of six years so passed over. Nevertheless I was thought well of and indeed esteemed beyond most of my brethren for my regularity, decency and endeavours to keep up external attendances, and somewhat or other in my public addresses. Would to God I were the only one entrusted with the gospel in these circumstances![42]

In a *Letter from a Clergyman* concerning the first question in the office for the ordaining of deacons, which was published in 1758, he shared more details about his pre-conversion ministry. His honesty and clarity are striking:

1. *Was I led particularly to attend to and observe the necessities of the people about me?*
As I was ignorant of the salvation that is in Christ Jesus and of my want of him in all his offices, so I had not taken the least notice of the spiritual state of others. It was to me as a thing I had no concern with, that sins of the grossest kinds were committed on every side of me. And after I was ordained I had no sight or thought of the condition my parishioners were in, though I had some desire that they should come to church and sacrament, and not drink, swear and the like.

2. *In view of the people's want, was I led and effectually inclined to preach the word of God to them?*
Having no view of the people's real wants concerning their souls, this could not be a principle inclining me to preach the gospel to them. I had not any inclination arising from views of usefulness to others, disposing me to undertake the ministry; nor indeed, any other concern about the matter of preaching than that I must do it somehow or other as a Sunday's talk. I remember, that the day I was ordained deacon, my conscience was something alarmed and forced me to this resolution, that I would endeavour to do my duty as a clergyman. But my thoughts were altogether confused, and it lasted then the ordination hour only, though at seasons afterwards I found the like remonstrances, which drove me to something like diligence, the short time they were upon me.

3. *Was the sole end I had before me the glory of God in preaching his word for the recovery and salvation of the people about me or others?*
It is most evident from the former considerations, and I am fully convinced of it as a certain fact, that I had not any such thing in view. The ends engaging me to go into the ministry were that my friends designed me for it, that therein I should get a livelihood at least, but I was most particularly pleased with this thought: that when I had passed the examinations, and was once ordained, I should be out of all restraint, might do as I liked, and be my own master.

4. *Was I so determined upon this work, that I was not to be deterred from it by any apprehension of danger, want or reproach, which I foresaw or expected in general?*

I had not the slightest apprehension that any of these things were likely to come upon me, so ignorant was I of the nature of man and the gospel. I had never observed any such thing falling upon the clergy wherever I had been. I dreamt of no danger, feared not want, and concerning reproach it was far from my thoughts. I doubted not I should make such an appearance as to get the esteem and praise of the world. And truly, had I gone on as I began, living vainly, preaching smooth things and not fretting myself to the work in earnest, I had lived and died without suspicion that a minister of the gospel in the Church of England should run any hazard or reproach, or worse, for preaching her doctrines and labouring to lead his people into the practice of them.

After the most attentive review, I must freely own my case was no other nor better than this. Wherefore, I feel not the least shadow of ground to suppose 'I was inwardly moved by the Holy Spirit to undertake the ministry'. For this my most sinful presumption, and for my after behaviour in many succeeding years, confirming that God had not sent me, I ought to lie low in the dust the remainder of my days.[43]

In spite of his 'most sinful presumption' and the spiritual ignorance in which he carried on his ministry, he still made an effort to serve his parishioners at Lanlivery, as the following example illustrates. In 1744 he contracted a violent fever. Fearing that he might not recover he dictated a letter to a neighbouring gentleman, which he asked to be transcribed and given to certain of his parishioners, whose names he wanted the gentleman to take down. These parishioners had paid little attention to his preaching and private admonitions and, with this last remonstrance, he hoped to bring about the reformation of character he had been seeking. However, God was pleased to restore him to health and the letter was never sent.

In the same year as his illness he replied to the visitation queries of the bishop. In his report he gave a few details of the parish and the various duties he performed:

> The number of families is ninety-nine, of which there are no Dissenters, excepting one family consisting of two persons, and a single person in another family, who are Quakers. The house of the former is licensed, and the few Quakers in the neighbourhood usually meet there on Sundays, but have no teaching, unless occasionally by an itinerant preacher... There is no charity school or almshouse... I serve the parish myself, but do not reside in the vicarage house... I perform divine service on the days of Humiliation and Thanksgiving appointed by the Authority, and twice every Sunday, with a sermon in the morning. The holy sacrament of the Lord's Supper is administered five times in the year, of which twice at Easter. I catechize the children during Lent, and the parishioners carefully send them.[44]

He served at Lanlivery for another two years in his unconverted state before he settled in Truro,[45] where his private life and public ministrations were so wonderfully transformed. At Lanlivery he observed the outward modes of worship, performed acts of kindness and benevolence, which earned him the respect of others, and abstained from gross sins and scandalous vices; whereas at Truro, after he had been brought into the light of the gospel, he was filled with an earnest desire to be conformed inwardly and outwardly to the image of Christ, to renounce his own will if it in any way opposed God's will, to fight for the cause of truth regardless of the troubles it occasioned, to win souls for Christ and to live solely to the glory of God.

James Hervey

William Romaine

All three men were at
Oxford with Samuel
Walker and were born in
the year 1714

George Whitefield
(Nathaniel Hone)

Some of the learned and knowing among men have had those things revealed to them of the Father in heaven, which flesh and blood do not teach: and of these, some who had gone into the modern notions, and had no other than the polite religion of the present times, have had their prejudices conquered, their carnal reasonings overcome, and their understandings made to bow to gospel mysteries; they now receive the truth as it is in Jesus, and their faith no longer 'stands in the wisdom of man but in the power of God'...

The virtuous and civil have been convinced that morality is not to be relied on for life; and so excited to seek after the new birth, and a vital union to Jesus Christ by faith. The formal professor likewise has been awakened out of his dead formalities, brought under the power of godliness; taken off from his false rest, and brought to build his hope only on the Mediator's righteousness.

William Cooper. [1]

4

A Gradual but Remarkable Change

In July, 1746, at the age of thirty-one, Samuel Walker accepted the offer of the curacy of Truro from the absentee St John Eliot, who had been instituted to the rectory of that town on 3 June, 1746. Eliot had matriculated at the same Oxford College as Walker on 17 May, 1738, aged seventeen. In 1749 he became rector of Ladock, and he held both incumbencies until his death at the end of June, 1761, about three weeks before Walker died. He did not interfere with Walker so long as he was paid half the pew rents, fees and offerings punctually. This enabled his curate to work in the parish and conduct the services of the church according to his own principles.

At the time of Walker, Truro, 'that town of dissipation and notorious for its worldliness and frivolity', as Polwhele described it, had a population of about 1600. Richard Pococke on his travels through England in the middle of the eighteenth century called Truro

> ... a small trading town, in which there are many good houses; and many wealthy people live here, who have got considerable fortunes by the tin trade, and also several merchants and shop keepers who supply the country, the town being pretty much in the centre of the tin and copper mines; there is also a great trade in supplying the tin works with timber and the fire engines with coal. The church [St Mary's] is a most elegant building of about Henry the VIII's time.[2]

Daniel Defoe called Truro 'a very considerable town', with a large wharf in the front of it, where the water made a good port for small ships. He knew of at least three churches in the town, but had not heard of a Dissenter's meeting house. In the return of 1744 that Joseph Jane, then rector of Truro, sent to the Bishop of Exeter in answer to his visitation enquires, he mentioned six or seven Presbyterian or Independent families in the parish. He also stated that there were two services at St Mary's on Sundays, with 'a sermon in the morning, on all public festivals and fasts, on all Wednesdays and Fridays, and on Saturday evenings monthly; that he had a monthly celebration of the Holy Communion and on Christmas Day, Easter Day and Whit Sunday two communion services'; and that the children of the parish were 'publicly catechised in the church every Sunday in the afternoon after the second lesson from the beginning of Lent to the beginning of August or thereabout'.[3]

Walker was delighted with the opportunity of going to such a populous town as Truro, the centre of fashion for the county, with all its festivities and amusements, and he wasted no time in participating in them. During his first year, 'His only ambition seemed to be that he might be courted for his gaiety, admired for his eloquence, and become the reformer of the vicious by the power of persuasion and force of example.'[4] There was no thought of winning souls for Christ or of bearing the offence of the cross. In many private conversations with James Stillingfleet of Hotham, he said 'that he was not actuated by the least measure of a ministerial spirit at the time of his first coming to Truro; but that his only motive in going to live in that populous town, in preference to any other place in the country, was the greater resort of company, and that he might take his pleasure at the assemblies, and particularly in dancing'.[5] In his preaching, which was based on a good education and extensive reading of mainly unregenerate theologians, he expressed what he called 'speculative and historical notions' of the leading doctrines of the gospel, but 'neither felt nor taught them practically'.[6]

One of the problems Walker encountered during the first year of his curacy was the question of his inadequate stipend, which had to be increased by voluntary subscriptions. Once a year he had to 'collect in the town'; that is, go from house to house, among the principal inhabitants, asking for money in order to boost his income, an ordeal he for years dreaded. But by 1757 he had overcome many of his apprehensions. On Wednesday 30 March of that year, he wrote in his diary, 'Tomorrow I am to collect in the town. Am I ashamed of that employment? Not as once. Am I afraid of the treatment I may perhaps meet? The thought has not been much on my mind. Am I prepared for a repulse? I should be careful neither to indulge anger nor distain.'[7] He also profited from an order of the Truro Corporation, dated 3 April, 1747, 'that £22 should be paid to the Rev Mr Walker, minister of the borough of Truro', £10 for a year's gift sermons and a further £12 donated by the borough, annually on the 9 November, 'until some further order be made herein'. However, it is clear that throughout his ministerial career he suffered financially. In a letter to Thomas Adam (9 March, 1757), he remarked:

> I am a curate, and by necessity a housekeeper, in a very dear country. I pay too much to my principal [probably for house rent] to make my own circumstances altogether suffi- cient, though I keep, by the way, on the right side of nothing. Were my income a little augmented, it would enable me to use more horse exercise, and at the same time to get assistance when I should need it.[8]

Basil Woodd recorded that Walker used to say in his later years: 'I have nothing to support me but the curacy of Truro. If I out- live my strength for this service, I am, as a parishioner, entitled to the workhouse, where I can still serve God and enjoy his service. Besides, I may still administer instruction and consola- tion to my fellow-paupers.'[9]

The remarkable change in life and doctrine that was wrought in Walker did not come about through the workings of his own imagination or the influence of high-ranking friends, but from a deep conviction, founded upon the word of God, that he had been acting from wrong principles. He found that his best deeds 'were full of sin in themselves and the result of bad or mistaken motives', and that in himself there was an 'absence of every-thing spiritually good, and a propensity to what is evil'. He saw that a corrupted nature lay at the bottom 'of those very actions which had gained him the applause of men' and 'had defiled and rendered them blameworthy in the sight of God'.[10]

This inward knowledge of himself, which led to his conversion from a pleasure-seeking curate to a devoted servant of Christ, was mainly brought about through his friendship with George Conon, headmaster of the grammar school at Truro from 1728-1771. Conon was a Scotsman, born in Aberdeen in 1701, and a Presbyterian layman, who graduated from Marischal College, Aberdeen University, in 1721. He arrived at the Truro school when its standards and reputation were low, superseding Joseph Jane, who remained rector of Truro until his death in 1745.

Conon, a 'rare and devoted Christian' and an outstanding teacher, soon raised the standards of the school and all the gentlemen's sons in the middle and western part of Cornwall were sent to Truro to be instructed by him. He paid close atten-tion to Christian morals and education, particularly on the Lord's Day, 'when divine worship was held twice, and the evening given over to learning the most useful catechisms', which he himself had devised. Joseph Jane recorded in 1744 that the boys in the school were 'carefully instructed in the principles of Christianity according to the doctrine of the Church of England and are brought daily to church, as the Canon requires'.[11]

Under Conon's tuition Thomas Haweis 'made rapid progress and distinguished himself both in Latin and Greek'. 'To his honour I wish to record it,' Haweis wrote in his autobiography, 'that his diligence to make us scholars was equalled by his zeal to make us Christians.' After his conversion Haweis was always thankful for his tuition: 'For the clear and unchanging views of divine truth which I have been favoured with ever since, I acknowledge myself much indebted to the instructions of my excellent master.'[12] Thomas Wills in 1755/56 was also placed under the care and tuition of Conon, during which time he had the 'privilege ... of sitting under the ministry, and frequently being permitted to visit that blessed man' Samuel Walker.[13] Another of Conon's pupils stated that his tutor's 'manners were not polished, but his worth was sterling'.[14]

Conon's openness in sharing the gospel with his pupils eventually led the corporation to withhold his settled stipend for many years and to the loss of nearly all his scholars, but he 'bore hostility with the truest Christian resignation, and carried himself with dignity and mildness that would have disarmed the rancour of all enemies, but such as abhor the image of the Saviour'. At a time when he was severely ill he spoke of the school and the treatment he had received in a letter, remarking: 'I am engaged in honour and conscience to do all I can for the good of [the school] and the public, and have forgotten, and most heartily forgiven all former bad treatment and even present unkindness.'[15]

It was a terrible shock when his friend and minister Samuel Walker died. Coupled with other circumstances that occurred later on, Walker's death caused him to move to Padstow, where he sat under the ministry of Thomas Biddulph,[16] with whom he became close friends, and where he taught a select group of students grammar, the Latin and Greek languages, and the first principles of the Christian religion, 'which he made it his constant practice on the Lord's Day evenings to explain and enforce with clearness and energy, during the whole year, while the children were under his care'.[17] He so enjoyed teaching that he often expressed the wish that, if it pleased God, he should die while so employed, and that suddenly. His wish was granted. 'One Saturday evening [27 May, 1775], after endeavouring to prepare the youthful minds of his scholars for the solemnities of the coming Sabbath, he earnestly prayed for a blessing on his labours, when suddenly the stoke of death silenced his voice of supplication, and changed it for that of ceaseless thanksgiving in the regions of eternal praise.'[18] He was buried in Padstow churchyard and his tombstone bore a Latin inscription believed to have been written by his friend George Burnett.

J. C. Ryle commented that 'Conon was one of those rare servants of God who, like Job, are found in places where you think no good thing could grow, and who serve to show that grace and not place makes the Christian.'[19] Skevington Wood called him 'at once a scholar and a saint', and Nicholas Carlisle spoke of him as 'a sound grammarian' and 'a Christian both in faith and practice'.[20] A letter he wrote from Truro to George Burnett on 19 June, 1766, while suffering a 'feverish disorder', well exemplifies the spiritual tenor of his mind:

> This late indisposition, I trust, has been and will be a great blessing to me. I valued health too much ... it pleased the Lord to show me feelingly, and in great mercy, the frailty and uncertainty of it. It was a gentle chastisement. I saw my heavenly Father's hand in it. I wanted it, and was enabled to kiss the rod and the hand that sent it. I bless my God in Jesus Christ, in whose merits alone was all my hope and confidence, for his inward support under it. I had more awful and solemn views of eternity than I ever had before. A sense of the love and goodness of God to me a vile sinner, through all my life, has frequently since overwhelmed me... Join with me ... in praising the Lord for all his goodness, but especially for his late mercy to me, the most unworthy of all his servants.[21]

'He knew but little of the world here below,' remarked Thomas Wills, 'but he was deeply versed in the things of the world to come... The great day only will disclose how very useful he was made, though not a minister, to some who were in that sacred office.'[22]

Walker's friendship with Conon began in an unusual way. Walker received a letter from the Truro school teacher in which there was an apology for troubling him and a sum of money, with instructions for him to take the money to the custom house and pay the duty on some French wines which he had purchased for the sake of his health. The wines had been smuggled into the country and sold to him duty free. Conon, uneasy at the thought of evading taxes, sought the assistance of Walker, whose reputation was such that he would be above suspicion of fraudulent dealings. Curious to meet a man with so tender a conscience and of such scrupulous honesty, Walker made the writer's acquaintance, and the outcome was a lasting and intimate friendship between them, in which the former never took any step of importance in the management of his parish, without first asking the latter's advice.

About a year after moving to Truro, when Walker was in the company of some friends, George Conon probably among them, and their conversation

... turned upon the nature of justifying and saving faith, he [Walker], as he freely owned afterwards, became sensible that he was totally unacquainted with that faith which had been the topic of the discourse, and also convinced that he was destitute of something which was of the greatest importance to his own as well as to the salvation of the people committed to his charge. He said nothing at that time of the concern he was brought under to any one of the company, but was ever afterwards, as opportunity offered, ready to enter upon the subject. He began to discover that he had hitherto been ignorant of the nature of gospel-salvation,

inattentive to the spiritual state of his own soul and the souls
of others, and governed in all his conduct not by the only
Christian motives of love to God and man, but purely by
such as were wholly sensual and selfish; he found that he
was a slave to the desire of man's esteem; and in short, as
he himself expressed it, that all had been wrong both within
and without.[23]

In a letter written to Dr Guise, he mentioned this dramatic if
gradual transformation:

It was at least a year after the kind providence of God brought
me hither, ere I fell under considerable suspicions or
uneasiness about myself and my manner of preaching; when
by the frequent conversation of a Christian friend [George
Conon] (verily the first person I had met with truly possessed
of the mind of Christ), I became sensible all was wrong within
and without. My uneasiness was rather abiding than violent,
possibly because my life had been free of gross sins, having
been used in a good measure to follow the direction of my
conscience, and the change wrought upon me was slow, till
under a variety of means I was brought to the knowledge of
the truth as it is in Christ Jesus.[24]

In later years, when he reflected on 'those days of blindness',
he could plainly see the motives behind his actions. After a
meeting of neighbouring clergymen, who met for religious
conversation, he said that he had lived for many years entirely
ignorant of a sinful nature, and though he had lived by certain
external standards of decency and regularity, he was 'influenced
by and acted upon two hidden principles', which were 'as
contrary to God as darkness is to light'. The first and dominant
principle was

... a prevailing desire of reputation and being esteemed,
which went through all I did, followed me into all companies,
dictated all I said, led me to compliance often in direct

> opposition to conscience, made me above all things fearful of being thought little of, directed all my sermons both in writing and in speaking them, and in short swayed my whole life.[25]

He struggled, more or less, with this temptation for the rest of his life. As late as 1756 he wrote in his diary for Tuesday 27 April: 'I have found myself this day greatly exercised by fear of men' and 'I experience a lurking desire of man's esteem,' which, when combined with his 'natural timidity', made him inwardly shrink back from any approaching trial in which he had to 'look in the face of persons of an angry and violent temper'.

> It is [he went on] to the free and mighty influence of the Spirit of God I owe it, that this fear has not dominion, and that in despite of it, I am enabled to persist in the ways of God and the discharge of my duties in opposition to this secret enemy. Yet I have reason to suspect that though it does not hinder me from doing, yet it cramps me in doing. I desire to wait with patience, to be humbled, to be thankful for the measure of liberty bestowed on me, and to believe always that his grace is sufficient for me.[26]

Again, in his diary for 1757, he lamented the 'desire of esteem' that rested upon his heart, and which evidenced itself in various ways:

> Among triflers it would make me light; and in a large company it would constrain my conduct that I might not be singular. It has a general influence, that wherever I am, and whatever I do, I am too much biased by it. Indeed I find it difficult beyond measure, to act with that freedom and particularity I ought in a wicked world. Beset with such an enemy, 'tis no wonder I am often deceived, and seldom act up as I ought, when brought to the trial. This has been my most obstinate adversary all along. The Lord deliver me speedily out of the hands of such a betrayer of his interest, and disturber of my peace! [27]

On Friday 25 April he wrote: 'I ought ... not to be biased by the
fears or esteem of an opposing world, as I find my corrupt heart
would needs be; and by which I am so far influenced, as, though
not to make much compliance, yet not to act up to the character
of a zealous Christian and minister.' And on Thursday 12 May
he grieved over 'the coldness and cowardice of my heart...
When shall I have zeal that will set me above the apprehensions of frowns? For 'tis men's furious faces I chiefly dread.'[28] In
a letter to Risdon Darracott, written on 15 December, 1757, he
again condemned himself:

> Could you see the bottom of me, you would see everything
> a man would abhor, particularly pride with two heads taller
> than the rest, I mean desire of esteem, and secret
> self-applause. These monsters continually thrust in their faces
> whichever way I look, and wherever I am they are sure to be
> of the company. Pretty often indeed they receive a stunning
> knock on the head, and then I seem to get rid of them a little,
> but even then I never look back but I see them dogging
> me.[29]

Occasionally, as intimated above, he felt a measure of victory
over this besetting sin. On Monday 11 April, 1757, when he
heard unexpectedly that he must meet his parishioners, he
panicked, writing in his diary, 'I am weak as water. When shall
I be able to look the world in the face? Surely, while possessed
with such animal fears, I am in perpetual danger of disgracing
my profession.' By the following day he was more at peace:
'My prayer has been heard, and I am in some sort delivered
from the fears of men.'[30]

The second 'hidden principle' that influenced his pre-
conversion ministry was 'a desire of pleasure, which rendered
me slothful, indolent, and restless out of company, eager after
amusements'. However, this desire was so subordinate to the
other that he had delighted in those entertainments in which he

excelled and could impress others, such as music and dancing. Both these principles had so ruled his heart that he felt at ease with them and regarded them as an innocent part of the life of a minister. These feelings of 'peace' were strengthened when he considered his own moral lifestyle, his attendance upon 'the forms of my ministry', and how he encouraged others to do the same.[31]

In the early months of his 'true Christian experience', he found it difficult to cast aside his previous way of life.

> Were I to say [he wrote some years later] with how many heart-felt pangs of fear and disquietude I have been brought during these latter years to any reasonable measure of indifference about the esteem of the world, I should describe the passages which have most engrossed my mind. The love of pleasure decayed first, but yet I could only part with it by degrees. And many things of that sort I continued in, when I had no pleasure in them, because I was ashamed to leave them.[32]

At length he decided to turn his back on worldly amusements and his former companions and to devote himself to the ministry in accordance with the new spiritual life he experienced. He applied himself diligently and with fervent prayer to the study of the Scriptures, 'to be a good Bible Divine', to use his own phrase, and was careful to assert nothing that was not found therein. However, he did not come to a mature knowledge of the truth overnight. He grew gradually in an understanding of the gospel and learned little by little to apply its message to his hearers' hearts.

One of the first sermons he preached after his 'enlightenment' was from Matthew 18:7: 'Woe unto the world because of offences! for it must needs be that offences come; but woe to that man by whom the offence cometh!' He had already preached this sermon on two previous occasions: on 7 December, 1746, and at St Olave on 5 April, the following year. The third occasion was at Truro on 9 October, 1748, some time after he had become suspicious and uneasy about himself and his manner of preaching. The sermon is clearly deficient in Evangelical application, without any explanation of the cause or remedy of human depravity, and is more like a moral address than a gospel sermon. He condemned outward immoralities and professors of Christianity who fail to practise their religion, admonished all who neglect attendance at communion, and declared: 'There seems to be a general conspiracy in the cause of wickedness, by which every man, one would think, was engaged to entice his neighbour into the unchristian practices which the world in one shape or other is guilty of.'[33] He uncovered the problem but offered no solution.

But as he grew in grace and in the knowledge of God he became convinced that the word of God is 'the only sure ground of a divine faith', that it uncovered 'the nature of man's spiritual disorder', and that in the gospel the remedy is supplied. In his preaching he condemned the empty pleasures in which his parishioners were involved and exposed the danger of resting on the mere formalities of Sabbath worship for salvation rather than on Christ. Repentance, faith and the necessity of the new birth became the doctrines of his new forthright sermons, joined with urgent appeals to turn from the wrath to come.

> Do you consider this, you who are yet in your sins, labouring after the meat that perishes, drudging in the nastiness of lust; you that are proud and high-minded and selfish; you that are lovers of pleasure, living without God in the world? Do you know that you are never the better for that Christ has died for you, rather much the worse – heirs of a blacker destruction, seeing you have denied so much grace and mercy! And you, too, who are setting up a religion of your own, who conceit that you are well enough, because you are not altogether so abandoned as your neighbour; you who content yourselves with doing no harm, and you who satisfy yourselves with the outside, the formality of holiness; whilst

you have never discovered the hidden iniquities of your hearts, nor put on the power of godliness; and you also who are at a stand, easy with just so much holiness as you imagine will carry you to heaven... Do you know that none of you have repented![34]

He then went on to show the true nature of repentance, how it 'convinces us of utter sinfulness ... brings us down to the dust, and makes us feel that we are nothing, and can do nothing to deliver ourselves'. It causes us to hate sin and to delight in holiness, to do all things, be they great or small, to the glory of God, and to be 'ready and zealous to every good word and work towards him and our neighbour. Such a repentance is the only proof that we have an interest in Christ.'[35]

It is hardly surprising that such preaching stirred up enmity against him, especially from his former associates. To hear him 'denouncing the very practices in which he had lately indulged himself, and pressing home the very doctrines which he had neglected or despised, was enough to make men's hair stand on end!'[36] His parishioners were shocked at this change in their minister. His choice of subjects and the manner of his address were offensive to them and they reacted against them. 'Hatred as an enthusiast, derision as a madman, and vehement opposition as the destroyer of harmless joys' were levelled at him. 'An infidel even went so far as to insult him in the pulpit, an affront he bore with extraordinary patience and dignity.'[37] In his own words he described the change that was taking place in himself and the effects it had upon his people:

By and by I began to deal with them as lost sinners, and beat down formality and self-righteousness, and to preach Christ. The fruit of this, by the mighty working of the Spirit, quickly appeared. It was a new way to them. They were surprised and grew angry, not without an evident fear resting upon them, and an interesting curiosity to hear me again on this matter.[38]

James Stillingfleet, in a summary of this part of Walker's experience, said:

> The work of grace went on gradually in his own soul. Nor was it without much self-denial and opposition to his fears and his connections in life, that he began to declare to others the convictions which had newly impressed his heart. Being caressed by all companies, wherever he went, as a man of good understanding and good manners, he was called upon to give up many of the choicest comforts of this life for the sake of the gospel; because he evidently foresaw that, unless his former companions should be brought to experience the same change which he had entered upon, they would at least look cool upon him, if not separate him from their company, or perhaps cast a slur upon his reputation. How great a trial this is to a man who is naturally fond of esteem, those only can be proper judges, who have themselves been under the same difficult circumstances. Yet in spite of every carnal and selfish motive, which the love of ease, the apprehensions of shame, or the fear of men's faces might suggest to the contrary, the Lord preserved him faithful to the light he had received, and emboldened him to make an open and unreserved profession of the truth, in proportion as he himself became acquainted with it.[39]

At length, the earnestness of his preaching and the striking reformation of his character, which was in unison with his precepts, produced a deep effect on many who knew him, and those who had at first railed against him grew silent out of respect. The crowds that soon attended his ministry were so large that the town appeared deserted during the hours of service. 'You might fire a cannon down every street of Truro in church time,' it was remarked, 'without a chance of killing a single human being.' Even out of the pulpit his presence was feared. When Sabbath loiterers saw him approaching, they said, 'Let us go, here comes Walker.'[40] The theatre and cock-pit were forsaken and given over to other uses and similar reforms extended to other parts of the neighbourhood through his instrumentality. When Walker looked back six years later, as far as he could judge, he thought that almost all of his hearers had been 'one time or another awakened more or less, although I fear many of them have rejected the counsel of God against themselves'.[41]

His first convert, in 1748, was a young soldier in the regiment raised by Lord Falmouth. This man had lived an immoral life, but was 'awakened and brought under great terrors' under one of Walker's sermons. Walker called him 'my first and as such my dearest child', and watched and rejoiced over him as a father over a son.

> His conduct [said Walker] drew the attention of the whole town. God left him about a year and a half with me; during which time, with an unshakeable firmness of faith and constancy in conduct, amidst perpetual oppositions and the strife of tongues, he lived, I trust, a Christian.
>
> About the end of that year, some other young men, convinced perhaps by his example, applied to me. And before his death, which was in June, 1750, their number was considerably enlarged; and both men and women, for the most part young persons, had some great concern about salvation.
>
> But I think the principal work began immediately upon his death, which begat a visibly anxious distress upon the whole town. I judged a sermon requisite upon such an occasion. The blessings of the Spirit were remarkably with the providence and word.[42]

As the numbers of enquirers steadily increased, so Walker had to consider carefully the most appropriate way forward.

Let it be my endeavour to deal with the hearts, rather than the heads, of sinners; and only to apply to their heads, so as to influence their hearts. This I am sure is the plain Scripture way.

An extract from Walker's diary for Monday 21 March, 1757.[1]

I would improve opportunities of serving Christ in the conversion of sinners. There is much knowledge of the way, at least in many; and Jesus is at least exalted in the mouth of such as yet do not appear to be closed with him.

An extract from Walker's diary for Wednesday 13 April, 1757.[2]

This being a public day, I have had occasion to see how the world lies in sin and security. I find nothing like the least sense of God in the hearts of most. This sight convinces me, nothing but the gospel preached can revive practical religion.

An extract from Walker's diary for Wednesday 20 April, 1757.[3]

5

Two Schemes of Private Instruction

After the funeral of Walker's first convert, the numbers that applied to him daily were so large that he was obliged to rent two rooms a fair distance from his lodging in the town in order to hold private conversations about spiritual things with them. Later, when he had his own house, he talked with them at home. In his letter to Dr Guise he described the work of God in the hearts and lives of these inquirers:

> The far greater part have been brought to the acknowledgement of the truth in a very gentle way. Very few have been struck into terrors, though some have. The most have been impressed with a sort of mournful uneasiness, and have been brought to Christ in a sorrowing kind of way. I have reason to believe their convictions have been deep, for though many have drawn back, yet I cannot find above one or two who have been able to this day to shake them quite off. Those whose convictions are most lively and lasting, have importunate desires after inward holiness, striving against indwelling sin.[4]

In the same letter to his friend in London, he gave further details of what he did when 'some more sensibly pricked in their hearts' came to him inquiring what they must do.

> The number of these [inquirers] continually increasing, I thought my utmost diligence was needful towards them. They were universally ignorant in the grossest degree. I was glad

to give them as many evenings in the week as I could spare, appointing them to attend me, after their work was over, at my house. As there was no knowledge of divine things amongst them, and in consequence thereof they were incapable of instructing one another; and withal, as they were marked out by reproach, and had every art tried upon them to draw them away, they needed from me both instructions and cautions, which I was obliged for these reasons to give them, either singly, or by two or three together. This I have continued to do to the present time, with no variation but that of using the help of those who had made any progress, to watch over beginners.

I had from the first engaged them frequently to converse together, and pray with one another, as I could put them together; and though the far greater part of them fell away from their awakenings, yet when a number of them seemed to be somewhat confirmed, they of their own accord met together in larger bodies in their own houses, to read God's word, pray, sing psalms, &c. This became pretty much practised about two years ago, and herein I have left them to themselves, only giving them directions as need required.[5]

Rather than relying on the thought of the moment, Walker drew up extensive plans for their systematic instruction. He devised two 'schemes of private instruction in the Christian religion', both of which exhibit his deep knowledge of the human heart and of the operations of the Holy Spirit that lead to salvation. The first is divided into three sections – conviction, faith and repentance – and supposes that the person seeking instruction 'is awakened to some general concern about his soul'.

Section one opens by saying that the inquirer must be 'brought to some sense of his guilt, and being liable to the wrath of God, without any refuge in himself'. Right at the beginning of the instruction Walker thought it useful to

... state the case of man generally, as born in sin and a child of wrath; and also to speak of that gracious and all-sufficient remedy provided in the gospel, both of them as certain truths on the authority of God's word, though acknowledged by none to good purpose, unless, and until, the Holy Spirit works them into the heart. The design of this caution is, that the encouragement of the promise may go along with conviction of sin. This is the Scripture way; repentance and remission are declared together.[6]

Birth-sin must then be carefully disclosed and in such a way as to show that man is 'by nature proud, and carnal, and filthy in the flesh and spirit'. Naturally we love this world because it is so suited to our natural inclinations. Our wills are perverted and biased against God, so that we are '*unwilling* and *averse*' to do any part of his will or to submit to his dispensations. We are 'entirely selfish' and our great aim is not to please him but ourselves. Thus the heart of man is 'naturally full of all manner of wickedness', and from there has sprung all the actual sins of omission and commission, which every man on earth has committed.

However, because the conscience is commonly awakened first by a sense of grosser sins, it is proper to begin with 'the *outward fruits* of birth-sin', to expose the general forgetfulness of God in which the person has lived; and then, when the conscience is more tender, to take occasion from the fruits to show the principle and cause in corrupt nature; 'which is not effectually done till he has such experience of himself as readily to trace every outward sin to the corruption which gave cause to it, and is completely acquainted with the whole body of sin'. This is true self-knowledge. With adults it is advisable to argue from the *effect* to the *cause*, but with the young it is often better the other way.

When the person's natural pride begins to make excuses, his conscience must be appealed to – 'he *practised* what he knew to be sin' – and his personal guilt insisted on. He must be taught to 'search after his sins', depending on the Holy Spirit, who convinces of sin, and he must be made sensible of the Scriptural promises relating to prayer and pressed continually on the matter. At the same time, something may be said of God's perfections, especially his holiness, justice and presence. He must be questioned about what sense he has of his sins or his heart – 'whether it be *abiding, with a desire to know more of them*, and full of concern' – and warned against those things that will lessen the impression and stop the work of the Spirit, 'as ill company, trifling conversation, amusement, above all, sloth in prayer and delay'.

The consequence of all this, the curse and wrath of God, must be fully opened next, without reason or argument, 'but the plain declarations of Scripture only insisted on'. If there is any resistance, he must be set to seek further into the sense of sin. Full conviction has only come when he can 'acquit God of cruelty should he cast him into hell, saying from the bottom of his heart, God has threatened sin with death, but *I deserve* to die'. If this is not fully acknowledged at this stage, 'there will be much leaning to self-righteousness perhaps ever after'.

The inquirer must be made sensible of these two things:

> First, that no future obedience, however perfect, could render God satisfaction for the sin he has done, to deliver him from the threatened wrath. Secondly, that by reason of the perverse bias of his will ... he has not the least power of his own to return to God and to serve him.
>
> Thus *full* in every particular must his conviction be, that the pride of his heart may be altogether beaten down ... and the way made plain and open for the Redeemer.[7]

Walker closed the first section by saying that though he had set out this work methodically, many 'workings of faith will often be discovered in the progress of *conviction*', for the 'Spirit works as he will and there is great variety'.

Once the sinner has been brought to a 'due sense of his guilt, danger and helplessness', he is ready to hear the promises of God. This is the opening to the second section.

The inquirer must be set to search out the Scriptures, with much prayer for the Spirit, so that he can come to a firm persuasion of Christ's sufficiency, which for a convinced sinner 'is the hardest thing in the world, and that also which the artifices of the devil will be above all things opposing'. The following must be observed by the instructor:

a. That the sinner does not deceive himself 'by a supposed conviction of the truth', which is based on merely human foundations such as he has 'always heard it was true, has been taught to assent to it from youth, nobody seems to doubt it, it is one of the articles of his belief, and all good people believe it'.

b. That the only ground of faith is God's word on which his belief must be built.

c. That there is a natural unbelief in his heart of Christ's sufficiency, which he cannot subdue by his own strength.

d. That it is the Holy Spirit who must show him Christ in the Scriptures. 'In opening this point, he must be made to see the purposes of God before the world to save sinners by a Redeemer, and the promises consequent to and issuing from that purpose.' He must be shown

> ... the fitness of the Redeemer in his double nature, his obedience to death, with the design, fulness and proofs of his atonement, his exaltation, dominion and intercession. He must be made sensible how, in the execution of this merciful contrivance, Christ has magnified the law, satisfied divine justice, taken away the curse; and how, the scheme being purposed at the instance of God's infinite good will towards sinners, planned by his infinite wisdom, and actually engaged for by repeated promises, all the perfections of God, his love, wisdom, truth and faithfulness, stand at stake for the performance of the whole and every part of it.[8]

Secondly, he must be 'assured of Christ's *willingness* to be his Saviour, and so be encouraged to make application to him'. Thirdly, he must see that

> ... this only is the way of salvation, and that the faithful God does certainly forgive and take into his favour all self-condemned sinners, who come to him by Jesus Christ, and that for Christ's sake only... Here the sinner must be guarded against self-righteousness, must be shown the workings of it in his heart, in those complainings he makes of the want of sensible and particular frames, which he seeks for to substitute them in place of Christ... This lies couched under the common expression, 'God for Christ's sake will forgive us our sins with *true repentance*'... [Here] repentance is made *the cause* of God's forgiveness, and is put in the place of Christ.[9]

At this point the person to be instructed must not try to understand the precise nature of justifying faith in case he is perplexed with notions or tempted to speculate. Nor is it important for him to know the time he first believed, though the instructor should be clear 'that it is such a persuasion of Christ's sufficiency, as determines the heart to rest wholly upon him, should separate in his own idea of it faith from feeling, faith from sight, faith from the fruits and proofs of it'. In all things the person to be instructed must be brought 'at all times and in all cases, in all frames, high as well as low, and low as well as high, in all attainments, and in all spiritual temptations to rest on Christ only, and so to give God glory by believing'.

Particular care must be taken that his faith is grounded 'only on God's declarations in the Scriptures', and so to this end the instructor must bring out the Scriptures 'on all occasions, making the express word of God suited to the case, the foundation of his advice and direction', without party prejudices.

The third section deals with the fruit of faith, that is, repentance, 'which is the heart choosing God in Christ as a master and portion, and refusing the services of sin and the delights and confidences of the world, and which is also called *conversion*. This must be distinguished from sanctification, 'which is the carrying forward by the Spirit that which was begotten in the soul by the fruit of repentance or conversion'. The person to be instructed must be made 'diligently and continually to attend to and regard what that mystery of redeeming love presents to him, in order that it may have a converting and sanctifying influence upon his heart'.

The instructor, if he is to manage this matter rightly, must have deeply experienced these things in his own heart and well digested them in his head. He must know that 'The real motive to delighting in God, and choosing his service, and the true ground of a due sense of the sinfulness of sin, of self-abasement, hatred of sin and actual rejecting it, is an *evangelical* sight of God.' When the Spirit impresses on the heart a sense of sin, rather than turning the sinner away, 'He drives him to Christ for mercy, and by enabling him to believe that God in Christ is a merciful, gracious and desirable God, does engage the heart to turn and daily to return to him.'

As to conversion, the self-condemned sinner must diligently pray for 'clear discoveries of God's love and compassion in Christ'; and, as he is made to grow into them, he will 'prefer God's favourable countenance to all manner of carnal delights, and the doing God's will to the following of his own'. Two cautions should be in the mind of the instructor at this point:

a. 'That no other motive can convert the heart but an evangelical sight of God.'

b. 'That inasmuch as conversion lies in the will, neither knowledge on the one hand, nor sense on the other, can be mistaken for it.' The deceived sinner will either rest on his knowledge of the gospel or in those passionate emotions and feelings that are often produced when gospel truths are first discovered to an awakened sinner. These strong affections are not to be discouraged, but dealt with wisely. Perhaps the safest way will be for the instructor to say little about them, and to go on describing conversion and sanctification.

Secondly, sanctification, which is a progressive work that 'contains the daily renewal of the graces on the one side, and the daily mortification of the body of sin on the other'. Three things must be noted:

a. The motive of sanctification is 'a sense on the heart of God's love towards sinners in Christ'. When this is lost, sanctification stops and, as we are apt to lean on the work of sanctification in us, we lose sight of Christ our righteousness. But when God's pardoning love is kept in sight, sanctification goes forward in us and we are kept sensible to the fact that we are not admitted to stand before God but in the merits of Christ.

b. The work itself is the 'growing up of the graces and the mortification of the lusts', the latter being a consequence of the former.

c. The means of sanctification are 'self-examination, prayer, the word and meditation'. The fruit of these exercises will not only be 'a growing sense of our vileness, but also a discovery of our insufficiency, by reason of the power of sin abiding in us, either to do good or resist evil, and so a more steadfast living by the power of Christ'.

Sanctification goes on with many discouragements, which are used by the Spirit to humble the heart, 'showing us our sinfulness and nothingness, and so bringing us to a more entire dependence on Christ'. These discouragements must be used by the instructor to show the person 'his exceeding sinfulness and insufficiency manifest therein'; to convince him of the unbelief of his heart; to stir him up to seek a 'stronger persuasion of Christ's power to justify the ungodly'; and to 'guard him against impatience and murmuring, because he is a corrupted creature', which tempts him to forget the 'free gifts already received, or does more dishonour to the faithfulness and power of God to fulfil his promises in Christ'.

On the other hand, there will also be consolations. From time to time the Spirit will be making gracious visits and 'witnessing to his work in the soul'. These times will be 'accompanied by deep abasement and thankfulness, and will be followed by a more zealous and close walking'. However, they must not take the place of Christ or be made an occasion of pride or security.

These three things, 'conviction, faith, and its fruit in conversion and daily sanctification, constitute a Christian'. In all that is taught, this general object must be kept in view: 'to humble the sinner and exalt the Redeemer', by leading the former out of himself to Christ in everything.

Walker concluded his first scheme of private instruction with a word concerning the communion, that only the truly converted are qualified to partake of it. But so that they will not rest on it, it should be a year after their first awakenings and then only under the direction of their instructor, who ought to be satisfied that they have a 'good work begun in them'.[10]

Walker wrote a 'Second Scheme of Private Instruction in the Christian Salvation', which appeared in the Christian Guardian for November, 1802, published at Bristol. It is a simplification of the first scheme and is set out in an interrogatory form for the use of his assistants. It is not necessary to work through it in full. The opening four sections only are presented below:

I. *To beget a sense of guilt and condemnation.*

(1) *You are a sinner;* either have lived careless and unconcerned about God, never having set in earnest about the business of religion; or else your own conscience will tell you, that you have many sins of omission and commission to answer for. Try yourself by God's commandments. You have broken them all; and, if you have lived carelessly, have been in a constant breach of them.

Question. Do you believe yourself a sinner, your heart convincing you?

(2) *You deserve to die*; and this whatever your conduct has been; for the wages of sin is death, of all sin. God is a just and righteous God and King, who will not suffer the breach of his law to go unpunished; and this punishment is eternal death.

Question. Do you think that you deserve this death? Or, that it is prepared only for greater sinners than you?

(3) *You cannot turn away this punishment*. For, should you sin no more, your past sins would be your eternal ruin. But your best endeavours will be imperfect; in the best day of your life you are impure and defiled.

Question. Do you think that you can make up the matter by doing better than you have done? Or do you see yourself unable to help yourself, and in need of a pardon as a condemned criminal?

II. *To stir up a sense of inability to do good.*

(1) *Sin is your greatest enemy*. It has consigned you to death, and made you unworthy before God; and especially it has made you unfit for heaven.

Question. Have you an earnest desire to be free from it?

(2) *You have no power of yourself to cast it off*. Your inclinations are all naturally evil; you cannot of yourself do good. So God tells us, and your own experience may do the same.

Question. What sense have you of this weakness?

III. *To set forth Christ's sufficiency.*

You see you are under *two great evils*; the wrath of God and the power of sin. Christ is able to relieve you in both, by the satisfaction of his death from wrath, and by the power of his grace from sin.

Consider how vast is the undertaking to satisfy God's justice in place of man's eternal punishment, and to work with the hearts of men to bring them to God. Observe the fitness of the Son and Spirit as divine persons.

Question. Do you believe that Christ is able to save you from wrath and sin? And on what do you build that sufficiency?

IV. *Of coming to Christ, or faith and repentance.*

(1) You must be deeply sensible of the need you have of a Saviour in both these respects; i.e., to save you from wrath and sin, and that none other than he can save you.

Question. Are you thus humbly sensible of your want of him?

(2) You must be willing that he should save you from wrath and sin too. He will not procure your pardon unless you be willing he should save you from sin; i.e., unless you be heartily tired of it and desirous to leave it.

Question. Are you willing to trust yourself to him? And would you that he sanctify as well as pardon?[11]

In his private conversations with the inquirers, Walker was particularly adept at detecting hypocrisy and 'instilling into his awakened hearers an acquaintance with themselves. Gifted with a peculiar penetration, he knew equally how to deal with the tender spirit, or to probe deeply into the corruption of the self-deceived or the deceiver.' On one occasion a young man called on him to thank him for the benefit he had received from his ministry and to seek his advice. When questioned by Walker as to the knowledge he possessed of his own heart, the youth responded by saying, in somewhat general terms, that he was an unworthy sinner. Doubting the genuineness of this conviction, Walker explained to him the nature of the sinner's character. With a personal reference to the youth he focused on 'his ingratitude to God, the evil nature of the motives which had influenced all his actions, the fruitlessness of his life' and 'the defilement even of his best deeds'. He then remarked, 'I fear you are secretly displeased with me, because I have not commended your good intentions and flattered your vanity.'

'No indeed, sir,' replied the youth. 'I feel extremely thankful for this striking proof of your kindness and regard.'

The next day the youth admitted that he had lied and that he had been displeased with Walker by the little account he had made of his profession. He had also 'secretly determined' not to expose himself again to such searching and uncomfortable questions, which unveiled 'his shallowness, and brought low the vain imaginations of his heart'. Nevertheless, Walker's discernment and straightforwardness were not in vain, for in due time the youth became a useful Christian.[12]

Walker realised that his converts, as well as receiving Biblical instruction in the Christian faith, must give evidence in their lives of its practical effects. Every effort was made to that end with the inquirers who came to him, a duty he performed with sound judgement and discrimination. By studying the workings of religion in his own heart, he developed an intimate knowledge of the deceitfulness of the hearts of others. He could detect weaknesses in the Christian's character that are often hidden by formality and external show, and from experience he knew the *real nature* of religious progress. Anything that withdrew the eye of faith from Christ was a deception too dangerous for him to ignore. With such a wise shepherd watching over the sheep and guiding them to the Saviour of sinners, many of his inquirers were not only converted but firmly established in the faith.

The outbreak of revivalism in Truro spread to the whole of West Cornwall, and by 1750 we find a Clerical Club established in Truro, comprising Evangelical incumbents from the neighbouring parishes of St Gluvias, Veryan, St Agnes, Gwennap, Lanlivery, Cubert and St Endellion. This pattern was followed elsewhere in the development of Evangelicalism. There was no concerted action on a national scale. There was no attempt to organize an influence. Here and there, as in Cornwall, clusters of Evangelical parishes were to be found.

Skevington Wood.[1]

6

The Clerical Club

Throughout Walker's ministerial career he was careful to use every legitimate means to establish his parishioners in the Christian faith, and to exercise an influence for good in the surrounding area. He avoided preaching in other parishes, deeming it an irregular practice; and, because of doctrinal differences, he would not unite himself with the Methodists. However, in order to realise his goal of strengthening Evangelicalism in the county, he brought into effect 'the design of a union among the pious clergy'. Several ministers in the neighbourhood associated themselves under the name of the 'Parson's Club', for 'mutual consultation and direction', in order to promote the great end of the Christian ministry.

The original number of members was six or seven, but it afterwards increased to eleven. All members were expected to be attached wholeheartedly to Evangelical principles and to the discipline and Liturgy of the Church of England. As a group they stood aloof from the Methodists, whose doctrines they tried to correct. Several of the Club members encountered 'strange opposition' from the Methodists, which weakened the effect of the revival in the county. Of the eleven, four died, two moved to a situation too distant to be able to attend, and two members fell away because of the opposition they encountered – all before Walker's death.

This was not the first time that such a clerical club had been formed, although it may have been the first gathering of its sort

in the country specifically for Evangelical clergy. In 1699 Archbishop Tennison had recommended similar clubs in a circular
addressed to the bishops of his province. 'It were to be wished,'
he observed, 'that the clergy of every neighbourhood would
agree upon frequent meetings, to consult for the good of
religion in general, and to advise with one another.'[2] In the
eighteenth century John Fletcher of Madeley drew up some
excellent rules for their management, and Henry Venn of
Huddersfield and James Stillingfleet at Hotham were also
involved in such enterprises. The Club Walker established was,
he said, based on 'the old principles'.

According to Sidney, Walker's group met for the first time
on 18 March, 1755. However, this is contradicted by Walker,
who said in the letter to Dr Guise dated November, 1754, that
the Parson's Club was formed 'not long after the commence-
ment of this work at Truro'.[3] Similarly, on Sunday 4 March of
the previous year, he noted this prayer in his diary:

> We entreated also your blessing on our society of ministers.
> Grant, O God, that it may be a blessed instrument of reviving
> true practical religion. Keep us from pride and debate and
> jealousy! Grant us to watch over one another in love! And
> be ever with us enlarging our hearts with zeal, constancy
> and charity, and mortifying the world and our lusts continu-
> ally; that as we are separated to the ministry, we may mind
> this one thing, to feed the sheep. And to me, O my God,
> give all needful direction that I may speak boldly and
> prudently among them, humbly and affectionately, without
> pride or resentment.[4]

There is no doubt from this prayer that the Parson's Club was
already up and running. This seems to agree with two other
statements by Walker. The first is again found in the letter to Dr
Guise: 'Our Club consists of six clergymen. We meet monthly,
except in the depth of winter. I have reason to hope something

from a clergyman or two who are not [of] our Club.'[5] The second statement is more precise. In a letter to Adam on 16 February, 1755, Walker wrote that the Parson's Club had been 'subsisting these five years'.

In a third letter dated 5 March, 1755, this time to Risdon Darracott, a Nonconformist minister of Wellington, Somerset, Walker confused the issue when he said, 'Pray for us, and for the divine blessing on our meeting, the 18th inst., which will be our first Club.'[6] Darracott must have known that 'our first Club' did not mean 'our very first Club ever', because he himself, referring to the Club, said in a letter to Henry Venn of the previous year (20 November, 1754): 'I find that there are six clergymen who thus regularly meet together to strengthen each other's hands in the work of the Lord.'[7] Adam too, writing to Walker on the first day of the same month (November, 1754), was probably pointing to the Club when he remarked: '[I] give up my heart and whole self to the brotherly unity of those clergy-men in your neighbourhood with whom you are in concert, and wish you good luck in the name of the Lord, and say to you in the power of a true love, go on through evil report and good report, and be of the few names in Sardis.'[8] It is clear from all this that Sidney's date is incorrect. In all probability the Club began in 1750, as Walker said in his letter to Adam, and the 'first Club' mentioned to Darracott was the 'first Club of that year'.

Before the first meeting Walker was prudent enough to seek the permission of his diocesan, and received a grudging consent – at least as far as the words 'do not forbid you' may be understood – from the wary Lavington, who suspected any such meeting of being infected with Methodism. He also drew up proper regulations for conducting the meetings with which the members of the Club agreed. The purpose of these meet-ings is shown in the following extract from a letter written by a Club member:

Mr Walker was the person who first proposed a friendly meeting of neighbouring clergymen, with a view to improve one another in Christian knowledge, for the better edification of the people committed to their care, and to encourage each other if, as it was likely, any difficulty or opposition should arise to either of them in the more vigorous discharge of the ministerial duty.[9]

According to Walker, all this was done 'with so much freedom, love and unanimity' that he was 'even astonished at the remembrance of it'.[10] The Club members' letter went on to give other details:

It was proposed to meet seven months in the year, on the first Tuesday after every full moon, at their several houses by turns; to meet at ten; to dine at two; to have two plain dishes of meat and no more; not to stay later than six o'clock; and that the person, at whose house the meeting was, should take care, that one only speaks at a time, and that no new matter be brought on the carpet, till the matter in question (whatever it were) should be satisfactorily adjusted.

Whatever subject the conversation turned upon, every member of the Club was desired to draw up his sentiments in writing against next Club day, either in the form of a sermon, or what other form each person saw fit, for the better assurance that the subject was well digested.[11]

Although Bishop Lavington had given his reluctant permission, an outcry was raised against this gathering by both clergy and laity on account of its similarities with Methodism, a charge that was totally unfounded as all the members, especially Walker, as his correspondence with Wesley proves, were zealously committed to the doctrines and discipline of the Church of England. This antagonism surfaced at Truro on 19 July, 1754, when Thomas Michell of Veryan, a member of the Club, was appointed to preach at Bishop Lavington's Visitation. The sermon was wrongly understood 'to be that of the Club', although the other members would have endorsed it whole-heartedly. As Walker's letter to Adam indicates, it was not well received:

> My friend [in his sermon] called on us to exert our ministerial function by preaching Christ, studying the Scriptures, &c. with a word or two on pluralities and non-residence. He spoke modestly but freely, and, as the bishop [said], falsely, who took occasion in his charge to mention the preacher, and insisted, contrary to what the sermon insinuated, that the clergy both preached Christ and studied the Scriptures. The matter was again resumed after dinner, when the outcry of the many was strong, and he was particularly attacked for speaking against pluralities. His defence was to appeal to the judgement seat.[12]

At the meetings, before the Club proceeded with ministerial business, the members offered up their joint prayers to God for his blessing in a form collected by Walker from the Liturgy, *The Whole Duty of Man*, and Jenk's *Devotions*. With his usual wisdom, and for the benefit and discipline of the members, he also drew up various searching questions, which each member was to ask himself on a regular basis:

> **1.** What is it that I have in view, or what is my mind chiefly engaged upon? Is it the setting forth of God's glory? Or is there some worldly meaner matter, which has as much room in my thoughts as that?
> **2.** When I sit down to make a sermon, or when I go into the pulpit to preach it, is my mind running on the performing of a talk, or on gaining esteem by performing it well? Or am I chiefly concerned to do something for God?
> **3.** Would I rather that the interest of Christ, whose minister I am, be advanced in the world, though I should thereby forfeit ease and other conveniences, than favour these to the neglecting of his interest?
> **4.** What is my view as a member of this society? How may I know, whether I am employing myself here to the best purposes, agreeably to the design of the meeting?

5. Do I continually look up for divine grace to accompany and prosper my ministrations? And, in this strength, am I often enquiring after the success of my ministry with anxiety? And, relying on gospel-promises for this strength, am I continually seeking it in prayer, public and private?

6. Am I satisfied with the answer that my conscience makes of these questions, as I could wish to be when I shall be lying on my death bed, when every thought will sink to the bottom of my soul, and when I am just to be called upon to render up my account of this important charge and ministry?[13]

As can be gauged from the above, the Clerical Club was very beneficial to its members, although it did not always live up to its originator's expectations. On Tuesday 10 August, 1756, Walker complained:

This Club day. I have not found such desire after it as formerly. This is a great fault. I am not thankful as I ought for such friends and opportunities; nor do I meet them with suitable desires of receiving and communicating good. I should regard the Club as a distinguished blessing, and as laying me under peculiar obligations; and be continually influenced by the expectations, which the world has from us.[14]

On Tuesday 19 April, 1757, Walker wrote in his diary,

Club very uncomfortable and unpromising. What I see in others, too much influencing conduct, let me fear it myself. Concern about a worldly character which I see plainly, and find also by my own heart, would needs set itself up, for a rule of action. This fills me with serious thoughts on my way home; and in the consideration of being left to stand alone, supposing some dead, and others gone back, I was sometimes fearful of apostasy; and then confident in Christ with regard to usefulness; with some I have missed the opportunity, I am condemned in [retrospection]. O what a dreadful state must I be in, if I should no longer have a heart to rejoice in the success of the gospel, and should be ready to think ill of its professors![15]

In contrast, a letter from Walker to Adam highlighted the spiritual prosperity and usefulness of its members:

> The Lord is still with us, and whatever we take in hand, he makes it prosper. Great things is he doing in a neighbouring town which I heartily praise him for. Their worthy minister, a member of our Club, speaks the truth boldly, nor is dismayed by the strife of tongues. Numbers flock together, as to hear him, so to converse and pray together in a house hired for that purpose. There is of them by this time a considerable number of names, and of such as hold forth the word of life in their conversion. Through much evil report we all gain ground; and I suppose there are not less than ten thousand to whom we preach the gospel, one and another of us.[16]

It is uncertain how long the Club continued, although it was still going in the summer of 1759. Nor is it known whether it carried on after Walker's departure from Truro. What is acknowledged is its extended influence. One of Walker's converts informed Risdon Darracott that God had blessed the Club 'to the awakening ministers, who from careless and formal preachers are become livers and preachers of the everlasting gospel'. In a second letter the same correspondent wrote that the 'good effects [of the Club] have already spread through their several parishes, and seems likely to diffuse its influence yet further amongst the clergy and laity'.[17] Darracott himself, writing from Somerset, reported that several clergymen were 'forming themselves in this county in somewhat of the same society as dear Mr Walker and his brethren in Cornwall';[18] and in 1790 Thomas Haweis recorded in his diary that the annual conference of Evangelical clergymen in the East Midland area met at Aldwincle. This Clerical Club was 'much on the lines of that founded by Samuel Walker of Truro'.[19]

It is not an easy task to ascertain exactly who all the members were. Three are known for certain, but the others are open to conjecture. Along with Walker there were Thomas

Michell of Veryan and John Penrose at Penryn. Of this trio
Haweis inquired: 'Could there be three more godly men?'[20]
Michell was admitted to his benefice on 1 October, 1743, and
remained there until his death thirty years later. He always
resided in his parish and worked conscientiously on behalf of
his people. By 1755 he had gathered around him a group of
'thirty zealous souls'. On 5 March of that year Walker expressed
a high opinion of his friend when he said to Darracott: 'You
would love that dear man could you see him.' Of his work
Davies stated:

> In 1744 ... there were two services on the Sunday, with a
> sermon in the morning and on Saints' Days. He read prayers
> daily and held eight Sacraments in the year. Out of 150
> eligible communicants, eighty came regularly, with 130 the
> previous Easter. Twenty years later, the number of eligible
> communicants had decreased to 130, with an average of
> sixty at each of the ten Sacraments held annually. The chil-
> dren were catechized in summer. An echo of his true feel-
> ings for his people occurs in the burial register between 15
> and 26 July, 1761 [the year of Walker's death], when six
> men were buried; after which appears his comment: 'Lovers
> of pleasure more than lovers of God. O may God convert
> and save this parish!' His confirmation candidates were
> numerous: 50 in 1749, 73 in 1754, 113 in 1765, 36 in 1768,
> and 35 in 1771.[21]

The third member of the Club was Penrose, a close friend of
Walker's from their school days together, and a man who
entered all the Club's projects with enthusiasm and energy. He
is confirmed as one of the original members by the testimony
of his grandson. From September, 1741, until his death in 1776,
he was vicar of St Gluvias, situated nine miles from Truro. In
addition to his regular ministry, he preached charity sermons in
accordance with the terms of various benefactors' wills; distributed books and tracts on behalf of SPCK (in 1772 his order of
books from SPCK amounted to 2892); catechized school children

after the second lesson every Friday in Lent; and administered the Sacrament on the first Sunday of each month and on the great festivals. When he baptised infants, if the child was illegitimate, he drew a hand with an outstretched index finger in the margin of his register. In the opinion of one writer, who was unfavourably disposed towards the Evangelical clergy, Penrose 'left a reputation of learning, of piety, and of all the virtues which adorn the clergyman'.[22] Miles Brown called him 'a forerunner of the Evangelical movement within the Church of England'.[23]

Walker's elder brother James, and Samuel Cooper, curate of Cubert; James Vowler and William Philp of St Agnes, and perhaps Henry Phillips of Gwennap, were members of or in some way associated with the Club. James Walker, Vivian, Philp and Cooper all officiated for Walker at St Mary's for marriages at various times from October, 1759, until the new rector Charles Pye arrived in 1761. Cooper and Philp also rallied around Walker during his illness in 1760. Other possible members include Mydhope Wallis of St Endellion and Thomas Vivian, vicar of Cornwood; John Turner of Week St Mary and George Thomson of St Gennys. Whether or not all these men were members of the Club is impossible to say, but at least it shows that there was a group of Evangelical clergy living within a short distance of each other.

James Walker, vicar of St Agnes with Perranzabuloe (1730-1793) and Lanlivery in plurality from 1752, who was also the brother-in-law of Thomas Vivian, proved his worth when he appointed three 'awakened men' to the curate of St Agnes: Vowler, Philp and later Thomas Wills, in spite of a likely confrontation with Bishop Lavington. John Wesley heard him preach an 'excellent sermon' in the morning before he gave Philp's funeral address, and another has described him as a first rate parish priest, although extremely deaf for the last ten years of his life.

Cooper could well have been a member. He arrived at Truro shortly before Walker left and was noted for his ability as a preacher. In September, 1760, John Wesley, who had received 'a pleasing account' of him from a gentleman of St Columb, heard him preach both morning and afternoon at Redruth, with much satisfaction, and in reference to him, exclaimed, 'Surely God has a favour for the people of these parts! He gives them so serious, zealous and lively preachers.'[24]

James Vowler, 'a capable, humble and prudent' pastor, was curate of Perranzabuloe (1750-1758) and curate of St Agnes from 1757. According to Sidney he was 'one of that faithful band of ministers who entered into all Mr Walker's projects of usefulness, with a kindred spirit of zeal and piety'.[25] On Sunday 4 September, 1757, Wesley heard him preach 'two such thundering sermons at church as I have scarce heard these twenty years. Oh how gracious is God to the poor sinners of St Agnes! In the church and out of the church they hear the same great truths of the wrath of God against sin, and his love to those that are in Christ Jesus.'[26] Wesley again referred to him after his death as an 'upright, zealous servant of God, and indefatigable in his labour'.[27] In a letter by an anonymous author, written on 25 June, 1757, the writer, who had enjoyed attending the ministry of Vowler at St Agnes, found there

> ... abundant comfort in the hopeful prospect he has been glorifying King Jesus in the salvation of sinners among that once barbarous people. Such a congregation I hardly ever beheld. He has in his parish upwards of fifteen hundred men, mostly common tinners, most of whom seem to receive the word with deep and solemn seriousness, while he displays, with persuasive language, the ways of sin, and the love of Jesus, the thunders of Sinai, and the mild still voice of Emmanuel, whose bowels yearn over sinners. Numbers inquire after Christ, and many, receiving him into their hearts, have peace and joy in believing.[28]

Walker mentioned the spiritual prosperity of Vowler and his flock in a letter to Thomas Adam on 7 June, 1758; and on 29 April of the same year, Fawcett, a Kidderminster clergyman, stated in a letter to Mr A. W. that at St Agnes Vowler

> ... is greatly blessed and the people flock to him every night in the week, but one, which he reserves for making his plain practical sermon. His house is full, and more than it can hold, every night, and by day (taking a bit of bread in his pocket) he walks round his large parish, about three or four thousand inhabitants, and inquires into the state of their souls; besides the people come to him for advice, three or four miles around him, not regarding wind or weather, and, by what we hear, a greater reformation among the common sinners was never known in any parish or neighbourhood. Mr Vowler ... was not long since a gainsayer, but by means of Mr Walker's acquaintance is become truly serious.[29]

Vowler died of a fever on 30 July, 1758,

> ... in full assurance of faith, and with his expiring breath poured out his soul in earnest cries for his dear people. The last intelligible words he uttered were an answer to Mr Walker's inquiry, how it fared with his soul in the near approach of the king of terrors? 'Ah, my friend,' says he, 'I thought I should have been in eternity before I could see you, but I rejoice that we have once more a meeting. I am near expiring, but blessed be God, I have the testimony of my conscience, and an interest in Christ, and I have nothing to fear.'[30]

He was buried in the chancel of St Agnes Church. A huge weeping crowd attended his burial and Walker preached a funeral sermon to the society at Truro.

His successor at St Agnes, William Philp, 'a man of a humble, loving, tender spirit', according to John Wesley, was probably a member in the later years of the Club's existence. 'Between him on the one hand,' said Wesley, 'and the Methodists

on the other, most in the parish are now awakened.'[31] Referring to him again two years later on 18 September, 1762, Wesley
called him 'a man eminently humble, serious and zealous for
God. He was snatched away by a fever three weeks since.'[32]

Henry Phillips, vicar of Gwennap (1743-1782), was possibly
a Club member. He lived near Truro and Walker held a very
favourable opinion of him. In a letter to Thomas Michell at
Veryan in May, 1754, Walker wrote:

> Let me tell you that I was, as proposed, at Gwennap, and
> surely I have never preached to a congregation where so
> many expressed an experience of the power of the Word,
> and all in a manner heard with a more than curious atten-
> tion. I was tempted to wish myself an assistant to my dear
> friend there, where the harvest is so plentiful and promising.
> May God direct his heart into the knowledge of all faith. He
> seems singularly fitted for his important trust by the more
> than ordinary measure of natural endowments which he is
> possessed of, and I am abundantly rejoiced in the proofs I
> see in him of a work of grace carrying on upon his soul.[33]

The following day, 22 May, he wrote to Phillips himself and
thanked him for the blessing he had experienced at Gwennap.
'I reflect upon your congregation with great satisfaction and am
fully persuaded of a plenteous harvest approaching under your
hand. May God in every way enable you for it! May you see
your works prosper! May you have many seals to your ministry, making your latter days full of peace, and brightening your
crown!' He went on with a word to check pride: 'I must take
leave to put you in remembrance, that whatever success you
have, God will take a thousand ways of showing you, that the
work is not yours but His.'[34]

Another possible member was Mydhope Wallis of St
Endellion, although he probably lived too far away to be anything more than an irregular visitor to Truro. He was 'an excellent classical and Hebrew scholar' of Balliol College, Oxford,

who was instituted to St Endellion and to the Prebend of Trehaverock in 1753. On 10 September the following year Walker wrote to him, having enjoyed his company at St Columb. 'I am willing,' he commented, 'to contribute what I may to the interests of Christ's religion against the violence it suffers, nor does anything so peculiarly rejoice my heart as an acquaintance with clergymen hearty in the same cause.'[35]

The last to be named in connection with the Clerical Club is Thomas Vivian of Cornwood, who in 1747 married Mary Hussey, the sister-in-law of James Walker. He is described by Polwhele as a man 'gifted with a very strong understanding', and who possessed 'an uncommon sweetness of disposition, partly owing to his natural temperament, and partly to the mild influence of Christianity'.[36] According to one of his published sermons, which supported Evangelical doctrines, his view of preaching was 'to deliver my own soul by using the opportunity my office supplied me with of speaking some necessary points plainly and freely'. His next publication was *Three Dialogues Between a Minister and one of his Parishioners*, which appeared in 1759, and which Walker described to Adam as 'a close little piece, very familiar, and remarkably calculated to awaken'. By 1788 it had reached its twenty-second edition.[37]

He was curate in charge of Truro for a few months after Joseph Jane's departure and before Walker's arrival in 1746. He then moved to Redruth, where he stayed less than a year. The reasons for his 'sudden and unexpected' departure from his second curacy are stated in a letter he wrote to John Wesley on 10 October, 1748. He acknowledged that to the 'writings' of Wesley he owed 'the blessing wrought on my soul'.[38] They had brought him to 'a clearer discovery of the nature of gospel salvation' and an '*experimental* knowledge' of practical religion. As a consequence of this new 'lively hope and faith', his 'speech was too plain and irksome to be suffered ... any longer at Redruth. My words were no longer tolerable, when I began to preach Christ crucified, and the necessity of an inward change, Jesus and the resurrection to a new life.'[39] He settled at Cornwood in Devon and remained there until his death in 1793. From Walker's correspondence with Charles Wesley and Adam, it is apparent that he and Vivian agreed theologically. This, along with his family connections, make it likely that he was an occasional visitor to the Truro Club despite the distance he had to travel.

It was with men of this calibre and experience that Walker conducted the Clerical Club. Only the imagination can wonder at the spiritual depths and heights of their discussions, and the sense of God's presence in their meetings, equipping them for their revival work. When these men returned to their respective parishes, encouraged and refreshed by their gatherings, they were ready to preach the gospel of Christ with new vitality and force, and to spread the Evangelical doctrines throughout Cornwall to a degree comparable only with the clergy in Yorkshire at this period.

Yes, and all who desire to lead a godly life in Christ Jesus will suffer persecution.

2 Timothy 3:12.[1]

Then Jesus said to them all, 'If anyone desires to come after me, let him deny himself, and take up his cross daily, and follow me. For whoever desires to save his life will lose it, but whoever loses his life for my sake will save it. For what advantage is it to a man if he gains the whole world, and is himself destroyed or lost? For whoever is ashamed of me and my words, of him the Son of Man will be ashamed when he comes in his own glory, and in his Father's, and in the glory of the holy angels.'

Luke 9:23-26.[2]

7
Times of Testing and Self-Denial

It was not long before those who did not appreciate what Samuel Walker was doing in Truro tried to curtail his activities. To meet this end, various accusations were made against him to the Bishop of Exeter, George Lavington (1684-1762), 'a strenuous opponent of Methodism' and John Wesley's bitterest antagonist. Walker's enemies knew that the bishop would not look kindly on what was happening in his diocese and interpret it as another example of Methodist fanaticism.

Lavington was consecrated at Lambeth on 8 February, 1747, two months after his predecessor Bishop Claggett's death. By then he was a staunch adversary of Methodism and in full agreement with the prevailing view that both Whitefield and Wesley were 'Jesuits in disguise', who intended to lead the masses into the Roman Catholic Church. Five years previously he had ranked Wesley 'with the most hated of the founders of Catholic orders, Dominic and Ignatius, and with the most despised of the mystics, particularly Bourignon'.[3]

His relationship with the Methodists was not helped by the fact that in 1748, after he had delivered a charge to the clergy of his diocese, a fictitious extract from that charge was printed, in which he appeared to support the doctrines and experiences of Methodism. Lavington was furious and accused in the public papers both Whitefield and the Wesleys of fraud. With the intervention of the Countess of Huntingdon their innocence was proved and the bishop was induced, albeit with great reluctance, to retract his accusations and apologize, and his letter was published in the leading journals of the day. As can be imagined, this 'disreputable fracas' only added to his animosity, especially when he learned that his humiliating recantation had been made public by the countess, 'and from that period he became a bitter and malignant reviler of her ladyship and the Methodist leaders'.[4] John Wesley, however, was not one to hold a grudge. After he had attended a service at Exeter Cathedral on 29 August, 1762, two weeks before Lavington's death, he said, 'I was well pleased to partake of the Lord's Supper with my old opponent, Bishop Lavington. Oh, may we sit down together in the kingdom of our Father!'[5]

Two years after his consecration he published anonymously the first part of his widely read work *The Enthusiasm of Methodists and Papists Compared*, in which he tried to make out that the Methodists were 'everything that is bad'. It was an attack, said John Rowe, 'from the secluded study by a man of considerable learning, but whose whole career had divorced him from the harsh realities of the world'.[6] In his preface, the bishop called the Methodists 'a set of pretended reformers – a dangerous and presumptuous sect, animated with an enthusiastical and fanatical spirit', and stated that his object was to compare 'the wild and pernicious enthusiasms' of the Papists with those of the Methodists. Their preachers, he alleged, were 'strolling predicants of affected phrases, fantastical and unintelligible notions, whimsical strictnesses, and loud exclamations. The windmill indeed is in all their heads.'[7] A second part of his work appeared later in 1749, again without the name of the author, in which he continued his attack. Methodist preachers, according to him, were 'either innocent madmen or infamous cheats', while Wesley had 'so fanaticised his own followers, and given them so many strong doses of the enthusiastic tincture, as to turn their brains and deprive them of their senses'.[8]

The final part was published in 1751 and the bishop made Wesley the almost exclusive object of his scurrilous pen. The latter was called 'an arrant joker' and 'a perfect droll'. 'Go on,' he challenged Wesley, 'and build chapels. One may be dedicated to the god Proteus, famous for being a juggling wonder-monger, and turning himself into all shapes; another to the god called Catius, because he makes men sly and cunning as cats.'[9] The three parts were published together in 1754, by which time the bishop had acknowledged authorship. The complete work was republished as late as 1833.

Lavington was also active in Cornwall to hinder the progress of vital religion. He did all he could to prevent the ordination of Thomas Haweis, one of Walker's converts.

[Haweis's] testimonial from Cornwall was signed by Samuel Walker, John Penrose [vicar of St Gluvias], and Thomas Michell [of Veryan]... When these testimonial signatures were submitted to Bishop Lavington of Exeter, he countersigned them and sent them on to Haweis. But the unscrupulous prelate, in his bitterness against what he regarded as enthusiasm, purposely omitted to add, as was customary, 'I believe them worthy of credit in this matter', thus rendering his signature valueless. Haweis being unversed in such legal procedure, was unaware of the trick that had been played upon him, and duly presented his testimonials. He was examined by the Bishop's Chaplain, Thomas Burton, and was highly commended. To his great surprise, on the morning when he was to go to the Cathedral to be ordained, he received a note from Bishop Secker to inform him that, since his county testimonial was not properly authenticated respecting the credibility of the signatories, he could not be ordained.[10]

Haweis learned from George Berkeley, son of the Bishop of Cloyne, that 'Lavington had written personally to Secker expressing his utter dislike of Walker, Penrose and Michell, and explaining that for this reason he had refused to testify to their credibility.' Later, when Lavington spoke to Haweis, he voiced 'the strongest disapproval of Walker and his work, with misrepresentations that Haweis could not interrupt to correct, his brother bishop [Edward Willes] joining in the chorus of defamation'.[11] As to the accusations that were made against Walker to the bishop, it was decided that on this occasion no action should be taken against the Truro curate, whose life and piety afforded his opponents no opportunity to substantiate their claims.

A man more easily influenced was the non-resident rector of St Mary's, Truro, St John Eliot, described by one as 'a pious young man of considerable property',[12] and by another as 'timid and irresolute'.[13] He resided in his other parish of Ladock. When some of the wealthiest inhabitants of the town approached him with complaints about Walker, demanding his dismissal from his cure, the rector was willing to listen to them. He promised to go to Walker and give him notice to leave his charge. When Eliot entered Walker's lodgings, he was received so kindly and with genuine courtesy that he felt too embarrassed to mention the reason for his visit. Instead, he directed the conversation to the ministerial office and character. Walker responded enthusiastically to this religious subject, 'with such acuteness of reasoning and solemnity of appeal to his rector as a fellow labourer in the gospel, that he retreated, overwhelmed with confusion, and unable to say a word about the intended dismissal'.[14] Eliot reported back to Walker's opponents and was rebuked by them for not fulfilling his promise. He went a second time determined to carry out their wishes. Again he returned without having dared to mention the dismissal. When he was urged to go a third time by one of his principal parishioners, he replied, 'You go and dismiss him, if you can, I cannot. I feel in his presence as if he were a being of a superior order, and am so abashed that I am uneasy till I can retire.'[15]

A short time later the rector was taken ill. He sent for Walker and asked him to pray that his health might improve. At the same time he acknowledged the uprightness of Walker's conduct as a minister and promised to support him wholeheartedly if he recovered. He did recover, but, as with his promises to his parishioners, he failed to stand by his curate. Walker was hardly surprised.

On a similar occasion, a 'fine gentleman', who had recently declared he would 'spend all he had in the world, in order to strip Walker's gown off his back', fell ill and lay on his death bed. He desired Walker's assistance. Walker, without hesitation, attended him 'constantly every other day', which, on account of the gentleman's previous attitude, quite 'alarmed the place'.[16] Such strength of character enabled Walker from this time to the end of his ministry to hold 'on his way without let or hindrance, though not, of course, without much hatred, opposition and petty persecution. But nothing that his opponents could do, or devise, was able to stop or silence him.'[17]

During these trials he received considerable encouragement from his ministerial brethren and others. Joseph Williams, a non-conformist tradesman from Kidderminster, 'a truly pious man', and a stranger to Walker at the time, wrote to him in 1754, wishing him 'God speed!' He had heard of Walker and his work through Risdon Darracott, who had urged him to write. In his letter, he said:

> You are engaged in the best of causes, but you have thereby enraged the worst of enemies. Does not Satan roar, since you have stricken his kingdom? He certainly will roar; therefore, 'take to you the whole armour of God'. Christ's gospel has in all ages made its way with greater success by means of reproaches and persecutions. God will cause 'the wrath of men' to praise him, and will 'restrain the remainder' thereof; and thus he defeats the old serpent. I doubt not but you have counted the cost. Count it again, and you will certainly see reason to 'count it all joy' to 'fall into divers temptations'...

May the Lord abundantly strengthen you for your work and
sufferings, and all your fellow-helpers in the Lord.[18]

Soon after Walker's arrival at Truro the trustees of his late
patron, Nicholas Kendall, had presented him to the vicarage of
Talland, a village on the south coast of Cornwall near Looe,
which he had accepted. His presentation date was 13 July, 1747.
He had also obtained leave of non-residence from the bishop
without any difficulty. Some time after this he began to enter-
tain serious doubts about whether he should accept the
benefits of this position, the duties of which he could not peform.
He weighed the matter in his own mind, with his usual calmness of judgement and deliberation; consulted various authors
on the subject of pluralities and non-residence, including Dr
Newton's well-known treatise; prayed earnestly about it, and
came to the conclusion that he should resign the benefice, which
he did in 1752. In a letter to Thomas Adam, dated 7 October,
1756, in which he sketched his early life, he remarked in the
third person:

> *Non-residence began to make him uneasy, as soon as God
> began to deal solemnly with his heart.* About four years ago
> the living he first held became vacant, and was offered him.
> He could not be reconciled to non-residence, and judging it
> most for the interest of religion that he should stay at Truro,
> he refused it, and also resigned the other. It was the happiest
> day of his life. He was eased of a grievous burden, and will
> never more undertake a charge to which he cannot
> attend.[19]

In a letter of 6 August, 1758, he said, 'I approve a living simply
to God's glory in the world, and in a disregard of ease, interest
or esteem, to maintain an interest in Jesus' kingdom.'[20] His
decision to give up Talland may have been influenced by the
success of his ministry at Truro and the new and spiritual
relation between him and his flock there; 'and accordingly it
became his settled judgement that he ought not on any worldy

consideration to leave them, unless providence should open to him a more extensive field of usefulness to the church of Christ, or he should be removed by superior authority'.[21]

This sacrifice was made in the full knowledge that it would place him in financial difficulties. Nevertheless, he made the decision without complaint and reported to his friends that a heavy weight had been lifted from his conscience. When he was no longer able to support the expense of housekeeping, he gave up his accustomed comforts and moved to smaller lodgings, where, 'though his board and habitation were of the most ordinary kind, yet, as his mind was wholly intent upon spreading the saving knowledge of the gospel, he lived in peace and calmness'.[22] While in this condition he received four offers of preferment, but refused them all, being unwilling to leave his flock in Truro for personal advantage. His successor to the vicarage of Talland was the notorious pluralist John Trist, who was instituted to that place on 8 November, 1752. Trist also held the livings of Crantock, St Stephens by Saltash and Altarnon, and in later years Kenwyn, Kea and Veryan.

Thomas Adam, recognising Walker's Christ-like attitude, wrote to him, saying, 'I am convinced that worldly accommodations have never been matter of considerations to you; but that you have conducted yourself with a view to usefulness, though with the loss of outward advantages.'[23] In a letter from Darracott to Henry Venn (20 November, 1754), Darracott quoted one of Walker's converts, who was struck with Walker's 'deadness to the world, both as to its profits and his reputation in it. [He] contents himself with a curacy for the glory of God when a living of £140 per annum in a very pleasant country has been offered to him.'[24]

In all this Walker epitomised his own words, taken from a manuscript sermon found among his papers, which contrast a poor but contented Christian with those 'great ones' who 'know not God':

No desire is there of other treasure but God, nor is there any want grievous while the light of God's countenance is enjoyed. This changes rags into purple garments, sweetens the coarse and homely meals, satisfies that the dwelling be narrow and inconvenient, and makes the heart dance for joy, while beholders regard, some with pity and some with scorn. O you poor great ones; poor, because strangers to God, poor and without quiet, how little cause have you to boast that you fare sumptuously! This man has delicates which you cannot relish, a continual feast he has satisfying his soul, while your very heart is troubled with all the contrivances of art to please, and all the elegances of luxury to indulge you; you cannot feed upon content as he does, because you know not God, for it is his privilege, having nothing, to be as if he possessed all things.[25]

In another instance of Christian self-denial and disinterestedness, Walker was again willing to forsake a life of worldly comforts in order to be more effective in the ministry. There lived in the neighbourhood of Truro a well-educated and religious young lady 'of accomplished manners, beauty, fortune and piety'. Walker described her to Adam as

... a person of distinction in this county, and I believe the best fortune in it. She had enjoyed all the advantages that education could give. Her natural parts were good. Her constitutional temper remarkably tender and humane. Besides all which, she was everything in religion but a Christian. The world, I think, has not often brought out a more finished production. About three years since [1753] she came in the way of my ministry; being some months on a visit in this place. It pleased God to open her eyes... The truth was discovered, and she is walking in it with eminent exemplariness. Indeed, she makes a noble profession, but it cost her the loss of all things. Her friends and relations have forsaken her, and her former acquaintances are afraid of her, though her conduct towards the one and the other is remarkably meek and forbearing... She was before universally

> esteemed among the best of women. You would be pleased
> to see how carefully she endeavours to improve this advan-
> tage to the honour of Christ.[26]

This lady, it was believed, would have readily accepted Walker's
proposal of marriage. A friend of Walker's, anxious to see him
relieved of his financial straits, urged him to make the most of
the opportunity. Walker did not reply immediately, probably
wanting time to think the matter over and to ask for divine
guidance, but a few days later he remarked:

> You spoke to me lately about Miss – [apparently the lady
> was Miss Aggis, a convert of Walker's, who later married
> John Archer of Whiteford, near Callington]. I never saw a
> woman whom I thought comparable to her, and I believe I
> should enjoy as much happiness in a union with her as it is
> possible to enjoy in this world. I have reason also to think
> she would not reject my suit. [At this point he paused and
> then added with feeling and seriousness:] Still it must never
> be – what would the world say of me? Would not they imagine
> that the hope of obtaining such a prize influenced my
> profession of religion? It is easy, they would say, to preach
> self-denial and heavenly mindedness; but has not the
> preacher taken care to get as much of this world's good as
> he could possibly obtain? Sir [he said with emphasis], it must
> never be. I can never suffer any temporal happiness or
> advantage to be a hindrance to my usefulness.[27]

Whether a happy marriage would have hindered or extended
his usefulness, or prolonged his life, is a question that is impossible to answer. He was certainly never charged with pursuing
material or worldly gain, or of putting his own comforts and
desires before the kingdom of God. From a life that gave
incontestable evidence that God and his service were the foremost desires of his heart, he could thus address his converts:

I know that you sometimes need such evident proofs, when
one how or other you are in doubt and sadness. Keep this by
you then, as a sure ground of confidence, that while you do
so choose God as to prefer him to all things, refusing them
all in comparison of him, you cannot but be his. This would
be one of the most common and also of the safest and most
profitable evidences of a good state. It is common, you may
always have recourse to it; it is safe, it cannot deceive you;
it is profitable, because it will always keep you on your guard
where you are most in danger, and put you upon a still greater
mortification of the law of sin you have in your members. [28]

His dedication to Christ was the fruit of a constant and intimate
communion with God. He was emphatically a man of prayer,
laying all things before his Saviour's feet. He once mentioned
to a friend, who repeatedly questioned him on the subject, that
he was 'sometimes favoured in prayer with such rapturous views
of the excellency of divine things, that he almost enjoyed a
foretaste of heaven'. He then added, with his keen spiritual
insight and thoughtfulness, that usually he did not mention these
experiences for three reasons:

First, it might have held out to my people a false standard of
religion, causing them to substitute feeling for holiness;
secondly, it might have discouraged some pious and
humble persons, who from various causes are destitute of
such enjoyments; and thirdly, it might have encouraged those
presumptuous enthusiasts, whose arrogant pretensions I am
always aiming to expose. [29]

This prayerful submission to and dependence on Christ is
further seen from extracts taken from his own papers. On Thursday night 14 September, 1752, he was visited with a sudden
and violent disorder that very quickly brought him to the edge
of the grave. On the following Sunday, when he was somewhat
recovered, he wrote about this experience and the lessons he

was learning from it. As in all his writings, there is a refreshing openness and honesty, and an expressed desire to 'cast off all dependence on myself':

[My illness] was God's good pleasure. It was his fatherly goodness hereby to give me a more practical and interesting sense of death and eternity. Hereby he has taught me the great importance of every hour I live; I can say now I feel it with a more active impression. May I number my restored days wisely! Nor may the things of this life ever more separate eternal things from before my eyes! May I live to his glory, who has thus lengthened my days!

Remember, my soul, in the confusion of the hasty hour, how little you could do; just no more than present a broken resignation of yourself into the hands of your heavenly Father. Remember how you were oppressed with a spiritual insensibility; all the objects of faith how dead and flat; how without either fear or hope or trust in any degree of lively exercise!

Ah, my soul, the dying hour is not for the work of religion, for gaining an interest in Christ. This must be the business of my healthy days. In these I must seek to humble my soul, renounce myself, cast off all dependence on myself, and on everything, which by the grace of God is wrought in me, and to work out my salvation drawn by the love of Jesus to yield myself to him the purchase of his blood. Now I must seek peace in believing in the Son of God, and prove that I have a title to justification through him by all the evidences of his Spirit working in me. Keep me in this faith, you Mediator, with whom I do heartily trust my soul. Yes, increase this faith in me. And let me know that I belong to you by the sanctification of my corrupt nature more and more.

Sunk as I am into the grave and death of sin, let me hear the powerful voice of your word, and feel your quickening influences upon my heart, and come forth and live in holy obedience to your call. Yes, let me live no more to myself. You have given me warning, a sufficient summons to be ready, that by and by I must be away. Let me live to you, that you may acknowledge me at your judgement.[30]

There can be little doubt in reading such a frank statement that Walker possessed an intimate knowledge of his own heart, a deep experience and appreciation of the inner work of divine grace, and a humble dependence on his Saviour. This is again illustrated by the comments he made on the sacrament Sunday of 4 March, 1753:

> By the endurance and goodness of God I am alive this day, and have been enabled, without disturbance, to renew the covenant of grace. Praise be to God, my mind was clear, my conscience quiet, and with due deliberation and without distraction, I was before the Lord.
>
> I must bless him also that the ordinance was with comfort. Faith seemed in exercise more than usual to see, receive and in some measure to appropriate Christ to me in communicating. Though always I have cause to complain of the hardness of my heart, yet now I could in some sort mourn and love. I found heartiness in my purpose of serving the glory and interest of God in Christ, and was forward to make a full surrender of myself, depending upon divine grace.
>
> It has been a day with me signally marked with divine favour. Notwithstanding the insensibility and unbelief of my heart, I am returned rejoicing. What shall I render to the Lord? It may be some greater trial than ordinary is at hand. Let me be mindful therefore of the vows I have this day made. Your peculiar suit, my soul, was that pride might no longer have dominion over us; that the loss of men's opinion and esteem might not fright on one side, nor the approbation of friends puff us up on the other. We sued also for a more enlarged spirit of love, that those who speak evil against us, or use us ill for the work's sake, may be entertained with compassion and forgiveness, without resentment or hatred. We sued for this charitable mind and demeanour towards those mistaken persons, who, prejudiced to their own opinions, represent us as not preaching the word of God soundly. Lord, it is your pleasure to try me with the reproaches of the wanton and careless; and with the misapprehensions of those who, having conceived unsafe evidences of faith, blame me that I speak not as they do, and ignorantly oppose themselves.

> Lord, keep me in a charitable temper to endure with meek-
> ness the outrages of the one and the prejudiced mistakings
> of the other of these, between whom my lot is fallen to me![31]

He concluded with a word of encouragement to his own soul: 'See now, my soul, the work before you; but shrink not. Remember how God has visited you this day. Be strong and of good courage, and yet be fearful in case you let anything of all this slip. Great Shepherd, leave me not. Amen.'[32]

One area that caused him much concern was his own walk with God, which he examined minutely almost on a daily basis. If he detected a worldly frame, an independent spirit, the risings of pride in his heart, a reluctance to seek God, or anything else that opposed the ways of Christianity, he would express strong disapproval of himself, but all the time keeping God's grace and mercy in view. In his diary for Wednesday 23 March, 1757, he wrote: 'How great the apostasy of my nature! I get a glimpse of God in prayer; and lose sight of him again as soon as prayer is ended. Indeed, I scarcely ever keep him continually in view through my devotions. If the apostasy be so great, I have greater cause of thankfulness, that I have any fellowship with God at all.'[33]

On Tuesday 5 April of the same year, he recorded:

> 'Seek and ye shall find.' So 'tis by experience; the more I
> seek communion with God, the more I enjoy it. What a sink
> is my heart! Such a shame of having spoke as became a
> Christian, immediately after, started up in my heart, as
> confounds me to think of. O this pride! And yet my pride is
> so great, it does not stop as it should, in the very sight of so
> much vileness. Lord, for thy mercies sake, make me vile in
> my own eyes.[34]

Ten days later, he complained, 'The thoughts of God are distant, cold and lifeless on my heart. I see him but through a glass darkly;'[35] and on 10 May: 'During this time [the last fifteen days] I have been exercised with denying Christ in the face of several trials I have gone through.'[36] There were brighter moments too: 'This morning [Tuesday 29 March, 1757] I had more than common of a steady believing frame, which, more or less, has attended me through the day – blessed be God!' Six days later, he wrote: 'Somewhat better satisfied with the day than usual, having enjoyed more impression of God upon my heart.'[37] Nothing gave him a deeper sense of peace and contentment than the presence of God in his daily ministry. It satisfied the longings of his soul and enabled him to do the work of God, which is by faith.

In all the trials he faced his trust in God remained steadfast, confident that divine 'grace is sufficient for me, that he will not suffer me to fall'. 'How needful such things!' he would say. 'They show me the vileness of my heart, and draw me nearer to Christ.'[38]

It is an observation no less true than common, that kindled coals, if placed asunder, soon go out, but if heaped together, quicken and enliven each other, and afford a lasting heat... If Christians kindled by the grace of God unite, they will quicken and enliven each other, but if they separate and keep asunder, no marvel if they soon grow cold and tepid. If two or three meet together in Christ's name, they will have heat; but how can one be warm alone?

George Whitefield preaching on religious societies in 1737.[1]

Be pleased, we beseech you, to bless all those societies, who in truth apply their hearts to your service and glory; we pray you, be pleased to strengthen, establish and settle both them and us in your holy faith, fear and love. Let nothing in this world discourage us from the pursuit of those holy purposes, which your Spirit has at any time put into our hearts and minds. But make us all faithful to you our avowed God and desired portion, even to death; that we may at last (with your whole church) be partakers of that eternal life and perfect bliss which you have promised through Jesus Christ, your only begotten Son, our mediator and redeemer. Amen.

Part of Samuel Walker's society prayer.[2]

8

Religious Societies at Truro

By the blessing of God 'the number of those whose conduct seemed to express a lively faith' in Truro became so large that it was impossible for Walker to give them the private advice and personal attention they demanded. So about the end of the summer of 1753 he decided to form his converts into a religious society, which after some delays was effected at the beginning of February, 1754. The number of members soon rose to seventy.

> While I was deliberating about this society [Walker wrote], which was to consist of such only as gave hopes of an edifying example, it was thought proper to call together as many others as were willing in my house once a week, as a sort of nursery for the principal society. And by talking and praying with them we seem to have found some establishment among those who are weaker.[3]

While the society he established was along similar lines to Wesley's societies which were springing up in various places, in drawing up the rules for its government he had chiefly followed the plan laid down more than half a century earlier by Josiah Woodward in his treatise *An Account of the Rise and Progress of the Religious Societies*, first published in 1697.[4] This little book contains a full and exact account of the remarkable growth of societies for prayer in London. Walker distributed it among his people when they first met together, 'purposely to remove every ground of prejudice, because in this tract the most considerable objections against religious societies are fully answered'.[5]

There were religious societies in the days of Beveridge, vicar of Ealing, and Anthony Horneck (1641-1697), who travelled from Heidelberg to England about 1661. He was a popular preacher at the Savoy Chapel, London, and 'a person of saint like life'. After preaching in 1678 what he called 'awakening sermons', several young men were 'touched with a very affecting sense of their sins, and began to apply themselves in a very serious manner to religious thoughts and purposes'.[6] They started to meet on a weekly basis in what became known as 'society rooms', 'to apply themselves to things wherein they might edify one another', and thus, inadvertently, they launched the first Anglican Religious Society. They were encouraged by the Church authorities and as the idea developed other societies mainly in and around London were formed. Horneck drew up rules for their government, at the head of which stands: 'All who enter the society shall resolve upon a holy and serious life.'[7] By 1740 these societies had waned in power and usefulness, although they still existed in many of the town parishes.

During Queen Mary II's reign (1689-94), and under her protection, similar societies were established in many parts of the kingdom. By the turn of the century there were thirty-nine in London and Westminster alone, and ten in Dublin – and all acted, generally speaking, according to the same rules and regulations. 'They met to pray, sing psalms, and read the Scriptures together; and to reprove, exhort, and edify one another by religious conference. They also carried out designs of charity.'[8] On a more personal level, the objects set before the members were, for example: 'to love one another; when reviled, not to revile again; to wrong no man; to pray, if possible, seven times a day; to keep close to the Church of England'.[9] Arnold Dallimore said that 'by 1730 nearly one hundred of these societies existed in London, and others – perhaps another hundred – were to be found in cities and towns throughout England. The societies' movement became, in many senses, the cradle of the revival.'[10] As the revival progressed, it was by means of these societies that new converts were directed and encouraged to propagate the faith by a practical testimony, which 'perhaps more than anything else promoted the growth of the movement among the masses'.

Risdon Darracott's society at Northampton was formed during the days of the Holy Club and in 1736 Howel Harris formed a society at Wernos,[11] which may be regarded as the first-fruits of Welsh Calvinistic Methodism. At this time he had not heard of the London societies and it is difficult to know from where the idea came – he did not read Woodward's book until three years later. His first plain reference to them in his own writings is in a letter to Griffith Jones, dated 8 October, 1736, when he said, 'We are beginning to set up private societies.'[12] These societies soon spread throughout Wales. The society at Fetter Lane, which belonged to the Church, was organized in May, 1738, and James Hervey founded a religious society at Bideford in 1743, which remained an Evangelical stronghold for over forty years. Hervey said: 'Woodward's rules we purpose punctually to observe, reading his exhortations distinctly and solemnly; offering up his prayers humbly and reverently; only with this difference, that some edifying book be substituted in the room of religious talk.'[13] His sole design was to 'promote real holiness in heart and life'.

In 1700 Wesley's father had published a plea for a more widespread adoption of societies and about a year later he founded one at Epworth. Following in his father's footsteps, Wesley's societies – 'a company of people associating together to help each other to work out their salvation' – were first formed towards the end of 1739. They had a strong Church tone and were modelled after those societies created at the end of the previous century. Concerning the rise of the Methodist United Society, a term adopted by Wesley to describe the emerging Methodist assemblies, he wrote that

... eight or ten persons came to me in London, who appeared
to be deeply convinced of sin, and earnestly groaning for
redemption. They desired I would spend some time with them
in prayer, and advise them how to flee from the wrath to
come... I appointed a day when they might all come together,
which, from henceforward, they did every Thursday, in the
evening. To these, and as many more as desired to join with
them (for the number increased daily), I gave those advices,
from time to time, which I judged most needful for them;
and we always concluded our meeting with prayer.[14]

Before returning to Walker, it must be noted that the Evangelical
clergy did not imitate the Methodist idea of establishing a new
organization around religious societies. While it is true that many
had Methodist sympathies and some worked in close conjunc-
tion with the Wesleys, others were unhappy at supporting their
societies, 'because of the danger of schism'. They rejected
Wesley's attempts to win them over, the stumbling block being
'their respective attitudes towards Church Order'. Nevertheless,
many remained on friendly terms with him, as did Walker, and
cooperated as far as differences would allow.

In a letter to his 'dear and much respected' friend Thomas
Adam, vicar of Wintringham, Lincolnshire, Walker gave further
details of his society. He first referred to his 'worldly' attitude
when he came to Truro and to his subsequent conversion, after
which he began to deal with the people 'as lost sinners – my
discourses were levelled at self-righteousness and formality, and
Christ was preached unto them'. From that time God poured
out his Spirit:

The number of those who have made particular application
to me, inquiring what they must do to be saved, cannot have
been less than eight hundred [out of a town of 1600, which
meant nearly the whole adult population], of whom, though
far the greater part have drawn back, yet I have the pleasure
of seeing a very considerable number about me, who, I trust,
are sincerely seeking God. The beginning of this year [1754],
it was found proper to form a religious society, the members

of which, being persons who have given some proof of their faith, are about eighty [afterwards the numbers greatly increased].[15]

He then mentioned that as a consequence of this success the 'eyes of the country are upon us, and the influence of what God has done here, has reached to many places near and at some distance'.[16]

The formation of the society was conducted with care and prudence. Walker first inquired into the religious state of the members and then divided them into two groups. One was made up of men, the other of married men, their wives and unmarried women. Into this second group single men were not allowed. Each class met every other week alternately on Tuesday evenings. At the opening of the society Walker laid before the members 'considerations' that expressed its threefold design: 'to glorify God, to quicken and confirm ourselves in faith and holiness, and to render us more useful among our neighbours'. To each design various 'cautions' were attached. Finally six 'motives' were read to encourage the members to observe the rules.

In the same month, February, 1754, under the direction of Walker, eleven 'orders for the religious societies at Truro', similar to Woodward's, were instituted, of which the following are examples:

> **3.** That the sole design of this society is to promote real holiness in the heart and life of all who belong to it, in a dependence on the Divine Power, and the conduct of the Holy Spirit, through our Lord Jesus Christ, to advance and perfect all good in us.
> **4.** That in order to our being of one heart and one mind, and to prevent whatever may engender strife, as well as to remove all occasion of offence being taken against us, no person be admitted a member of this society, or allowed to continue such, who is a member of any other religious meeting, or follows any other preaching than that of the established

ministry in this town. That none be admitted members, but
such as are inhabitants here and communicants, and that
no person at any time be introduced but at the
request of [Walker] the director.

5. That the members of this society do meet together at
a convenient place, one evening in every week, and that
they go home at nine o'clock.

6. That every member endeavour to give constant
attendance, and be present at the hour of the meeting
precisely, and that whoever absents himself four meetings
together, without giving satisfactory reason to the society,
shall be looked upon as disaffected to it.

7. That to prevent confusion, no person be removed from
the society but by the director... and that a disorderly
carriage, or a proud, contentious, disputing temper ... be
sufficient ground for ... removal.[17]

A 'disorderly carriage' to Walker meant 'not only the commission of gross and scandalous sins', but also matters such as a
'light use of the words *Lord, God, Jesus* in ordinary conversation... The buying and selling of goods which have not paid
custom. The doing needless work on the Lord's Day. The
frequenting ale-houses or taverns without necessary business.'
Perhaps remembering his own worldly beginnings at Truro, he
then cautioned the members against participating in 'vain
amusements' such as 'cards, dancing, clubs for entertainment,
playhouses, sports at festivals and parish feasts'. The ninth
order allowed members, with the concurrence of the director,
to make new orders, when needed.

10. That every member do esteem himself peculiarly
obliged to live in an inoffensive and orderly manner, to the
glory of God and the edification of his neighbours; that he
study to advance in himself and others, humility and meekness, faith in our Lord Jesus Christ, love to God, gospel
repentance, and new obedience, in which things Christian
edification consists, and not in vain janglings. And that in all
his conversation and articles of his faith, he stick close to
the plain and obvious sense of Holy Scripture...

11. That these orders shall be read over al least four times a year by the director, and that with such deliberation, that each member may have time to examine his own conduct by them.[18]

During the course of the meeting Walker kept close control and performed the devotional exercises himself. He drew up what he called the 'office of devotion' for the weekly meeting, derived mainly from Woodward's *Prayers*, though part was original. He opened by reading six sentences of Scripture and three Collects. The congregation then sat and a portion of the Bible was read, followed by the Confession from the Holy Communion service and the Lord's Prayer, which they all said on their knees, after which Walker offered up a prayer, three portions of which are given below:

O most holy and blessed God, the creator, governor and judge of all, who hates falsehood and hypocrisy, and will not accept the prayer of feigned lips; but has promised to show mercy to such as turn to you by true faith and repentance; vouchsafe, we pray, to create in us clean and upright hearts, through an unfeigned faith in your Son our Saviour. To us indeed belongs shame and confusion of face; we are not worthy to lift up our eyes or our voice to heaven; our natures are depraved and our ways have been perverse before you. O let not your wrath rise against us, lest we be consumed in a moment; but let your merciful bowels yearn over us, and vouchsafe to purity and pardon us through your all sufficient grace and mercy in our Lord Jesus Christ; since it has pleased you to offer him up as a sacrifice for sinners, vouchsafe, we beseech you, to cleanse us from all iniquity through his blood...

Give us the deepest humility, without which we can never be accepted of you, our infinitely condescending God. Make us continually to tread in the steps of our blessed Lord and Saviour Jesus Christ; being of a meek and quiet spirit, always influenced by the highest love of you our God, and by the most charitable disposition towards all men...

> Glorify, good God, your strength in our weakness, your grace in our pollution, and your mercy in our salvation. May our holy religion be grounded and settled in our hearts, that out of the good treasure of a gracious heart, our speech may be savoury and our conversation exemplary; that we may be fruitful in all good works, even to our old age, and to our last day...[19]

After the director's prayer all stood and sang a psalm. Next, Walker, or someone appointed by him, read a sermon or 'an instructive treatise', followed by further prayer. The congregation then 'stood in silent attention to hear an exhortation to humility, drawn up for the purpose by their minister'. They sang another psalm and the director said, 'It is very meet and right...' &c. They all joined in the Sanctus and finally Walker closed the meeting with the Grace.

Although this society resembled the Methodist gatherings, there were significant differences. Walker adhered closely to the forms of the Church of England and used extracts from the Book of Common Prayer. His aim was not to create a new church, but to enhance true Christianity within the Establishment and to uphold Anglican authority. He alone officiated, and that more strictly than in the Methodist societies, and there were no extempore prayers. His own prayer, composed by him, was the only unusual feature. The success of these meetings, which was comparable to the Methodist societies, Walker ascribed to the somewhat Draconian measures he adopted and to his own personal direction. In the main assembly he did not allow the members to share their religious experiences, insisting on the supremacy of the minister. In this way the arguments, petty jealousies and rivalries that can arise when members are permitted greater freedom were avoided.

The blessing that attended these meetings was described to Risdon Darracott late in the year 1754 by one of Walker's young converts. 'The use and success of this happy meeting,' he wrote, 'is very apparent, being every week more delightful and profitable to its members, who all love and watch over each other with a brotherly affection and care, and more awakening to the careless and profane.'[20] Walker himself, writing to Dr Guise at the same time as the above letter, acknowledged that the society

... appears to have been very instrumental to the establishment of the most of those who are members of it in saving knowledge and practice. It is my endeavour that none be admitted into it, but such as have given some good proofs of a good faith by an orderly and self-denying conversation; and my hope is, there are not many of it, concerning whose sincerity I have reasonable question.[21]

J. C. Ryle in his short biography of Walker is more than enthusiastic about his subject's success in this area:

He seems to have been deeply impressed with the necessity of following up the work done in the pulpit, and with the desirableness of stirring up real Christians to be useful to one another. There can be no doubt that he was right... The best and wisest manner of conducting meetings for mutual edification is a subject of vast difficulty, and one on which good men differ widely. Scores of excellent ministers have attempted to do something in this direction, and have completely failed. It was precisely here that Walker seems to have been eminently gifted, and to have obtained extraordinary success.[22]

In Thomas Adam's reply to Walker's letter detailing the Truro society, the vicar of Wintringham, asked, 'How do you manage to avoid disputes in your society? What method have you of terminating them amicably when they do arise?' His intention was not to 'dampen the design', but admitted that the whole 'is a delicate affair, and requires all the steadiness, prudence and piety of an able conductor, to keep the members of it knit together in the bonds of Christian love, considering the variety of tempers and the frailty of the heart'. He hoped very much that God would make it a 'blessing ... in the pious examples, Christian lives and brotherly charity of all who belong to it'.[23]

Walker read part of Adam's letter to the members of the society and enforced his observations upon them with the aim of promoting love and unity. With thankfulness he then reported to Adam

> ... that we have had no disputes among us, which, under God, we ascribe to the nature of our constitution, which is *that no one is to be talking there but myself*. That private persons should be speaking in a large company, we had observed from the Methodists, to be so great a temptation to conceit (and the next step to that is always envy, strife in the heart and contention) that we dared not venture upon it. Our way is, to take advantage of one passage and another of Scripture, to give and impress some piece of advice suited to a society, which office I ever take upon myself. Conversation they have enough elsewhere.[24]

So that members of his society could have the opportunity of talking about their trials, consolations and experiences, and of receiving the benefit of mutual advice in a free conversation, Walker instituted smaller assemblies (not less than five persons, no more than eight). They were not limited to any particular day or hour, but appointed at the most convenient time for all concerned – sometimes before the Sabbath service or between services, and also after work on a weekday, so as not to interfere with their worldly businesses. The persons present were 'to exercise an affectionate inspection of each other's conduct', and to encourage or rebuke accordingly. Members met according to age, condition, circumstances and sex. The reason for this breakdown was that those who endured similar trials, would be better able to strengthen and exhort each other. Therefore, the 'married men met together by themselves, the unmarried by themselves, and so the women in like manner'.[25]

Walker was not present on these occasions, but to avoid confusion and to promote the ends designed by such a meeting, he drew up a little treatise for their instruction called *Regulations and Helps for Promoting Religious Conversation among Christians*, 'for improving each other in Christian knowledge and practice by the grace of God'.

Regulation

I. That every person come to the meeting now proposed with a prepared heart, expecting through divine grace to receive improvement in saving knowledge, self-conviction and edification.

II. That the conversation be introduced and ended with prayer.

III. That they speak freely and lay open their hearts, as far as their own case, or that of others, may require.

IV. That they beware of conceit in delivering their sentiments, and of diffidence in being afraid to speak of them.

V. That in the spirit of meekness and humility, counting others better than themselves, they do warn each other of their faults, freely and affectionately examining everything thoroughly.

VI. That the conversation be confined to the state of one another, and that all prying curiosity be excluded.

VII. That each person be allowed to speak in turn, and that as briefly as possible – that none be interrupted while speaking, and when all have delivered their sentiments, that the enquirer may then apply what has been said to his own case, and nothing further be said on that subject, unless the enquirer should desire any person more fully to explain himself.

VIII. That each person do carefully examine and watch over his heart, that no disgust be taken against any who have spoken freely to his case, or may seem to have more knowledge or experience than himself.

IX. That they often ask their own hearts whether they have a desire to come to such conversation, and if not, why.

X. That afterwards each person carefully recollect and endeavour to improve the conversation.

XI. That what passes in such conversation be not divulged elsewhere.[26]

The members were 'to correct faults, warn of dangers, relieve despondency, and stimulate Christian progress'. Inconsistencies in others were to be mentioned so that an explanation might be offered or the error corrected. Each filled in turn the position of *enquirer* for the day, and part of his duty was to close the meeting with prayer, which was occasionally followed by singing. Annexed to these regulations were proper inquiries concerning 'growth in humility, faith in Jesus Christ, the love of God and of our neighbour', and other interesting points to stimulate conversation.

To help his people Walker wrote *Some Hints for Prayer for the Society in their Private Meetings, by the Director's Orders.* In the seven paragraphs he urged the leader to plead for 'an awful and reverential sense of the presence of God' so that in some measure he might 'lose sight of his fellow-worshippers' and 'that his desires may the more sincerely ascend to God'. He exhorted the society to humble themselves at the sight of their sins, and to pray that, as a result of their 'unseemly behaviour' and 'unfruitfulness', the Lord Jesus would not 'remove his gospel in its power, purity and fulness'. He urged them to pray for their minister 'that he may eminently hold forth the light of the glorious gospel in doctrine and conduct, wherever he is or wherever he goes'; to pray ardently for the grace of the Spirit to attend the ministration of the church and to bless the means to the profiting of their own souls; for the salvation of their ungodly neighbours and to be 'ready to do them good for evil'; for strength to remain steadfast in the faith; and for 'sincere and unaffected love to one another', for 'without this we shall fall to nothing'.[27]

The success of this scheme was 'so complete' that Thomas Adam urged him to watch over his own heart in case he became 'puffed up' by his achievements. Walker received this admonition with humility and encouraged his friend to continue his 'seasonable and acceptable' advice, observing,

> When we are grown up to a becoming disregard of the reproaches of the world, it is but too easy a step to become vain of them. Perhaps it is more dangerous still to be in the direction of a number of serious persons, and yet worse again to hear of the commendations which injudicious zeal will be throwing in our way. I have indeed much need to watch over my spirit, perhaps more than a high degree of preferment would have called upon me to do.[28]

The influence of Walker's society spread into other parishes in Cornwall and beyond. Both Michell and Penrose followed Walker's example. In March 1755, Walker wrote to a friend in Somerset and told him that Michell's 'company is advanced to thirty' and that 'Penrose too has a larger number about him'.[29] Thomas Haweis, one of Walker's converts, founded a society at Oxford in 1757, which 'met regularly to read the Greek Testament, discuss theology, share their Christian experience, and join in prayer'.[30] One of the members of this fellowship was Thomas Biddulph, vicar of Padstow, and later friend of George Conon. John Wesley in the latter half of 1757 spoke of preaching to a large congregation at St Ewe, 'many of whom were in Mr Walker's societies'.[31] And James Hervey no doubt spoke for many when he commented:

> I am much pleased with the account of the religious society at Truro, of which Mr Walker is the founder and present director. It is an admirable plan! I would have endeavoured (had my health permitted my attendance) to have formed one of the same kind at Northampton. I heartily wish so useful an institution was more known, and well established in all the principal towns in this kingdom; as I am persuaded such a society must be productive of great good, and in some degree revive the drooping interest of Christianity, wherever it was prudently managed.[32]

[The Church Catechism] is a summary of that whole salvation for fallen creatures, which is in the Redeemer Jesus Christ. Every part of it has the most direct eye to him, as the all in all of lost, fallen man. The baptismal covenant is entirely founded in his merits; the baptismal renunciation stands upon his kingdom and grace; the Christian faith points him out to us as the Author of all our pardon, acceptance and fellowship with God in time and eternity; the law in the ten commandments sets him before us as our righteousness, and the Procurer of that grace, by which we are restored to that image of God and conformity to his blessed nature and will, which is the substance of the law; prayer, finally, and the sacraments, which are the means of our access to God as our Father, and of our receiving from him the full assurance of his love and favour, with all needful supplies of his Spirit; these are not otherwise acceptable to God, or profitable to us, but in the faith of Jesus Christ, and through his mediation. Christ then is the sum of this Catechism.

Samuel Walker.[1]

9

Teaching a Growing Church

By the end of 1754 the work at Truro and its influence on the surrounding area was deepening, with several remarkable conversions. One circumstance that Walker related in a letter of 14 January, 1755, occurred at the beginning of 1754. It concerned a young man, about twenty-six, who lived in the parish about twelve miles from Truro. One day he

> ... came to the shop of one of my people (for so they are called), thinking of nothing so little as his soul. As his custom is, the man who keeps the shop gave him some serious advice with the goods he had purchased. The poor creature having never heard much of the matter before, seemed to be attentive, which encouraged the other to be more particular with him, and to ask if he were willing to spend half an hour with me. He consented. They came to me together; he was ignorant of everything, and satisfied that all was well with him. I both talked with him and sent home some books with him. As business has brought him hither, I have seen him from time to time, and always to my great comfort. He told me last Saturday, that there are now many in the village where he lives, whose eyes seem to be opening. They are meeting together for prayer, reading and religious conversation, and are actually forsaking their gross sins.; and that many more in the parish are evidently struck, nor can find themselves easy to live as they were wont.[2]

Other 'surprising instances of the grace of Christ' were related by Fawcett of Kidderminster in a later letter (29 April, 1758).

On the death of a careless young man Walker made the most
of the opportunity by giving a free lecture to a numerous
congregation. All were deeply affected and many were in tears,
and two of the youth's friends, who had walked with him in the
ways of sin and who had carried his body to the grave, having
previously resisted the gospel, 'returned to their Father's house'.[3]
A more remarkable instance is the following:

> One of the most obstinate and incorrigible sinners who about
> two months since, among the carousing herd, threatened to
> spend all his fortune, which is £500 or £600 per annum, to
> pull Walker's gown from his back, for refusing to bury his
> drunken companion, is now ... crying out in the bitterness of
> spirit, 'What shall I do to be saved?' He frequently sends for
> Walker, owning him his best physician, and receiving with
> his whole heart, his free and friendly admonitions. And though
> he has for thirty years led the van in iniquity, yet Mr Walker
> is not without hope concerning him.[4]

Darracott in his letter to Henry Venn called the awakening
under Walker 'a glorious work', and at the close of 1754 Walker
himself rejoiced in the gospel's success: 'Never was there such
a day of grace with us as of late, and it grows brighter continually... Truly publicans and sinners, some of the most vile and
profligate, are amongst us... Some are melted, some
confounded, while I persuade them by the terrors of the Lord,
and beseech them to be reconciled to God, pouring out all my
soul, and more than all my strength, to them and for them.'[5] In
January, 1755, Walker declared that 'within these two months
perhaps, near two hundred of the lower people ... had fallen
under convictions and impressions', and Satan's strongholds
were under attack, with the Truro curate 'daily getting advantage'
over the old adversary. The display of the power of Christ among
his flock was 'most admirable' and in every way they were
upheld by his grace. 'From the beginning,' said Walker, 'we
have been supported, yes emboldened, yes enlarged. In spite

of an universal discountenance, of a powerful opposition, of the grossest ignorance, and vice in reputation; in spite of our own inwardly backsliding hearts, we still increase, and many are added to us daily of such, I trust, as shall be saved.'[6] Not only that, but the gospel was getting into several other pulpits of 'regular' clergy in the county, so that Walker could confidently expect that 'the little stone will become a mountain'.

In a letter of 8 February, 1755, Fawcett wrote that from the accounts he had received he thought the 'new and glorious revival in the county of Cornwall' was 'as remarkable in its kind as that at Cambuslang, or Kilsyth, or any places in America'. He observed how the Lord was 'stirring up the spirits of several clergymen to preach Jesus Christ in their own parishes', and how he had 'already given them to see hundreds of souls under the most serious impressions'. Samuel Walker, noted Fawcett, 'is the instrument whom the Lord has principally been honouring with his presence, power and blessing'.[7]

To enforce the doctrines and disciplines of the Bible on his growing church, Walker introduced the neglected custom of catechizing, which he regarded as vital to the spiritual health of his people. Appended to a letter Walker wrote to Adam, which the latter sent to a friend and which exemplifies the importance of catechizing in Walker's mind, was the following question: 'Walker asks me what I think of his writing to the Archbishop of Canterbury, to represent to him the low state of *Catechizing* in the Church of England, and the necessity of applying a suitable remedy. What do you think?'[8] This friend was believed to be the archdeacon of Stowe, William Bassett, Adam's neighbour and one of the few enlightened Church dignitaries of the time. From 1729 to his death in 1765 Bassett was vicar of Glentworth, a parish situated between Lincoln and Scunthorpe. When he was made archdeacon of Stowe in 1751, it was an early example of an Evangelical in the Church of England receiving higher preferment. Adam described him as 'an industrious labourer in

Christ's vineyard, exerting himself to the utmost to revive the antiquated doctrines of the Church of England, for which he does not escape scot-free; but he is a stout champion for the truth, and has grace enough to fear nothing'.[9] Walker also regarded him as a true servant of Christ, referring to him as a 'plain, open-hearted and tender' man.

The system of catechizing was little practised during this period, and Walker believed that more than 'by any other thing, the kingdom of darkness and sin was established in England' because of its neglect. In Truro the young people were divided into three classes: under twelves, from twelve to fifteen, and from fifteen to twenty years of age. The classes were instructed privately at set times and then catechized in the church 'an hour after sermon' before a large congregation of up to 500 people, who were 'for the most part impressed'. After that, and in order to influence their daily conduct, Walker took just one point which he explained 'as shortly as possible, enforcing it afterwards as largely and warmly' as he could. In this way he not only instructed the young people, but also their parents, who had come to church to hear the performance of their children. This exercise lasted at least an hour. About halfway through, he stopped and questioned the young people as to what they had heard, and again at the end. In a letter to Adam, Walker wrote:

> The young people are without fear or shame; and at that age so quick, that if anything I have said has slipped them (which is very seldom), I find it has been through my defect rather than their fault. I have had the unspeakable pleasure of seeing many of them brought into a very serious way under this means; particularly I remember in the first year, about fifteen of them, whom I had seen in the beginning of the season trifling and laughing, while I was speaking to them.[10]

Walker kept up the catechizing twice a year, each Sunday evening from six to eight from the beginning of February to the end of April and again from the beginning of August to the end of October. It was, from all accounts, 'greatly blessed'. 'The good effects of this work,' enthused Walker, 'are manifest both upon the old and the young. I heartily wish this were practised in every congregation in England. I know not how we of the Establishment can evade the express injunctions for that purpose.'[11] Darracott said it 'laid a happy foundation for future blessings in the rising generation',[12] and in later years Thomas Haweis adopted Walker's method of catechizing.

Walker always made good use of the 'seasons' of the church, taking these opportunities to 'arouse slumberers and quicken the awakened to increased activity'. On 30 January he made solemn reference to national sins; at the beginning of Lent he called his flock to personal repentance; on church holidays similar applications were made; and his lectures in the afternoon on some portion of Scripture at Christmas, Easter and Whitsuntide were of 'a character so heart-searching, that when they failed to convert, they awed the sinner into outward decorum... Strolling players, cock fighters and others of like description ceased from the streets of Truro during these seasons, and its inhabitants became ashamed of open desecration of such solemn occasions.'[13]

His sermons, which were always carefully written, were read on Sunday evenings in the society meetings and were often transcribed by the members, who handed them from one to another. In this way the preached word was imprinted on the minds of his hearers and the knowledge of religion spread more widely. In addition to his Sunday morning sermons he occasionally preached 'gift sermons' on some week days. In summer he gave a lecture every Thursday and during the winter quarter he lectured on the Sermon on the Mount every Sunday evening. On Mondays he gave a lecture to every person who would attend in the society room – 'by this many careless persons are every week awakened into a concern for their perishing souls'[14] – but it so impaired his health that he was eventually persuaded to give it up. His own room for private advice was visited every day except Saturdays. Overall he calculated that about one thousand inhabitants of Truro, as well as many from adjacent areas, had received his private counsel concerning the state of their souls. Saturdays were set aside to prepare for the Sabbath. The mornings were for humiliation and solemn prayer in preparation for composing his sermons in the afternoons and evenings. Add to all these labours the many hours of letter writing, visiting the sick, conversing with friends for the benefit of their souls, and it can be understood that before long he became so busy that he had little time to study the works of other men, and the Bible became the only book from which he drew that deep and practical know-ledge which he was always ready to impart.

During the last two years of his ministry, so many young people were awakened that he organized a private evening lecture for them in his own room twice a week. These meetings were crowded and very hot, and his friends noticed that his strength was being drained by them, so much so that unless he desisted his life would be shortened. However, the undertaking was so useful to the young converts, and Walker was intent on it, that they did not try to press him to stop. 'Indeed,' remarked one of his biographers, 'his compassion to the souls of perishing sinners appeared to be his shining grace, insomuch that when in conversation any hardened and impenitent sinner was mentioned, he seemed to express an inward pungent distress of soul.'[15]

In his teaching he wanted to impress on his people the importance of the devotional aspects of worship and of joining in the prayers of the church, so he preached a series of sermons on the nature and use of prayer, which he described as consisting of confession, praise, petition and thanksgiving. He wanted his congregation to participate in public worship 'in a manner becoming the majesty of the God they served, the decency and dignity of his house and family, and highly improving and profitable to the begetting and confirming religious habits within them'. He also explained to them the *Daily Service*[16] and the *Litany* [17] to 'show the spirit of devotion with which their several parts ought to be performed, and also how expressive they are of the sentiments with which a pious heart is warmed and enlivened'.[18]

In his lecture on the daily church service, he showed how the four parts of prayer are 'united *in order* in the morning and evening services'.

> **1. *Confession*.** Now, let us suppose ourselves, in the first place, approaching publicly the divine presence, that with one mouth we may confess the vileness, which, upon comparing *ourselves* with *God*, and our *actions* with our *duty*, we do every one of us at heart lament and bewail, and earnestly beseeching infinite goodness to avert the punishment we so well deserve...
>
> **2. *Praise*.** It was before remarked, that the more intimate consideration of God's excellences, whilst the mind was engaged on its own imperfections and vileness, afforded matter of confession; but that [God's excellences] looked upon in another point of view, and regarded as being altogether lovely and adorable in themselves, become the subject of praise. This ... might very naturally follow upon confession; inasmuch as the reflections suggested to us by the incomparable goodness of God, so ready to pardon the great and crying offences of his creatures, must of course lead us to consider more attentively his other perfections, the event of which must needs be the offerings of praise...[19]

There is nothing that sets us free to exercise our minds in the pleasing duty of praise more than 'God's gracious promise of absolution and remission'. Walker defined praise as

... an exaltation and triumph of the soul, on a nearer view of God's excellences; the understanding being swallowed up by God's immense perfections, the will most strongly engaged to dwell upon and enjoy them, and the affections with a kind of holy violence, struggling to express the exceeding great and awful joy, with which they are carried forth towards a being so unspeakably desirable.[20]

The third part of prayer is petition. On the one hand, we must be thoroughly convinced of our wants, both temporal and spiritual, and our inability to supply them. On the other hand, we must have every confidence – a confidence that stems from our meditations on God's perfections – that God is the only fountain of all our blessings and that he is able and willing, on our earnest request, to meet our needs.

We have ... placed God before us in his most endearing relations to us as Father, Redeemer and Sanctifier; we have considered him as the bestower of our daily bread (all things of every kind we need) upon us, and we have made a general representation of our wants, infirmities, weakness and dependence. These ... are the principal qualifications of *petition*. Let us, therefore, under this persuasion of God's loving-kindness, pour out all our necessities in his presence, lay before him the various wants we experience, and earnestly and faithfully implore his help...

4. *Thanksgiving,* [is] the expression of a grateful heart, upon reflection on the great blessings, both temporal and spiritual, which it had experienced at God's hand; the use of which, besides the returning to God the thanks so justly due to him, and the increasing our love and reverence, was observed to confirm upon our hearts a faith and hope and confident resignation with regard to God's future dealings with us...[21]

Having presented the four parts of prayer in a natural order, and in a way that 'cannot but engage us highly to esteem the church service, and most carefully to make use of it', Walker closed the lecture by saying:

The sum of the whole is in the last words of the concluding prayer of St Chrysostom. We must so enlarge the notions we have of God, and so represent them before him, that God may mercifully accept the 'desires' and longings of our souls after him, and 'fulfil our petitions' for the things we stand in need of, so that the knowledge of God and his truth may be growing upon us, and we may thereby become more fit for, and draw yet nearer and nearer to, the life everlasting.

If this whole service has been gone through with becoming attention and devotion, if we have been in earnest in what we have been about, and really laid ourselves open before God in all integrity of heart, nothing can be more comfortable than the blessing which God graciously gives to quiet, cheer and support us. This being, as it were, God's answer of acceptance to our faithful prayers, must be received with all reverence, the people in the primitive church being directed to bow their heads when it was pronounced to them. Let us then receive this prayer of benediction with all joy and thankfulness, and let us add our hearty Amen, thereby to make it our own, so that 'the grace' purchased for us by the death 'of our Lord Jesus Christ' may procure our pardon, the love of the Father may put his seal of acceptance to that sacrifice, and 'the fellowship' and communication of the graces 'of the Holy Ghost', may perfect our sanctification; and that all these may 'be with us now' and continue with us 'all evermore'. To which blessed Trinity, even the Father, Son and Spirit, be ascribed all honour and obedience, 'world without end. Amen'.[22]

Walker was also careful in directing his people to understand and appreciate the *Litany*, a general supplication 'of all the people under the pressing sense of some evil'. This service is 'altogether expressive of the earnestness and importunity with which a nation, under the visitation of God's hand, would with one voice call upon him to compassionate their miseries, and turn away his wrathful displeasure from them';[23] and, at the same time, 'the most lively method, whereby to remove or prevent any misery which may fall upon or threaten us, and also a most lovely exercise of the highest Christian virtues, faith, hope, resignation, patience and charity'.[24] 'An affecting sense of danger and utter want of divine protection' is the true spirit of the *Litany*, which helps to secure from us 'a most passionate and affecting address to Almighty God'. With his usual urgency he exhorted his people

> ... not to pass over so admirable a service, with a cold insensibility and an unaffecting indifference, but to join in it with fear and trembling, yet with assurance and faith, that our addresses to God may be as warm and lively as our necessities are urgent, and that we may find rest, when it can only be had in making our requests known to God. May he so enlarge our hearts in the use of this most excellent duty of prayer, that by a constant communion with God, we may be transformed into his likeness, and prove by our own experience what is that good, acceptable and perfect will of God.[25]

As far as baptism was concerned he instructed his followers that the sum and substance of their duty under the baptismal vow, was 'solemnly to deny sin in the life, and reject it with the heart'. He advised parents, who presented their children for baptism, to choose godparents that were 'judged fittest for helping to bring up the child like a Christian, without regard had in any means to interest, convenience or grandeur'. 'Baptism you may be sure is no trifling matter,' he remarked. Therefore, on 'such solemn seasons', 'all due moderation and decency' should be used in the entertainment of friends; for on that day

> ... do you not dedicate, present and offer up the fruit of your body to God, to be made partaker of God's mercy through Christ? Do you not call upon God to receive him into the ark of Christ's church, to wash him and sanctify him with the Holy Ghost, that he may be delivered from God's wrath; and

do you not earnestly plead with God that he may be steadfast in faith, joyful through hope and rooted in charity; that
he may so pass through this world as to come to everlasting
life? Are not these matters of more serious concern to you
than how you may acquit yourselves in the entertainment of
your friends, which, it is likely, too much engages your
thoughts at these times?[26]

He called the Lord's Supper 'the feast appointed to strengthen
the faith and refresh the spirits of pilgrims, who are going through
a dangerous and tempting world towards a better country'.[27]
He taught his people that a person partaking of it

> ... does profess Christ to be his Saviour and Lord, does
> profess himself to be his servant and soldier, undertakes his
> service, and engages in his cause, and does publicly
> declare this in the face of men, whether friends or enemies
> to his master, and before angels, whether light or darkness.
> He does declare and desire that, henceforward, he may be
> regarded as Christ's servant, as one ready to all the toils
> and all the works of a Christian.[28]

Seeing so many 'who had bound themselves by this very oath
of loyalty and service, the communion, [but] did either not
understand it or not observe it', he thought it necessary to
compose sermons on the nature of the communicant's profession. In these *Sacramental Sermons* he not only described the
Christian's duty towards God, but explained that at the Lord's
Supper believers are 'considered as united to each other' as
they gather around the Master's table, whose 'banner over them
is love'. It is therefore the duty of all to exhibit an inward and
holy spirit of love 'in their conversation', that love 'must qualify
all their conduct, and give a lustre to the daily business of their
lives'. Walker explained the temper and offices of Christian love
in his *Five Sermons on Brotherly Love*.

He took the administration of this ordinance very seriously and his preparation for it was accompanied by much soul-searching. His diary for Sunday 3 April, 1757, reads:

Sacrament day. Last night my heart did not cordially acquiesce with God's sentence against sin; and though that matter be pretty well cleared up in my mind, yet I ought to seek carefully more light upon it. I would go to the table like a pardoned rebel, who is *still* half a rebel: with great humility and thankfulness, to remember the great means of salvation represented in this ordinance. Thanks be to God. I heartily approve of this way; and do as heartily desire, and, through grace, determine, *not only for wrath, but also for conscience sake*, to lead my life conformably with the words of Christ, as a member of his kingdom, in the midst of a wicked world, with which I would make no compliances to get its esteem, or to avoid its displeasure; and this I regard as the only method by which I can glorify God.[29]

His views on marriage are illustrated in two letters he wrote on that subject. The first was written from Truro on 18 August, 1756, to Miss – –, on her intended marriage with Mr William –. He opened the letter by reflecting on the grace that had endeared them to one another, 'that heaven-born ornament which will grow more beautiful with age'. He urged Miss – – to be thankful that she had been delivered 'from the greatest curse in this world, an ungodly husband'. He instructed her to weigh carefully the duties peculiar to the married state before she made the solemn matrimonial vow. The substance of her duty as far as it regarded her husband was 'a willing subjection to him in the Lord'. He outlined further duties – 'to be a follower of godly matrons, to look to your house, and to take care of your children' – and encouraged her to make notes of what her present views were of the matrimonial vows and duties 'to keep your heart against those temptations which the ease and other delights of a newly-married state bring with them, and by which

I have usually seen the minds of the most serious a good deal hurt'.[30] He then told her to make

> ... a reasonable estimate of the trials and troubles which must or may attend you in [the married state]; such as the sickness or death of your husband before you; the want or loss of children, together with the possibility of their turning out ill; disappointments in worldly things, &c. &c. You know not how God may please to try you in this state...
>
> I wish you carefully to correspond with that great design of matrimony, the being a helpmate for your husband, which imports not only a helping with your husband in his labours, trials and troubles, but also with his soul... Watch over him in love, warn him continually and without reserve, do not think him so established, as that he shall not need greatly your watchful eye: this will endear and keep you dear to him. There should be the greatest confidence between you, and in that view I particularly beg you to be faithful in keeping all his secrets.[31]

The second shorter letter, also from Truro, was addressed to the newly weds and is dated 22 September, 1756.

> MY DEAR – AND –,
> I have not time to say much, but do you love one another? How do you know that? Your souls, I mean. Is Christ the bond of your love? Is it his image you love in one another? Or is your love too much carnal? Do you watch over one another's heart with a loving jealousy? Are you free, unreservedly so? What, every day, letting nothing pass? I would have you to begin well. Open your hearts every evening; I beg you will. It will be a blessing to you a thousand ways. Methinks I should esteem such an opportunity the greatest blessing of a married state. Well, but do you also pray for one another, yes, and do you pray with each other, yourselves alone? Have you done so often? Do you delight to do so? Also are you seeking God's glory in this state, and not your own pleasure? Are you aware of the danger you are in from *enjoyment* and *independency*? There is

nothing more dangerous than the latter, because it is so agreeable to our *own* will, and especially dangerous upon a charge, when from being dependent we become our own masters, and that most especially when we are first become so.

I could say much more, but this is enough for once, and I am just going to church. If I mistake not, there is no one more cordially yours than,

S. W.[32]

With the teaching that Walker imparted to his flock, the whole of Truro seemed to prosper and the general awakening spread to other parts of the county.

John Wesley ... is beyond doubt the great figure in later Cornish history. If we live in Cornwall we cannot escape him; if we are Cornish we would not. His fame is in all our Churches and his influence pervades our civil life. John Wesley is a founding father of modern Cornwall.

For two centuries Cornishmen were acutely conscious of the debt they owed him and, for many, its acknowledgement was their proudest boast. Devotion to the Wesleys and their principles was among the standards by which a Cornishman was measured. They did not think of John as a great historic figure, a somewhat despotic evangelist and reformer, revitalising their religious life and redeeming their society. He was their father; their individual example and guide. The veneration was intensely personal, a filial bond felt by all sorts and conditions of Cornishmen.

John Pearce.[1]

10
Methodism in Cornwall: The Beginning

Parallel to and yet distinct from the awakening in the Established Church in Cornwall was the Methodist movement in the county, headed of course by the Wesley brothers. Both revivals, or rather the two branches of the same revival, inevitably overlapped at various points, but on the whole they progressed independently. John Wesley, who regarded his work as complementary to that of the Established Church, did not preach, unless invited, in places where there was an Evangelical ministry. There was a group of Anglican Evangelicals in the north east of the county who were sympathetic to him and he preached in their churches, but he did not form Methodist societies there, preferring to leave the work in the hands of the resident clergy. However, Wesley did form Methodist societies in some Evangelical parishes, refusing to put his converts under the care of the local clergy, even when they were godly men, and his followers, with an inordinate zeal, were guilty of encouraging Anglicans to leave the Establishment, which inevitably caused tension between the two groups.[2]

He avoided preaching in Truro altogether while Walker was alive, because he did not want to clash with the Evangelical work in the town. He did, however, preach and form a society at Bezore, only three miles away. On Wednesday 21 September, 1757, he preached at St Ewe and many in the congregation were from the society at Truro. This was probably before Walker's followers separated from the Methodists. Surprisingly, on the many later occasions Wesley visited Truro – the first of these was in September, 1762 – he made few references to Walker's societies.

John C. C. Probert, in trying to understand the unpopularity of the Methodists with the Anglicans, and how in early Cornish Methodism 'revivals and declines often set in with feverish rapidity', said,

We might well ask what an Anglican clergyman might think of a case such as Medrose. He would have seen an outside clergy-man, Wesley, come into his parish, gain a great following and form a strong society, some of whose members would be claiming that Christ had saved them from all sin. Within a few years the majority might well have backslid. We can sympathise with the comment of John Collins, the rector of Redruth, in 1745: 'People are better for the present ... by-and-by they will be as bad.'[3]

A less cynical appraisal is adopted by Miles Brown, who reck-oned the dominant outlook among the clergy at the time was 'one of self-satisfied contentment with things as they were and opposition to change... The mass of Churchmen settled down into an attitude of unconcealed dislike of all Dissent, or of any-thing at all likely to lead to its strengthening, which probably affected profoundly the view of many towards Methodism.'[4]

It was this sense of novelty rather than stability among many of Wesley's converts that caused Anglican clergymen to look upon the movement with suspicion. Walker and his Club members, for their part, while never directly opposing the work of the Methodists, at least endeavoured to correct their doctrines and irregularities so that they might remain within the Established fold. With Walker's concerns in mind and in view of his protracted correspondence with the Wesleys, their disagreements and subsequent divergence, it is necessary, as an introduction to this period of our subject's history, to examine the establishment of Methodism in Cornwall and the changes that occurred in the county as a result of its influence.

Walker was still an unconverted vicar, striving to serve the people of Lanlivery, when the Wesleys first visited Cornwall in 1743. At that time there was a religious society at St Ives, which had been formed by clergymen, and their aim was to strengthen and increase its membership by the faithful preaching of the gospel. It was discovered by Joseph Turner, a Bristol Methodist sea-captain, when he visited the town early in 1743. Turner was 'agreeably surprised to find a few persons who feared God and constantly met together. They were much refreshed by him, as he was by them.'[5] This society consisted of Catherine Quick and eleven others, who gathered for prayer and to read Burkitt's *Notes on the New Testament*. (This society had grown considerably by the time of John's first visit.) Turner returned home and made known what he had found, and two lay-preachers, Thomas Williams, a convert of Charles Wesley, and William Shepherd, were sent to investigate the possibility of starting a Methodist work in the western part of the county. Later in the year, on the invitation of Catherine Quick and her associates, and moved by the needs of industrial Cornwall, the Wesleys arrived at St Ives.

> This pre-Methodist society [wrote Thomas Shaw] was ... adopted into Methodism, and became the first Methodist society in the town, and the first in Cornwall. [John] Wesley visited Cornwall each year from 1743 to 1750 to carry out his declared policy of developing the Cornish work 'little by little' from St Ives. During these formative years societies were built up in nearly thirty places in the mining areas in the west, and there were small isolated ones in the north-east, at Port Isaac, Camelford, Trewint and Launceston. Preaching was often in the open air, but the societies met either in private houses or, in the more populous areas, in 'society' or 'preaching' houses.[6]

Many in the county were astonished when the Wesleys visited Cornwall that two such educated Oxford men should leave their large London congregations to preach the gospel to the poor in so distant a place, notorious for its barbarity. But preach they did, and both men extended to the full their mental and physical powers in an effort to win the lost for Christ. Countless meetings were held, scores of sermons preached, and every attack from their enemies was rebuffed with calm courage as they travelled almost incessantly on horseback over rough terrain. One writer remarked about John that although 'high honour, learned ease, and literary fame were all accessible' to him, he 'chose to travel in hunger and weariness over the commons of Cornwall, and then, after the day of unparalleled labours, to sleep on a hard floor'.[7] John Nelson, in an account of these hardships (1743), wrote:

> All that time Mr Wesley ... lay on the floor; he had my great-coat for his pillow... After being here near three weeks, one morning, about three o'clock, Mr Wesley turned over and finding me awake clapped me on the side, saying, 'Brother Nelson, let us be of good cheer, I have one whole side yet, for the skin is off but on one side.' One day ... Mr Wesley stopped his horse to pick the blackberries, saying, 'Brother Nelson, we ought to be thankful that there are plenty of black-berries; for this is the best country I ever saw for getting a stomach, but the worst that I ever saw for getting food. Do the people think we can live by preaching?'[8]

As the Wesleys preached with uncommon power, the stagnant religious life of Cornwall began to stir. At first the poor, shocked by what they heard, did not know how to react. Should they believe and follow these men, or should they silence them with blows? The clergy too were taken by surprise. Some welcomed the newcomers – George Thomson, John Bennet and John Turner opened their pulpits to them – others remained apathetic. A third group, fearing a loss of authority if these men were not stopped, went on the offensive, and stirred up their parishioners against them, although there does not appear to have been any organized opposition. They resented interference in the work of their parishes from outsiders. So they closed their pulpits, and refused to allow their congregations to sing Methodist hymns. Malicious rumours were spread to blacken their reputation and other more violent methods adopted to stop them preaching. 'In Cornwall,' said John Wesley, 'the war against the Methodists was carried on with far more vigour than that against the Spaniards.'[9]

The opposition to the Wesleys and Methodism in Cornwall occurred at a politically sensitive time when the Young Pretender to the English throne, Romanist Charles Stuart, was preparing to invade England. The magistrates, unsure of the support he commanded in the county, were nervous, and especially so when they found societies being formed in mining populations, whose loyalty to the crown they suspected. They imagined that these societies were to prepare the way for an invasion of the county, a fear that was heightened because of Cornwall's geographical position, poor communications, and a rocky coastline that was thought to be a perfect landing place for the French armies. In 1745 Wesley was told that 'All the gentlemen of these parts [Tolcarn in Wendron parish] say that you have been a long time in France and Spain, and are now sent hither by the Pretender, and that these societies are to join him.'[10]

The agitation of the Cornish officials was not lessened by a rumour, apparently started by the master of the ferry boat at Tilbury, that a large store of arms was laid up in the Penzance district, ready for any group or society to use. In addition, the clerical magistrate Walter Borlase, 'one of the fiercest persecutors of Wesley and the Methodists in Cornwall',[11] discovered that large quantities of arms and ammunition from the wrecked privateer, the *Charming Molly*, had been sold to those sympathetic to the Jacobite cause, for which there was considerable support. There was also a rumour that the Young Pretender was in hiding in Boskenna, and, to make things worse, various letters were circulated, accusing the Methodists of 'subversive activities'.

The excitement in the church was increased when the Bishop of Exeter, Nicholas Claggett, urged the clergy under his juris-diction 'to bestir ourselves, with all possible diligence, in our several stations, at this time, for the preservation of our religion and liberties, now attempted to be ravished from us'. He wanted them to 'excite in the minds' of all under their care a hearty zeal for all the blessings they enjoyed under 'his most gracious majesty King George the Second', and to set before them, 'in the strongest light, the vast differences which there is between the Protestant Religion and a Free Government on the one side, and Popery and Arbitrary Power on the other'.[12]

Wesley's reputation in the county was not helped by a sermon he had preached on 11 June, 1734, before the Univer-sity of Oxford, 'the home of Jacobitism' early in the century, which was called by his brother 'his Jacobite sermon', for which he was 'much mauled and threatened' by the west-country colleges Exeter and Wadham. 'Such a sermon at such a time was not likely to go unnoticed in the west country, or unremembered by the Whigs when the Oxford don began itinerating among the Cornish tinners.'[13] Charles too was accused of Jacobite sympathies, especially when in 1746 one of his travelling companions James Waller was identified as the Pretender! In the same year Charles wrote in his diary that suspicion of Methodist disloyalty to the crown had become so deep-rooted that a 'law is to come from London to put us all down and set one hundred pounds upon my head'.[14]

During John's second journey to Cornwall in 1744, Borlase, 'a person of unquestioned sense and learning', as John graciously described him, regarded the followers of the new sect as 'a parcel of mad, crazy-headed fellows', while William Hoblyn, 'the hot-headed curate of St Ives',[15] represented them 'as enemies of the Church, Jacobites, Papists and what not!' At Morvah some of the brethren were shaken by two rumours: that John Wesley had been seen a week or two ago with the Young Pretender in France, and that he was in prison in London. John himself was accused of bringing the Pretender with him to St Ives the previous autumn under the name of John Downes and of impersonating the real John Wesley, who everyone knew was dead![16] With these and other rumours circulating, it is not surprising that by 1745 many of the gentry of west Cornwall were convinced that the Cornish Methodists were in liaison with the Pretender. It was only after the battle of Culloden and the fading of the Jacobite scare, that the clergy and gentry were less hostile to the Methodist cause.

In the meantime Borlase and others feared that the Methodists were endeavouring to re-establish Popery in England, and that their 'secret' societies were 'seditious and traitorous assemblies, and hotbeds of Romanism'.[17] The antagonistic clergymen seized on these suspicions and, in order to heighten their people's mistrust, portrayed the leaders of the new sect, especially John, as Jesuits in disguise and recruiting agents for the exiled Stuarts. On Monday 25 July, 1743, the Mayor of St Ives, who went to great lengths to protect Charles, reported to him that the ministers were the principal agitators of all the evil, continually representing him and his co-workers in their sermons as Papist emissaries and urging the enraged crowds to stop them in whatever way they could. As a result there were times when they were stoned as 'Popish incendiaries'.

This 'Papist' accusation, levelled at both Wesleys during the early days of their itinerant ministry, was given impetus by misinterpretations of what the two brothers said. Charles, for instance, once prayed that God would 'call home his banished ones', which was understood to refer to Charles Edward Stuart. In his reply, Charles said, 'I had no thought of praying for the Pretender, but for those who confess themselves strangers and

pilgrims upon earth.'[18] John, on the other hand, had published
an appreciative account of the societies formed by the Count
de Renty in Roman Catholic France, which, according to some,
was proof positive of his Papist tendencies. Both the Wesleys
insisted on, for example, weekly fasts and good works, which
laid them open to further accusations. Cennick and others at
Bristol (February, 1741) claimed they had 'often heard both
Wesleys preach Popery';[19] and in his diary for 28 March, 1743,
Wesley wrote that a Dissenting minister at Newcastle affirmed
publicly that we were 'all Papists and our doctrine was mere
Popery'.[20]

Almost immediately upon Charles's arrival in Cornwall in
mid-July, 1743, he complained that the priests stirred up the
people and prejudiced their minds against the brethren. He was
opposed by two of the fiercest clerical opponents of Methodism,
William Symonds,[21] vicar of Lelant and Zennor, and Hoblyn,
'the fire-and-faggot minister', as the local mayor labelled him
on account of his zeal in rooting out 'heresy'. Hoblyn thought
justification by faith alone was a 'damnable Popish doctrine'
and was often heard to say of Wesley and his like: 'They ought
to drive them away by blows, not arguments.' His advice was
taken literally, for when Charles preached at Pool 'in the heart
of the tinners', a drunkard tried to push him down a hill, but he
was rescued by the congregation, who took him by the arms
and legs and quietly handed him down from one to another
until he was outside. On Friday, 22 July, at St Ives, he had just
named his text (Isaiah 40:10) when 'an army of rebels' broke
into the meeting. He described what happened next in his Journal:

> They began in a most outrageous manner, threatening to
> murder the people, if they did not go out that moment. They
> broke the sconces, dashed the windows to pieces, tore away
> the shutters, benches, poor-box, and all but the stone walls.
> I stood silently looking on; but mine eyes were unto the Lord.
> They swore bitterly I should not preach there again; which I

disproved, by immediately telling them Christ died for them all. Several times they lifted up their hands and clubs to strike me; but a stronger arm restrained them. They beat and dragged the women about, particularly one of a great age, and trampled on them without mercy. The longer they stayed, and the more they raged, the more power I found from above. I bade the people stand still and see the salvation of God; resolving to continue with them, and see the end. In about an hour the word came, 'Hitherto shalt thou come, and no farther.' The ruffians fell to quarrelling among themselves, broke the Town-Clerk's [John Stevens Jnr, the son of the Mayor] (their captain's) head, and drove one another out of the room.[22]

The day after this disturbance Charles preached for the first time at Gwennap 'to near two thousand hungry souls, who devoured the word of reconciliation'. The following day at Towednack after the evening service he was again attacked, this time by 'the minister's mob', who 'fell upon us, threatening and striking all they came near. They swore horribly they would be revenged on us, for our making such a disturbance on the Sabbath-day, our taking the people from the church, and doing so much mischief continually. They assaulted us with sticks and stones, and endeavoured to pull me down.' Charles witnessed ten ruffians beating an unarmed man with clubs until they had bashed him to the ground. He himself walked slowly on, with the rabble behind, but under the protection of an invisible hand.[23] In various towns some of his people retaliated against this kind of violence, but Charles urged them to suffer patiently all things for the sake of Christ. In this way some of their bitterest enemies were won over.

On Sunday 7 August he rode to Mitchell on his way to London, having been called there by his brother to attend a conference with the heads of the three branches in the revival: the Moravians, the Arminian Methodists and the Calvinistic Methodists, in order to cultivate a better understanding between them. Owing to a misunderstanding the meeting never took place. According to one author, 'This abortive conference had the immediate effect of determining John Wesley to visit Cornwall,'[24] which he did on Monday 29 August, 1743, with John Nelson, John Downes and William Shepherd. Nelson worked at his trade as a stonemason and preached when opportunities arose; Downes became ill with a fever and was not able to preach at all or leave the house, which gave rise to the rumour that he was the Young Pretender in hiding; and Wesley stayed three weeks and preached about forty times.

On arriving in Cornwall John immediately headed for St Ives, where he spoke to the members of the society, which had grown to 'about one hundred and twenty', a hundred of whom had 'found peace with God'. At Treswithian Downs he preached to 'seven or eight hundred waiting', and again after dinner to 'about a thousand'. It was here that he first observed 'a little impression made on two or three of the hearers; the rest, as usual, showing huge approbation and absolute unconcern'. In the evening he again met the society at St Ives, 'where two women who came from Penzance fell down as dead, and soon after cried out in the bitterness of their souls',[25] manifestations that were to become less frequent as the years went by. In the first three days he delivered six sermons and rode over fifty miles.

Wesley's congregations soon increased. At St Just, where both Wesleys had been preceded by a St Ives sailor named Williams, who preached on the green without a book, Wesley proclaimed the gospel to a thousand listeners on Saturday 10 September, and the next day to 'the largest congregation that ever had been seen in these parts', so he was informed. As he preached the people trembled and remained still, and John 'had not known such an hour before in Cornwall'. After returning from the Isles of Scilly, where he had preached to almost all the inhabitants of St Mary's and where he had handed out some books that were so eagerly received that the inhabitants 'were ready to tear both them and me to pieces', he preached at St Ives and Satan was aroused. 'The mob of the town burst into the room and created much disturbance, roaring and striking those that stood in their way as though Legion himself possessed them.' John received only one blow to the side of the head and after a while managed to quieten the mob.

He preached to the largest congregation he had seen in Cornwall at Morvah; to 'two or three thousand' at Treswithian Downs; and at Gwennap to 'ten thousand people', who showed the deepest attention, 'none speaking, stirring or scarce looking aside'. On 21 September he was awoken between three and four in the morning by a large company of tinners, who had gathered round the house and were singing and praising God. After preaching to them he rode with his travelling companions to Launceston and out of Cornwall.

John returned on 2 April, 1744, and 'found the whole countryside greatly excited over the news of Admiral Mathew's victory over the Spanish fleet. The crowd at St Ives could think of no more congenial way of giving expression to their joy and thanksgiving than by demolishing all the windows and furniture of the Methodist preaching room.'[26] He visited the society that met in John Nance's house and was well received. The persecution they had suffered had only driven three or four away – a persecution he blamed, in great measure, on 'the indefatigable labours of Mr Hoblyn and Mr Symonds'. On 12 April, James Wheatley, a cobbler by trade and an itinerant preacher since 1742, was set upon by the mob, who soon turned their attention to John Nance's house. 'The cry was "Bring out the preacher! Pull down the house!" And they began to pull down the boards which were nailed against the windows.' Only after the mayor's intervention did the mob disperse. After preaching at St Just, Wesley noted in his Journal that the people there 'were the chief of the whole country for hurling, fighting, drinking, and all manner of wickedness; but many of the lions are become lambs, are continually praising God, and calling their old companions in sin to come and magnify the Lord together'.[27]

Five days after the beginning of Charles's second journey (July, 1744), he reported in his Journal the encouraging progress of the gospel:

> I came, by nine at night, with Mr [John] Bennet [whom he had met in the north and found him to be an acquaintance of his father] and Meriton, through the pits and shafts, to our host near Gwennap.
>
> Here a little one is become a thousand. What an amazing work hath God done in one year! The whole country is alarmed, and gone forth after the sound of the Gospel. In vain do the pulpits ring of 'Popery, madness, enthusiasm'. Our Preachers are daily pressed to new places, and enabled to preach five or six times a day. Persecution is kept off till the seed takes root. Societies are springing up everywhere [in the far western areas]; and still the cry from all sides is, 'Come and help us.'[28]

At St Just upwards of two hundred were settled in classes, most of whom had experienced the pardoning grace of God, and at Morvah one hundred and fifty had joined together in a society. This growth encouraged the Methodists to build a society house, which served them until 1867, when a new building was erected alongside.

In his Journal Charles mentioned the continuing antagonism and opposition of Walter Borlase, particularly in his parishes of Madron and Morvah, and how the clergy in many parts 'are much enraged at our people's being so ready in the Scriptures. One fairly told Jonathan Reeves [one of the first lay itinerants in England and Ireland] he wished the Bible were in Latin only, that none of the vulgar might be able to read it. Yet these are the men that rail at us as Papists!'[29] At St Just he preached to 'a larger congregation than ever', and on 1 August in a new place to 'near two thousand listening strangers'. At Gwennap, where the awakening was 'general',

> ... very many who have not courage to enter into the society have yet broke off their sins by repentance, and are waiting for forgiveness. The whole county is sensible of the change; for the last Assizes there was a jail-delivery – not one felon to be found in their prisons, which has not been known before in the memory of man. At their last revel they had not men enough to make a wrestling match, all the Gwennap men being struck off the devil's list, and found wrestling against him, not for him.[30]

John returned to Cornwall in 1745, a few weeks before the Young Pretender landed in Scotland. On this journey he preached in no fewer than four churches with the consent or at the invitation of their respective ministers. He was invited by the rector of Week St Mary, John Turner, to preach in his church and wrote in his Journal that he 'had not seen in these parts of Cornwall either so large a church or so large a congregation'.[31] A week later at St Just he preached to what he called 'the largest congregation I have seen since my coming'.

The opposition of previous years continued, with Borlase and others harrying him at every turn and doing all in their power to impede the progress and spread of Methodism. On one occasion at Gwennap, as John was reading his text, one of the Beauchamp brothers dragged him from his preaching position and led him three-quarters of a mile down the street before releasing him. At Falmouth, while visiting a 'gentlewoman who had been long indisposed', a raging crowd forced open the outer door of the house and then broke through the inner door in their efforts to attack him. As the door fell back into the room Wesley immediately marched into their midst, speaking to them 'without intermission'. He was only rescued when a clergyman, two or three gentlemen and an alderman of the town intervened.

He escaped by boat to Penryn. In referring to this episode, he said:

> I never saw before ... the hand of God so plainly shown as here... Although the hands of perhaps some hundreds of people were lifted up to strike or throw, yet they were one and all stopped in the mid-way; so that not a man touched me with one of his fingers: neither was anything thrown from first to last; so that I had not even a speck of dirt on my clothes. Who can deny that God heareth the prayer or that He hath all power in heaven and earth?[32]

Charles Wesley began his third journey to Cornwall on Tuesday 24 June, 1746. He found the society at Gwennap 'in a very prosperous way' – in fact, four societies had sprung up at Gwennap. His evening congregation at that place was over five thousand and he felt the people sink under God's power. At Sithney he showed more than a thousand sinners the love and compassion of Christ. He preached to a 'huge multitude' at Wendron, and again at Gwennap to near two thousand. His largest congregations were at Redruth, where there were 'more than eight thousand', and at Gwennap, where a crowd of 'nine or ten thousand' listened with all eagerness.

> The whole country finds the benefit of the Gospel [Charles enthused]. Hundreds who follow not with us, have broke off their sins, and are outwardly reformed, and though persecutors once, will not now suffer a word to be spoken against this way... At St Ives no one offered to make the least disturbance. Indeed, the whole place is outwardly changed in this respect. I walk the streets with astonishment, scarce believing it St Ives. It is the same throughout the county. All opposition falls before us, or rather is fallen, and not yet suffered to lift up its head again.[33]

On Sunday 20 July he wrote that 'near one hundred of the fiercest rioters' of a few months ago, expecting a disturbance, came to fight *for* him, declaring their readiness to lay down their lives in his defence.

Charles spent time exhorting, rebuking and encouraging society members wherever he found them. At Stithians he scolded the society sharply and 'gave them a fortnight to know their own mind, whether they will serve God or Mammon'. At St Just he exhorted the members 'to cast up the stumbling block of sin, to turn unto the Lord with weeping and fasting and mourning, that the Gospel-door might be again opened among them'; while at St Ives he expelled 'a disorderly walker', the first of the kind. In the society at Trewellard he experienced 'more of the power of God than ever' and at Gwennap he 'never had ... so large an effusion of the Spirit as in the society'.[34]

By the time of John's fourth journey (1 September, 1746), the threat from the Young Pretender had disappeared and with it the more serious opposition to Methodist preaching. John found 'no society in Cornwall so lively' as the one at Trewellard, yet he reproved a few members for 'negligence in meeting'. He again preached to large congregations, particularly near Porkellis, and at Gwennap and Laneast.

His fifth journey began on Monday 29 June, 1747, and he immediately reported from St Ives on how 'strangely has one year changed the scene in Cornwall! This is now a peaceable, nay, honourable station. They give us good words almost in every place.'[35] James Roberts, the drunken and violent tinner, was a reformed character; John Rogers, the Camborne persecutor, was nowhere to be seen; and even some of the gentry came to hear him at Penryn. At Redruth, he noted, 'There are now scarce any in the town (but gentlemen) who are not convinced of the truth,' and at Brea the 'scoffers are vanished away. I scarce saw one in the county.'[36] At St Agnes

   ... another man, learning that Wesley was about to preach, said, 'If he does, I'll stone him,' and forthwith began to fill his pockets with the needful missiles. He reached the spot. Wesley took his text, 'He that is without sin among you, let him first cast a stone at her.' The man's courage failed him, stone after stone stealthily dropped from his well-filled pockets, and he went away with the impression that the preacher was something wonderful.[37]

From St Ives on 18 July, 1747, John wrote to Ebenezer Blackwell:

Here is such a change within these two years as has hardly been seen in any other part of England. Wherever we went we used to carry our lives in our hands; and now there is not a dog to wag his tongue. Several ministers are clearly convinced of the truth; few are bitter; most seem to stand neuter. Some of the gentlemen (so called) are almost the only opposers now – drinking, revelling, cursing, swearing gentlemen, who neither will enter into the kingdom of heaven themselves, nor suffer any others if they can prevent it. The most violent Jacobites among these are continually crying out that we are bringing the Pretender; and some of these worthy men bear His Majesty's commission as Justices of the Peace.[38]

When John left Cornwall on Wednesday 29 July, 1747, the years of persecution, which ironically helped the growth of Methodism and consolidated the societies, were over. He had survived malicious rumours, personal threats and violent opposition to win the day, and to ensure the future success of Methodism in the remotest part of England. Although in the years that followed the 'growth of Methodism was phenomenal, especially after 1780', the effects of those early years were not quite as spectacular as many have suggested. Undoubtedly there were many transformed lives during that period, but the rough Cornish population did not become respectable citizens overnight. Probert concluded that the evidence 'suggests little more than the fact that the Methodists were no longer suspect and were therefore left alone. Wesley's Journal bears witness not so much to the changed character of the Cornish, but to their changed opinion.'[39] However, as the years went by, progress was made and the membership increased, particularly during the 'revival' of 1764. By 1767 there were 2160 Methodist members, divided into two circuits, east and west, of which three-quarters lived in the west.

In the visits that lay ahead for John Wesley – he made thirty-two in all[40] – he could look forward to the formation of many societies, to the appointment of new preachers, to the building of Methodist chapels, and to the day when Methodism would become the living and vibrant faith of the common people, and when his evangelism, along with the industrial revolution, would be regarded as the central theme of eighteenth century Cornish history.

John Wesley

Charles Wesley
after the painting by Thomas Husdon, 1740
(by courtesy of the Methodist Archives)

Samuel Walker, curate of Truro, produced an effect for good on the inhabitants of that town more unmixed than Methodism ever produced anywhere.

Frederick Hockin.[1]

Many are praying, and some are working. The Methodists have the lead among the latter. I suppose if God spare the land, we shall be principally indebted to them. Nevertheless, I could wish their foundations deeper laid, without which they will generally come to nothing. I converse with many of them who come in my way, freely and affectionately, and see cause to lament in them their utter ignorance of the depths of apostate human nature. Some will hear, others will not; for a discovery of natural corruption throws the evidences of faith into another channel than that of feeling, and so gives a shock to their favourite assurance, which they still preach as the one thing needful.

A preacher among them, who himself is in the humble way, told me he asked a travelling preacher about a month since, what foundation he had for preaching that doctrine as he had been just doing, and was answered, 'tis our way, yet he hoped well of others who had not that assurance. It would be a good thing to set them right, if it could be done. I have attempted it with some success on a few of them.

From a letter of Walker's to Adam, 9 March, 1757.[2]

11

Walker Disagrees with Some of the Practices and Beliefs of the Methodists

While Walker strengthened the cause of Christ in Truro and the neighbourhood, he kept a keen eye on what was happening in the church in other parts of the country, and noted with pleasure the success of the gospel in rousing a slumbering people. He watched with interest the development of Methodism and the ministry of the Wesleys, not only up and down the land, but more closely in Cornwall. His attention was particularly drawn to the proceedings of John Wesley – his intrusion, as he saw it, into the parishes of the county and the setting up of Methodist societies in both Evangelical and non-Evangelical areas – and the effect of his doctrine on the Church. Wesley was beginning to discover that his Cornish converts needed a strong arm to hold them together. As long as he was present to direct their affairs, all went well. But if he was away for any length of time, confusion arose and declension set in. In 1760 Wesley wrote to the rector of Roche: 'I am now entering into Cornwall which I have not visited these three years, and consequently all things in it are out of order.'[3] During his absence the membership had declined from 1700 to 1200.

It was not long before Walker, whose opinions represented and largely determined those of the other Evangelical clergy in Cornwall, became concerned about some of the Methodist tenets and practices, and his own temptation to yield, on grounds of expediency rather than principle, to the views expressed by Wesley's lay preachers to separate from the Established Church.

He was worried 'that evils affecting the whole community must arise from the bursting forth of a flame of zeal whose fuel was a mixture of enthusiasm, vanity and passion, and which refused to be circumscribed by Scriptural restrictions, enabling it to enlighten, but preventing it from spreading desolation'.[4] Perhaps he had also heard reports that in 1747, out of the eighteen Methodist exhorters in the county, 'Three of these had no gifts at all for the work, neither natural nor supernatural; that a fourth had neither gifts nor grace, but was a dull, empty, self-conceited man; and that a fifth had considerable gifts, but had evidently made shipwreck of the grace of God.'[5]

It was not that Walker undervalued the Methodists' instrumentality or deprecated their excellences, for he freely acknowledged the benefit conferred on thousands by the Methodists' fervour and diligence. In a letter to Thomas Adam, he said:

> There is no doubt I owe somewhat to their zeal, though my case has been different from the most of those who have been brought to the knowledge of the truth these late years. *Their light has either reproved or directed us all*. Like you, I have, and do, and will converse with them freely as they come in my way, though, as yourself, I suffer reproval for so doing.[6]

Again, although he could not agree with the Methodists on certain issues, he added:

> In this day of darkness and licentiousness, it becomes all the friends of the Gospel to bear with one another; and while they differ in opinion and denomination, to unite together in heart and endeavour, for the support of the common cause. It is my great comfort there are good men of all persuasions, who are content to leave each other the liberty of private judgement in lesser things, and are heartily disposed to unite their efforts for the maintaining and enlarging Christ's kingdom. This I take to be the most promising symptom of our day, and I am hoping great things from this spirit of moderation and peace.[7]

On the one hand, he had a genuine 'desire to love' the Methodists, but on the other, he entertained 'many reasons against joining' them. In a letter to Mydhope Wallis of St Endellion, dated 10 September, 1754, he wrote, 'I am no Methodist, tho' I think the Methodists as a body a sincere sort of people, yet they have mistakes and irregularities about them which I have no authority to countenance.'[8] His conduct with regard to them was 'upon the plan of Gamaliel's advice; for though there appeared a zeal and boldness in them which might very justly engage my heart to them, yet I could never persuade myself that their proceedings were justifiable... Nevertheless, I trust they have been the means of kindling gospel principles among us.'[9]

Not only did Walker cautiously respect the Methodists' 'light', but by conversing with them he hoped to 'see in practice the various influence of their way of stating things, and my own', and to hear all they had to say 'for their proceedings and sentiments'. He soon understood that, because of Wesley's definition of faith and assurance, which he regarded as Biblically unsound, most of the Methodists he talked to 'thought believing to be feeling' and placed faith in the affections instead of the heart; the 'consequence of which has been doubting when the stir of the affections has been less'.

> If [as Wesley taught] faith be a certain *sure confidence* of God's love to *me*, then previous to any sanctifying evidence, there is assurance of my acceptance; and that inward immediate assurance is the witness of the Spirit... If a sure confidence of God's love to me be the essence of faith, then whoever want it are unbelievers; whereas, if faith be the sinner's trusting his soul with Christ, from a persuasion, first of his own misery, and next of Christ's sufficiency, then this trust will be rather manifested as the first grace of the new heart, when the other graces, which always accompany it, become so.[10]

It did not matter whether a man had 'sure confidence' or not. What mattered was the disposing of the heart to serve God and a 'true self-denial and mortification of inward sin'.

In a letter to Adam he expressed his concern over a young member of the Truro society, who, with one or two others, was keen to promote the Methodists' 'feeling assurance'. According to Walker, this young man was 'of a peculiar turn, remarkably warm in his constitution, not humbled in such a manner as to be patiently waiting for salvation, and therefore ready to catch at anything which may minister present comfort'. He 'seems to have lost all apprehension of the power of godliness, but as consisting in sensible feelings'. All the Methodists with whom Walker had talked, who had been zealous on this point of 'sensible feelings', had possessed a similar constitution and temper as the young man, and they 'cannot think well of those who either are without it, or speak not of it in the way themselves do'.[11] As late as October, 1759, Walker told Adam: 'It will be a nice matter neither to quarrel nor join with [the Methodists]. They are in our parts hot, and must be treated with much forbearance.'[12]

In a private letter to Charles Wesley (16 August, 1756), Walker said that he considered John Wesley's views on faith, or the witness of the Spirit, which he had thoroughly examined, 'to be unscriptural and unsafe'. He found 'no warrant of God's word whereon it is built'. He went on:

> I do not quarrel at sensible feelings, they are proper in their place; but faith and feeling appear to me direct opposites, and feeling alone cannot be the witness of the Spirit. I do not say that people that make more of sensible feelings than I do are not right, or suppose there may not be a true work under them; but as the thing is stated, it seems to me dangerous and often uncomfortable. That we are justified by faith alone, or by the merits of Christ applied by faith, is as clear as the sun. But then what is that faith and the witness of the Spirit? I wish this matter might be reconsidered.

> I think there are many ill consequences arising from this
> manner of stating it. I fancy, were this matter regulated, the
> Methodists would be more useful, and in their classes more
> benefited. Believe me, dear Sir, I say not this from a spirit of
> opposition; but simply for the promoting the interests of true
> vital Christianity among the Methodists and by them.[13]

Walker had examined John Wesley's other writings, and in
particular the minutes of some conversations between Wesley
and others, printed at Dublin in 1749. On reviewing this tract
Walker was 'surprised at the inconsistency and unscriptural
assertions which run through the whole of it'. According to their
view, 'religion in the heart seemed to be nothing else but a
continuation of rapturous impressions, and the whole of it
founded upon their description of faith'. In these minutes two
things in particular were remarkable: 'One, that they express
not the least sense of the apostasy of man's will; and the other,
that by rejecting the imputation of Christ's righteousness, they
ascribe the merit of our justification to faith, and not to him.'
Thus, by this scheme, 'we are justified by works'.[14]

In all this Walker was reluctant to oppose the Methodists,
'who had been made so great instruments' in the cause of Christ.
However, he wanted to see them standing on a 'more scriptural and reasonable foundation'. He therefore proposed to write
to Wesley, who he thought a 'weak and warm, though honest
man', and to tell him about 'the trouble his people are bringing
upon me' and to give him 'a few hints upon these matters', not
to generate an argument, but to point his ministerial colleague
in a more Biblical direction. This appears to be the first sign in
Cornwall of a disagreement between the Methodists and the
'enlightened' clergy, which, sadly, would become more
obvious and difficult, and end in separation. Walker's gracious
yet firm approach to these differences kept his personal relationship with Wesley on a warm and friendly basis, as their correspondence, characterized by goodwill and courtesy, shows.

A further disagreement between Walker and Wesley was over the doctrine of perfectionism, which did not become part of general Methodist preaching until after Walker's death. Although Walker did not expressly mention Wesley's opinion in his correspondence, the controversy was evident from what the two men taught. In reference to his Cornish converts, Wesley wrote:

> The more I converse with the believers in Cornwall, the more I am convinced that they have sustained great loss for want of hearing the doctrine of Christian Perfection clearly and strongly enforced. I see, wherever this is not done, the believers grow dead and cold. Nor can this be prevented but by keeping up in them an hourly expectation of being perfected in love. I say an hourly expectation, for to expect it at death, or some time hence, is much the same as not expecting it at all.[15]

Wesley believed that by a simple act of faith, perfection, or entire sanctification, was immediately 'wrought in the soul', thus cleansing the heart from all sin; whereas Walker taught that 'perfect holiness' was a divine work, beginning in regeneration, and carried on progressively until it 'grows up towards that perfect state to which it shall be advanced in the future world'.[16]

Along with Adam, James Hervey and others, Walker disapproved of the Methodist practice of itinerancy, regarding it as 'a mark of insubordination, a breach of Church order, and an unwarrantable interference with the parochial system'.[17] Interestingly, a few months before Walker's death Wesley admitted to James Rouquet that the 'grand breach is now between the irregular and regular clergy'.[18] Walker was also disturbed by the first Methodist lay preachers and their 'spirit of separation', some of whom were already in Cornwall. Miles Brown stated that at about this time, and unbeknown to Walker, 'Not very far from his Truro sphere of labour there were four officially appointed lay persons supplying the Church service in the smaller Isles of

Scilly.'[19] According to Wesley, the leaders of Methodism, who 'had taken no step in their whole progress so reluctantly as this', originally felt the 'deepest prejudices' against lay preachers, 'until we could not but own that God gave wisdom from above to these unlearned and ignorant men, so that the work of the Lord prospered in their hands, and sinners were daily converted to God'.[20]

At the Leeds Methodist conference on 6 May, 1755, the main debate centred around the thorny question: 'Ought we to separate from the Established Church?' The two Wesleys and William Grimshaw were the only ordained men present, although Charles had tried to persuade others to attend, and the general conclusion to which they all 'fully agreed' Wesley noted in his Journal: 'That whether it was *lawful* or not [to separate], it was no ways *expedient.*'[21] However, their agreement was only a short-term solution, as Charles intimated to his wife when he wrote: 'All agreed not to separate; so the wound is healed slightly.'[22] Soon the 'spirit of separation' again prevailed and Walker took his stand against it. Walker's attitude did not go unnoticed by Wesley, who first mentioned him in his Journal, 30 August, 1755. He was riding through Truro when 'one stopped my horse and insisted on my alighting. Presently two or three more of Mr Walker's society came in, and we seemed to have been acquainted with each other many years; but I was constrained to break from them.'[23]

During this visit to Cornwall, which probably occasioned the first meeting between the two men, Wesley had the opportunity of seeking Walker's advice about a pamphlet he had written for the press, which had been discussed in full at the Leeds conference, on the topical question of a separation of the Methodists from the Church of England. Rather than give a detailed reply immediately, Walker 'earnestly sued for light and direction', and waited until the opening weeks of September, 1755, before writing on the subject. According to Walker's judgement, nothing could 'be of more importance to the interests of vital Christianity in these kingdoms' than a Biblical view of separation.

The main question to be addressed, said Walker in his reply, was 'whether it be unlawful for the Methodists to abide in the Church'. After advising him not to publish his pamphlet – 'it can do no good, and will probably do much hurt' and 'set all the world a disputing' – he exhorted Wesley to 'lay the matter before God and search the Scriptures' for an answer. If he came to the conclusion that separation was unlawful, what should be done with lay preachers?

> Now, if the laws of the Church of England admit not such preachers, then herein is a step made in separation... Either you will not be able to stop a separation or must somehow or other stop these preachers. As long as they remain, there is a beginning of separation...
>
> If you say, 'I dare not separate from the church,' what will you do with the lay preachers? If, 'I dare not lay aside the lay preachers,' how will you prevent a separation in part begun already in them? You must needs come to some resolution on this point, and I pray God to direct you to that which be most for his glory. That middle way you have trod, of permitting, not appointing them, puts the matter quite out of your hands, and deprives you of all your influence. If you are persuaded that they are extraordinarily called, and that there is such a necessity as justifies a separation and departure from the laws of the church in this particular, why should you not appoint them to preach, and so keep them under your direction? If you are not satisfied whether the necessity of them or their call might justify your appointing them to preach contrary to the law of the church, ought you not to tell them they are doing what you cannot judge lawful, and therefore that you dare not encourage them in it? As long as they are either permitted or appointed, you seem to stand upon the brink of a separation.
>
> I take this matter of the lay preachers to be the leading enquiry. Their permission or appointment is in fact a partial

separation from the Church of England, the essence of which considered as such, consists in her orders and laws, rather than in her doctrines and worship, which constitute her a Church of Christ. I have always thought this matter might have been better and more inoffensively ordered from the beginning, and doubt not but that a method might still be fallen upon, which conducted with prudence and patience, would reduce the constitution of Methodism to due order, and render it under God more instrumental to the ends of practical religion.[24]

He beseeched Wesley not to be unduly influenced by others, but to do 'the thing which is right and fear no consequences'. He reminded him of the feeble grounds on which his friends pleaded for separation: that the administration of the Church of England was bad, that they would be a 'more compact body if separate', and that a step towards separation had already been made in the appointment of lay preachers. He then considered whether separation would promote or hinder the interests of Christ's kingdom. He asked:

1. Will it be likely to make the body of Methodists more confirmed Christians? If it be said, yes, for hereby they will not hear God's word badly taught, nor be present at a slovenly performance of his worship, and will have the word and worship in Gospel purity and simplicity; it must be weighed on the other hand, how many will be lost who will not go in with a separation, how many will be hurt by dispute, how teachers sufficient in number and ability, may be found for the several congregations, how discipline can be preserved so as that the word and worship shall be done to edification? Whether the Methodists will not be more apt to decay, being then either left quietly alone, or attacked for their separation, not their practice, as now, which will have an evident tendency to make them rest upon their separation, &c. &c.?
2. Will it render the Methodists more useful to others? There is not the least appearance of it, but just the contrary...

3. What effect will it probably have upon bystanders?

(1) Upon those ministers who are zealous for the power of godliness? Will it not throw a prodigious objection in their way, and put it more out of their power to preserve the interests of religion by any schemes which are not common, particularly by societies?

(2) Upon those who are coming nearer the truth; can it be expected they will not stumble at it?

(3) Upon the infidels and Socinians; will they not be glad they are fairly rid of you?

(4) Upon every man in England who would do service; will it not be a bar to him?

(5) Upon every careless sinner; will it not supply him with somewhat to defend himself?

On all these accounts, a separation seems inexpedient; but on the other hand there is a strong expediency:

1. That the Methodists should remain in the Church, and *with the strictest observance possible, of all the laws of it*. The more regular they are, the readier access will they gain, and the more evidently will the difference appear, where we should always endeavour to make it seen, in the power and practice of godliness.

2. That if any of them depart, you, Sir, do not follow them, but declare publicly against it.[25]

He concluded the letter by advising Wesley that if he was determined to print his pamphlet, he should 'first lay it before some judicious person who is not immediately connected' with him, such as Thomas Adam of Wintringham. Walker himself desired to see 'a good many things' left out of it, particularly 'that clause about the Athanasian Creed'.

On 18 September, 1755, he wrote to Adam and told him about Wesley's pamphlet and sent him his written response to it. He noted his request to Wesley that before he published it he should 'seek farther light', and wrote that he had mentioned Adam 'as one likely to help him to it'. Wesley sent word that he would apply to Adam. 'By the very next post' Wesley sent a copy of his pamphlet to the vicar of Wintringham, although he had already decided not to publish it, as he was convinced by Walker's arguments against the expediency of such a step. In his reply to Walker from Bristol (24 September, 1755), he gave four reasons why those who 'plead for a separation from the Church' assert that 'it is not lawful to abide therein', reasons that Wesley himself could not answer to his own satisfaction. 'So that my conclusion,' said Wesley, 'which I cannot yet give up, that it is lawful to continue in the Church, stands I know not how; at most without any premises that are able to bear its weight.' The reasons are:

> **First**, with regard to the liturgy itself ... they think it is both absurd and sinful to declare such an assent and consent as is required to any merely human composition... Though they do not object to the use of forms, yet they dare not confine themselves to them. And, in this form (the book of common prayer), there are several things which they apprehend to be contrary to Scripture.
>
> **Secondly,** as to the laws of the Church, if they include the Canons and Decretals (both which are received in our courts) they think, 'the latter the very dregs of popery, and that many of the former, the Canons of 1603, are as grossly wicked as absurd'. And over and above the objections which they have to several particular Canons, they think, 'that the spirit which they breathe throughout, is truly popish and antichristian; that nothing can be more diabolical than the *ipso facto* excommunication so often denounced therein; that the whole method of executing these Canons, the process used in our spiritual courts, is too bad to be tolerated, not in a Christian, but in a Mahometan or Pagan nation'.
>
> **Thirdly,** with respect to the ministers, they doubt 'whether there are not many of them whom God has not sent, inasmuch as they neither live the gospel nor teach it; neither indeed can, seeing they do not know it'. They doubt the more, 'because themselves disdain that inward call to the ministry, which is at least as necessary as the outward'. And they are not clear 'whether it be lawful to attend the ministrations of those whom God has not sent to minister'.
>
> **Fourthly,** the doctrines, actually taught by these, and indeed by a great majority of the Church ministers, they think 'are not only wrong, but fundamentally so, and subversive

of the whole gospel'. They therefore doubt 'whether it be lawful to bid them God-speed or to have any fellowship with them'...

My difficulty is much increased by one of your observations. I know the original doctrines of the Church are sound. I know her worship (in the main) is pure and Scriptural. But, 'if the essence of the Church of England, considered as such, consists in her orders and laws' (many of which I myself can say nothing for), 'and not in her worship and doctrines', those who separate from her, have a far stronger plea than I was ever sensible of.

At present I apprehend those, and those only to separate from the Church, who either renounce her fundamental doctrines, or refuse to join in her public worship. As yet we have done neither, nor have we taken one step further than we were convinced is our bounden duty. It is from full conviction of this, that we have: (1) preached abroad, (2) prayed extempore, (3) formed Societies and (4) permitted preachers who were not episcopally ordained. And were we pushed on this side, were there no alternative allowed, we should judge it our bounden duty rather wholly to separate from the Church than to give up any one of these points. Therefore, if we cannot stop a separation without stopping lay preachers, the case is clear – we cannot stop it at all.

But if we *permit* them, should we not do more? Should we not *appoint* them rather, since the bare permission puts the matter quite out of our hands, and deprives us of all our influence? In a great measure it does; therefore to appoint them is far more expedient, if it be lawful. But is it lawful for presbyters, circumstanced as we are, to appoint other ministers? This is the very point wherein we desire advice, being afraid of leaning to our own understandings.[26]

He concurred with Walker's view that a resolution should be found, 'and the sooner the better', and rejoiced to hear that his friend thought the matter 'may be better and more inoffensively ordered'. 'I must ... beg your sentiments on this head,' he concluded, 'and that as particularly as your other engagements will allow.'

Walker replied to Wesley's letter on 20 October, 1755, ten days after Adam had written to Wesley. He referred to the objections raised by those who pressed for a separation: 'the assent and consent required to the Liturgy' and 'because they dare not confine themselves to forms' – objections that the Dissenters had made, and that, in Walker's view, were being used by those 'willing to take hold of anything whereby they may persuade themselves it is unlawful to continue in the church'. The compilers of the Liturgy never thought their work infallible and so its assent and consent should be in such a manner 'agreeable to the Scriptures'. The Bible is the only book in the world without defect. 'If the unavoidable defects of men were a sufficient ground for separating from a church, it is easy to see there would be no abiding under any establishment that could be invented.' He then threw out this challenge:

> And how is it they *dare* not confine themselves to a form in public ministrations? This is going far indeed. Appeal to their consciences; they cannot say this in the presence of God, that they dare not confine themselves to a form in public worship, wherein only they are required to do so as I can find? Upon the whole I ask, did the first thoughts of separating arise from this difficulty with regard to the Liturgy? I dare answer in the negative. That must have sprung from a supposed necessity of having ordained ministers over the Methodists. And if this were the case, what is there more in this objection than the sophistry of a deceiving heart, by which they who make it may have been too easily led astray? When we have a mind to do a thing, experience shows how easy it is to find a reason for doing it, and to deceive ourselves out of the truth.[27]

He then answered the second objection: 'because of the laws of the church, if they include the canons'.

> If the canons were never authorized by act of Parliament, they cannot be properly part of the Church Establishment,

which as such is merely a civil thing. The Church Establishment binds the conscience as a civil institution, which it
becomes by the authority of government; wherefore, whatever is not so established (I mean by the king, lords and
commons), not being an act of government, cannot bind the
conscience... Such a submission has never been exacted to
the canons, as has been to the Rubric and Liturgy, which I
take to contain the laws of our Church.

As to the spiritual courts, may not a man lawfully remain
in the Church because of them? If discipline be lost, we
lament it; but, surely, nothing shall revive discipline but a
revival of vital religion, for which we ought to pray and
labour in our several places.[28]

Again he saw Wesley's friends 'seeking occasions, whereby to
satisfy themselves in doing what they have before set their hearts
upon'.

The third and fourth reasons for a separation – 'because
many of the ministers are bad men, disclaim an inward call,
and preach contrary to the gospel' – showed further evidence
of a 'factious unsubmissive spirit'. But, argued Walker, 'these
are not the establishment':

We must separate from the notions and practices of all such,
and thereby show ourselves true members of the Church of
England. Were the faults of ministers a sufficient cause of
departing from a church, there could be no such thing as
remaining long in any church whatever. Yes, and what security is there that by and by for the same reasons, it should
not be as necessary to separate from the Methodists themselves? Such a principle can possibly produce nothing but
confusion as long as the world lasts, since it would lay every
private man under an obligation of conscience to leave his
church, when he thought many of the ministry belonging to
it did not live and preach as they ought. You can hardly think
of anything which would be more destructive of love, peace
and order.[29]

He placed the blame for this spirit of separation squarely at the feet of those who would aspire to be preachers themselves. They 'persuade themselves and you it is not lawful to abide in the Church, by such arguments as would never have got into their heads, had not a conceit of themselves, and an ambition of being ministers, first got into their hearts'. 'A lurking vanity and pride of heart' were the real foundation of their 'unkind contest' with Wesley.

> What I have said [continued Walker] on the second head will make my assertion, that 'the essence of the Church consists in her orders and laws, not doctrine and worship', more easy to you; though perhaps not altogether so, by reason of that point – lay preachers. I cannot think it any how authenticated for a few clergymen to take upon them to establish a church and ordain ministers. What you have said concerning the impossibility of laying aside lay preachers, entirely defeats the scheme I hinted at. However, you shall need maintain your ground with constancy... Sure I am you have much cause to stand firm to your first principles upon this occasion. Many of the clergy up and down are speaking the truth. Should you be deserted by some, there will not be wanting such as will support you, or rather the cause of vital Christianity I am persuaded you have at heart.[30]

Walker sent copies of his last two letters to his friend Adam, with the comments: 'And now what think you? Will he be able to stand his ground? For my part I think not. I fear he has too high an opinion of Methodism, and imagines it will be lost if the preachers leave him, which I am fully persuaded they will do, if he will not go with them.'[31] When he wrote to Charles Wesley the following year, he stated that he 'was fearful of going any further with [John] at that time, lest while I was arguing against a separation upon such arguments as entered into the heart of the matter, I might unwarily drive him into it'.[32]

John Wesley wrote again to Walker from London on 20
November, 1755. He had written most of the letter three weeks
earlier, but 'the dangerous illness of my wife' prevented him
from finishing it sooner. In the opening paragraph he mentioned
Adam's letter to which he had replied on 31 October.[33] He then
noted that two Methodist preachers had 'gone from us', while
none of the others 'have at present any desire or design of
separating from the Church'. This is followed by four observations, which reveal more clearly his personal views, the first of
which is given in full:

> Those ministers who truly feared God near an hundred years
> ago had undoubtedly much the same objections to the
> Liturgy which some (who never read their works) have now.
> And I myself so far allow the force of several of those objec-
> tions that I should not dare to declare my assent and con-
> sent to that book in the terms prescribed. Indeed, they are
> so strong that I think they cannot be safely used with regard
> to any book but the Bible. Neither dare I confine myself wholly
> to forms of prayer not even in the Church. I use, indeed, all
> the forms; but I frequently add extemporary prayer either
> before or after sermon.

He could not allow the authority of many of the canons or the
justification of the spiritual courts. Nor could he answer to his
own satisfaction whether it was lawful to attend the ministrations of a man whom he knew had not been sent by God to
minister. He was concerned that listening to these men may be
'bidding them God-speed, the strengthening their hands in evil,
and encouraging others to hear them till they fall into hell
together'. He was still keen to know Walker's opinion on how
the present work of God could be carried on without lay preachers. He had read Walker's volume of sermons entitled *The Christian*, and 'in the great points I cannot observe any difference
between us. We both contend for the inward kingdom, the mind

that was in Christ Jesus, the image of God to be new stamped upon the heart,' although he bemoaned how little of this he found in himself.[34]

As has been stated the correspondence between the two men was always conducted with respect and civility, with room for friendship to develop. Ultimately both men were seeking the same end – the glory of God and the extension of Christ's kingdom – but had different views on how that end should best be achieved. For all his industry and zeal, Wesley did not fully appreciate or understand the difficulties his itinerant lay preachers were causing some Evangelical clergy within the Church of England; whereas Walker, a precise and logical thinker, whose faith rested on sound Evangelical principles, weighed everything by the word of God, and no step was to be taken, especially an 'irregular' step, unless the Scriptures pointed clearly in that direction.

In the eighteenth century, when religious thought sought to undermine conservative Christianity, Walker was fighting not so much over methods or numbers, but for the purity of the church and for doctrines he regarded as essential to the Christian faith. He respected the Methodists and esteemed their leaders, but he was not prepared to compromise what he believed to be the truth, a compromise that would have led, in his eyes, to a weakening of the Evangelical position and to confusion over Biblical salvation. At times, it is true, he was too rigidly bound by the laws of the Establishment, but for him that Establishment was the nearest representation of the Scriptural ideal and so worth striving to uphold.

My expedient was, as lay preachers would hardly submit to be laid aside, that as many of them as were fit might be ordained and fixed on cures; and the rest might have their mouths stopped by being used only as inspectors over the societies. You will see by John [Wesley's] unaccountable answer, how little good I am likely to do them. For which reason I have not, nor shall have any more to do with them, than to give them my opinion when they ask it.

Samuel Walker in a letter to Thomas Adam dated 7 October, 1756.[1]

12

Walker Opposes Separation from the Church of England (part 1)

The revival of religion under Walker's preaching continued to feed his Truro flock and to equip them to serve Christ. On 28 March, 1755, John Newton, then a layman in London, who had read two 'charming' letters of Walker's, 'breathing the best spirit', mentioned in a letter 'the extraordinary work of grace which is carrying on in the Establishment in Cornwall by Mr Walker and others'.[2] 'Here is a troop,' wrote one eye-witness at the end of 1755, 'who are willing to subscribe unto the Lord, and own before the whole world that they belong to him.' During this layman's stay of 'two delightful days', one a Sabbath, the word reached into his heart and for many days he felt its reviving influence. On the Monday evening, at a meeting attended by near two hundred, most of whom were just awakening out of a careless state, Walker fixed on the parable of the prodigal son for illustration, and each step of the prodigal's journey was considered and applied to every one present. 'We were all called upon to cry out, "Lord, we are the men!"' 'Several parts of the discourse,' said the visitor, 'drew tears from my eyes and melted my heart. I wished to take down in short-hand every word.'[3]

Walker himself, in a letter to Adam (25 March, 1756), said, 'The Lord is with us still and the work prospers greatly under my two friends, Mr Michell at Veryan, and Mr Penrose at Penryn. At this place we are still advancing. The society thrives and has peace. The formalists are generally confounded, have given over gainsaying, and are forced to own themselves sinners.'[4] In another letter he wrote later in that year (21 September, 1756), he remarked, 'We have much need of books, there being a good deal of impression on the minds of many about us, who therefore much needs such helps, which nevertheless we are not able to supply them with.'[5]

In the letter to Adam, Walker mentioned his 'engagements' and the 'many extraordinary incidents' that had prevented him from replying to letters. One of these extraordinary incidents was the loss of another Club member, who had died of a fever. He had only been a member for just over a year and had left Walker 'without all manner of assistance in a place where there is so very much to do'. He also thanked Adam for writing a preface to his work *The Christian*, and, as a 'small token of my respect and gratitude', had ordered six copies for him, one of which he hoped Adam would present to 'worthy' Archdeacon Basset. He returned Wesley's letter of 31 October, 1755, which Adam had sent him for his 'perusal and observations', with the comment: 'It is indeed a strange one.' Along with Adam's caution, probably for Walker to guard against high-mindedness in the dispute, Wesley's letter determined him to 'drop the correspondence, lest I might do mischief where I had no prospect of doing service'. He continued:

> There has been such an aberration from the old principles, that those who would do true Christianity service, know not with any distinction, what the vital truths of it are, nor where to find it. I have too much cause to fear, there is not one of those zealous persons in London, who speak with so apostolical a freedom and boldness, that is not puzzled, confused and either overrunning or falling short in some capital point, except perhaps Mr Murden and Mr Whit[e]field. And the matter is possibly more deplorable near Bath and Bristol, where there are no less than eight clergymen now lately joined together in a club, for mutual establishment in preaching the Gospel. They are all young men, their hearts

full of zeal for Christ; but they have among them so much
mysticism, Moravianism and Methodism, and not any of them
capable of setting the others right, that at the present there
is not much to be expected from them. I have a correspondence with three of them; and by means of the youngest of
those, Mr Brown, who is a sensible, modest and teachable
person (I suppose the most so of any among them), I am not
without hope of doing them some service.[6]

To help these young men, Walker, at the time of writing, was
drawing up some papers for Brown's use, which he hoped he
would communicate to the others. He encouraged Adam to
write a 'short treatise for the instruction and direction of young
clergymen, which might be handed to them in a private
manner, in manuscript, and perhaps, hereafter be published'.
Such a treatise would serve a useful purpose, not only in Bath,
but also in Cornwall, where at least four young clergymen, with
whom Walker had some connection, 'show a gracious disposition', along with 'others who are near the ministry'.[7] One of
these young men, said Walker, 'has a happy mixture of zeal
and prudence, the latter remarkably beyond his age. The Lord
is blessing him already, and my confidence is great that he will
be a considerable light in his day.'[8] All this suggests that Evangelicalism was animating more clergymen in the mid-eighteenth
century than many thought, although the young men Walker
mentioned needed to be taught more clearly the truths of the
gospel.

Another source of encouragement for Walker was a 'spirit of
catechizing' that had sprung up in many places. This exercise
pleased the people, who, in most places, were calling for their
ministers to practise it. Walker knew of two gentlemen who had
used Adam's lectures to introduce themselves and the people
into catechizing, and another who read them before his
congregation. This filled him with hope, for he regarded
catechizing as 'the most profitable part of my ministry'.

Walker set a very high value on Adam's 'communications', which helped protect him against 'secret pride which would persuade me I am something and do something, when indeed I am nothing; and when anything is done God does it himself'. 'Of all the others,' he remarked, 'I find it the hardest lesson to preserve a humbling sense of my vileness and insufficiency.'

> When I lose the sense of my sinfulness, conceit meets with a more feeble opposition; and as the sense of my insufficiency is remitted, I stumble. Also unbelief goes on in equal pace with my pride; the objects of faith are hidden from me, nor mix themselves in my heart, constraining it to heavenly-mindedness and communion with God, to a care of pleasing him in all things, to submission, patience, &c. Everything goes wrong with me, as pride is unmortified. Yet it continually pleads for indulgence, and while I am writing to you, would suggest to me a desire of your commendation.
>
> But what gives me most cause to quarrel with this pride of my heart, is that it still contends for the esteem of men, and raises up in me certain fears of men's faces which I would give the world to be rid of. The esteem of men was once my idol; I courted it every way, and was so unhappy as to get a great deal of it by the basest compliances. You will hardly imagine what it has cost me in inward pangs to get the mastery of it, if yet I may say it is in subjection; for sometimes I am in circumstances, in which I find myself under a constraint, which I have reason to believe I do not always oppose as I ought.[9]

This refreshing frankness to his best friend confirms his statement that there is 'none of all my brethren I can so join with in a perfect conformity of sentiments, and with whom I desire to be more conformed in practice' than Adam.

Humility and his battle against the desire for men's esteem were constant themes of Walker's life as he endeavoured to serve God in a godly and upright manner. In his diary for Tuesday 27 April, 1756, he reflected:

How hard is it to be angry and sin not! as much as self mixes, it is sinful. I think not more than twice in my life have I been angry without plainly seeing sin. I suppose true gospel *ΖηΛοs* does not ruffle the temper, nor leave any perturbation behind it. It must be perfectly consistent with meekness, and is sinful if not accompanied with compassion. *He looked about upon them with indignation, being grieved at the hardness of their hearts.* Surely our zeal and meekness bear proportion to our humility. I have most zeal and least wildfire when I am most humbled in the sense of my sins. Lord, make me humble. Lord, keep me humble.[10]

Two weeks later he told his friend:

My constitutional turn is timidity, wherewith the desire of man's esteem shamefully cooperated in the former years of my life. Both together made it a mountainous difficulty to look opposers in the face, and maintain the boldness of a Christian profession. You will not conceive what pain and grief, conflicts and struggles, this has cost me. To deny it has often been like cutting off a right hand, and often it has prevailed. To this day, though I am hoping it has not power enough to make me do what I should not, yet it sometimes, in particular circumstances, restrains me from doing what I ought. I mean, when among a company of carnal persons, I am often too like Samson shorn of his locks, without that freedom which God's honour and their case plainly demand. This is the great thorn in my flesh which earnestly, perhaps impatiently, I want should be drawn out; while at the same time I see the justice of God in leaving it there, and have, I think, some of my clearest evidences and most plentiful matter of praise and thankfulness, from the success given me against it.[11]

On 10 May, 1756, Walker again wrote to Adam, with whom he concurred that 'the matter of our justification and the principle of gospel obedience' rests 'in the righteousness of Christ'. In an allusion to the Wesleyan view of imputed righteousness, and with his penetrating knowledge of the human heart, he said, 'As far as any depart from making Christ their righteousness, I plainly see they are defective in humility, and hunted with doubts and fears, and their conduct is actuated by the narrow principle of self... From the cross I would derive all my comfort and my principles of action.' He repeated his call for Adam to write a 'short treatise for the instruction and direction of the young clergymen', explained to his friend how he became 'providentially' acquainted four or five years previously with several Dissenters (including Winter and Fawcett), and offered practical advice about which Dissenting bookseller Adam should use for his lectures. He then mentioned that Thomas Haweis and his friend George Burnett had returned from Oxford.

> Their fortunes, nor indeed opportunities of improvement, would not admit of their long continuance there. They purpose studying with me and my friend and father, Mr Conon, the schoolmaster of this place, till next spring, by which time, we doubt not they will be well qualified. They are both scholars, and have a tolerable foundation in Hebrew. I have no doubt of their heart qualifications for the work. In truth, they are lovely and promising young men.[12]

Haweis boarded in Truro for ten months until he returned to Oxford the following January (1757).

At the time of writing Walker heard that Wesley was dying in Ireland and had left the care of his people to Whitefield and his brother Charles.[13] However, Wesley recovered and towards the end of 1756 he published a tract of thirty pages entitled *An Address to the Clergy* – 'plain, affectionate and powerful; breathing at once the spirit of an apostle and the feeling of a brother', according to one of his biographers. In it he considered what gifts and grace a minister ought to possess, before he answered the question: 'Are ministers what they ought to be?' The latter portion of this pamphlet pleased Walker, who said, 'He does not do so well at head work – but his heart! That reproves and confounds me.' Wesley's aim in writing was twofold:

'**1.** To give a new impulse to the Church of England, to awaken its dormant zeal, to infuse life into its lifeless ministers; and thus prevent the necessity of a separation.

'**2.** To curb the ambition of his own lay preachers, by setting before them a ministerial standard, of which, in some respects, most of them fell immeasurably short.'[14] In this way he hoped to 'lead the way to the performance of duties which the State had blindly overlooked, and the Church had scandalously neglected; thus would he become the Author of a second reformation, whereby all that had been left undone in the former, would be completed!'[15]

Wesley's *Address* was not well received by all. William Law, in a letter dated 10 April, 1757, called it 'empty babble'; and an unknown clergyman accused Wesley of 'spiritual pride and presumption'. Walker, however, was not so rash or condemnatory in his judgements. Sadly, Wesley's warning went unheeded, which, if anything, gave further impetus to his lay preachers to press him to separate from 'the dead establishment'.

Before *An Address to the Clergy* was published Wesley was expected with his preachers in Bristol for the autumn conference (August, 1756). Charles Wesley, in some anxiety of mind, wrote to Walker from Bristol on 7 August, 1756, about the forthcoming conference, to which William Grimshaw, 'a man after Walker's heart', was travelling to strengthen John's hands. Although the journey would take him four or five days, Grimshaw wanted to attend for he 'felt the issues were of great moment, both for himself and Methodism'.[16] Charles agreed with Walker that his brother '*must* come to a resolution; *must* know his own mind and act consistently for the residue of his days'. He urged Walker to 'speak a word in season' to confirm him in his calling, as he was 'almost overcome by his preachers'. Foreseeing the consequence some time before, Charles had his

brother, along with four lay preachers, sign the following agreement:

> March 10th, 1752. We whose names are underwritten,
> being clearly and fully convinced:
>   **1.** That the success of the present work of God, does in a
> great measure depend on the entire union of all the labourers
> employed therein.
>   **2.** That our present call is chiefly to the members of that
> church wherein we have been brought up, – are *absolutely
> determined* by the grace of God:
>   (1) To abide in the closest union with each other, and
> never speak, do or suffer anything which tends to weaken
> that union.
>   (2) Never to leave the communion of the Church of
> England without the consent of all whose names are
> subjoined.

> CHARLES WESLEY   JOHN JONES
> JOHN WESLEY   JOHN DOWNES
> WILLIAM KENT   JOHN NELSON.[17]

But for this agreement, which Charles thought 'every preacher
should sign or leave us', he would have broken off from the
Methodists and his brother. In his letter he then expressed what
he wanted his brother to do:

> **1.** That the unsound, unrecoverable preachers should
> be let depart just now.
>   **2.** That the wavering should be confirmed, if possible,
> and established in their calling.
>   **3.** That the sound ones should be received into the strict-
> est union and confidence, and as soon as may be, *prepared
> for orders*.
>   To this end, my brother ought, in my judgement, to
> declare and avow in the strongest and most explicit manner,
> his resolution to live and die in the communion of the Church
> of England.

1. To take all proper pains to instruct and ground both his preachers and his flock, in the same. A treatise is much wanting on this subject, which he might write and spread through all his societies.

2. To wait with me on the archbishop who has desired to see him, and tell him our whole design.

3. To advise, as far as they think proper, with some of our brethren the clergy as know the truth, and do nothing without their approbation. I was advised long ago by Lady Huntingdon to write to you on this subject, but could not do it till now. Your concern for the cause of God will, I doubt not, induce you to do all you can to promote it, and to hinder the work from being destroyed.[18]

As a result of this letter Walker wrote to John Wesley in the hope that, at the Bristol conference, 'the constitution of Methodism [would be] put on a footing that shall render it more serviceable to the Church of Christ and the Church of England'. He wanted Wesley to do something effectual about his lay preachers during his lifetime, and not to leave the situation in confusion and uncertainty at his death. 'The restraint of your authority gone,' remarked Walker, 'some of your preachers will be separating, and others will be disputing, to the evident ruin of Methodism, to the new disgrace of the Church of England, and, what is worse than both, to the dishonour and hindrance of practical godliness.' The importance of Wesley being determined to come closer to the Church of England was paramount and would influence many of his followers. Walker then offered Wesley some general advice:

Follow your own conscience without any regard to consequences, which are altogether in God's hand... Keep your eye on the word of God, and forget not your office as a minister of the Church of England ... and then give way to the dictates of your own mind, without regard to any consideration whatsoever... Your must carefully distinguish between conscience and prudence, lest while the former bids you act, the latter engage you to delay or temporize.[19]

Walker then turned his attention to more particular counsel:

> **1.** I would have you to keep full in view the interest of Christ's church in general, and of practical religion, not considering the Church of England or the cause of Methodism, but as subordinate thereto.
>
> **2.** I wish you to keep in view the unlawfulness of a separation from the Church of England, considering it on the whole as a sound branch of Christ's church.
>
> **3.** I would wish you to declare yourself without the least reserve on the point, as one satisfied therein, and fully determined to dispute that matter no more with any who dissent from you in opinion.
>
> **4.** I would wish you immediately to act with vigour, in consequence of such declaration; requiring your preachers to declare themselves, suffering such to depart as will not join you herein, and making all your societies acquainted with what you have done.
>
> **5.** I would wish you to do this at the approaching conference. You may never have another. Delays will make matters worse. The disaffected will grow upon you, corrupt others, and imagine you are afraid of them; while also in so unsettled state of things, nothing can go forward, the enemy has advantage, and the interests of vital religion must suffer.
>
> **6.** I would wish as many of your preachers as are fit for it, might be ordained, and that the others might be fixed to certain societies, and that in my judgement, as inspectors and readers, rather than preachers.[20]

Walker also wrote to Charles Wesley (16 August, 1756), and expressed his concern about his brother's conference with his lay preachers.

A church of Christ [Walker argued] is a congregation of Christian people, where the pure word of God is preached, and the sacraments duly ministered. A particular church is that where these things, essential to the being of a church of Christ, are executed with such appointments as are peculiar to that particular church. Consequently, the essence of a particular church is not that wherein it agrees with all the churches of Christ, but that which is particular to itself. And so it is by submitting to these particular rites, that a man professes himself a member of that particular church; whereas to depart from them is to separate from it. All that can be left to a particular church is to settle government and modes of worship, because all other things are settled already by Christ. If this be well considered, it appears that lay preachers being contrary to the constitution of the Church of England, are as far as that point goes, a separation from it... Is lay preaching agreeable with the constitution of the Church of England? And if not, is it not a separation in part, inasmuch as it offends against one of the greatest ends of our Church Establishment?...

It appears that lay preachers are found at the head of so many distinct bodies of people, to whom they minister the word, and who only want the sacraments at their hands, to be as much particular churches as any other... The thing is plainly inconsistent with the discipline of the Church of England; and so in one essential point setting up a church within her, which cannot be of her. You easily see what an impossibility there is [that] a ministration of the word in a manner contrary to the Establishment, should be consistent with that Establishment, where one of the two great points that constitute that practical Establishment, is its peculiar way of appointment respecting the ministration of the word... The consequence of this is, lay preaching is a separation in part. When, therefore, it is asked, shall we separate from the Church of England? It should rather be asked, shall we make the separation we have begun, a separation in all forms? And if we do not think ourselves allowed to do this, shall we unite with her? We do not, unless lay preaching is laid aside.[21]

Unless the case of lay preachers be laid aside, you will 'live on
the brink of a perfect separation', and cause there to be 'two
disunited ministrations of the word in the same place' – one
from the regular clergyman, the other from a lay preacher – 'by
people who yet do call themselves of the Church of
England'. Walker then mentioned a scheme of his, which he
thought could settle the issue, with which Vivian of Cornwood,
who was with Walker, agreed. With it he hoped to 'promote
usefulness on one side and to remove difficulties on the other',
and to keep the lay preachers, many of whom were in danger
of becoming a law unto themselves, within the bounds of order
and discipline. He felt strongly that if men were being raised up
to preach, they must be raised up by God, not by selfish ambition, and where possible be ordained according to the laws of
the Church of England. He passed on to Charles an incomplete
sketch of the scheme, which he had outlined to John:

> **1.** That as many of the lay preachers as are fit for, and
> can be procured ordination, be ordained.
> **2.** That those who remain be not allowed to preach, but
> be set as inspectors over the societies, and assistants to
> them.
> **3.** That they be not moved from place to place, to the
> end they may be personally acquainted with all the mem-
> bers of such societies.
> **4.** That their business may be to purge and edify the
> societies under their care, to the end that no person be
> continued a member, whose conversation is not orderly and
> of good report.[22]

Walker was endeavouring to keep the ministry of the word pure,
and free from men who would promote themselves to that
office. He was not curtailing the proclamation of the
gospel. If the objection was raised that this scheme would
prevent lay preachers from 'preaching abroad' and much good
stopped, he suggested that an inquiry be made to see if these

preachers, many of whom 'started up of their own heads' and were 'raw, disqualified and sadly misbehaved', had been 'so much to the honour or interest of religion or Methodism, as may be supposed. I remember when it first began, I said and thought lay preaching would be the ruin of Methodism.' With this letter Walker enclosed a private note – it seems that Charles did not want his brother to know he had written to Walker – in which he told Charles that it would be a vain exercise to get the preachers to subscribe to the agreement of 10 March, 1752.

As soon as Charles received these letters he replied from Bristol (21 August, 1756) before his brother had arrived for the conference. This letter, only partially and incorrectly quoted by Tyerman, is one of the most important he ever wrote. 'Lay preaching,' he said, 'is a partial separation, and may but *need* not, end in a total one. The probability of it has made me tremble for years past, and kept me from leaving the Methodists. I stay not so much to do good, as to prevent evil. I stand in the way of my brother's violent counsellors, the object both of their fear and hate.' He agreed wholeheartedly with Walker's regulations, but knew his brother would 'not hear of laying aside his lay preachers'.

> All I can desire of him to begin is: (1) To cut off all their hopes of his leaving the Church of England. (2) To put a stop to any more new preachers till he has entirely regulated, disciplined and secured the old ones. If he wavers still, and trims between the Church and them, I know not what to do. As yet it is in his power, if he exerts himself, to stop the evil. But I fear he will never have another opportunity. The tide will be too strong for him, and bear him away into the gulf of separation. Must I not therefore enter my protest and give up the preachers formally to him? *Hoc Ithacus volit*, and they impatiently wait for it. The restless pains of bad men to thrust me out from the Methodists seem a plain argument for my continuing with them. I want light, would have no will of my own, but prove what is that good and perfect will of God.[23]

Within a few days Walker wrote again to Charles Wesley and expressed his fears over 'the issue of this conference'. He was worried that John Wesley's uncertainty about what to do would mean he would not 'exert himself' and so hand the advantage to the preachers. On the one hand, Wesley did not want to lose his preachers – 'he had too great a hand in setting them up to think of pulling them down' – and was apprehensive that if he did not separate, they would 'leave him and the work come to the ground'; on the other hand, his conscience would not 'digest a separation'. He commended Charles's 'single eye', but was worried that 'the perverting influence of party, self-conceit, reputation and honour' would make the meeting 'of little purpose'. He then criticised the

> ... forwardness of an unhumbled spirit among the preachers, who however highly they may think of themselves, are but poor judges of what they are called to confer upon, and will make a very sorry figure at the head of a separation, should they obtain it. I fear the meekness of wisdom is not among them; if it were, they would know their place better and be subject. It has been a great fault all along to have made the low people of your council; and if there be not power enough left in your brother's hands to do as he sees fit, they will soon show him they will be their own masters.[24]

The rule in this matter, according to Walker, was:

> *If it be not sinful to abide in a particular Church, it must be sinful to separate from it.* And if this be granted, it is not easy to be seen how a separation can be considered on the footing of expediency; for to question if it be expedient to abide or to depart, is to ask if it be fit to do what is unlawful, or not to do what is duty, seeing I ought to depart if it be sinful to abide. Evidently this is the whole of the matter... Everyone should consult his own conscience with much fear and prayer, and to prevent mistakes that might arise, all might confer upon the duty or sinfulness of abiding; which done, such as

are satisfied in conscience before God it is sinful to abide,
should depart; and they who judge it not sinful to abide, must
remain.[25]

Walker conceded that this method was not easy to pursue
'because of our own will and worldly respects, which will be
exceedingly apt to rise up and blind or bias the judgement,
under the colour of bad or good consequences to be expected
from this or that conduct'. Only true faith acts obediently without worrying about the consequences.

If Walker's rule was right and the preachers were not guided
by it, they could not be depended on, because they did not
make abiding or departing a matter of conscience. If that
happened, Charles's conduct would have been 'a bearing
witness for the truth, a leading the way to others of like simplicity,
and a seasonable reproof of those whose will is their guide'. He
wanted Charles to obey his conscience without respect to
consequences. Walker could see many benefits from the
Methodists' closer union to the Church 'and a thousand ill
consequences from a separation'. What was intended by it? 'To
separate for the sake of separating is strange work! To separate
because it is sinful to abide is something; but to be fishing for
reasons to justify a separation, when one means nothing by
that separation but to please one's self, or raise a party, this is
strange work.'[26]

We know Mr Piers, Perronet, Manning and several regular clergy-men who do preach the genuine gospel, but to no effect at all. There is one exception in England, Mr Walker of Truro. We do not know one more who has converted one soul in his own parish.

John Wesley in a letter to Thomas Adam dated 31 October, 1755.[1]

Surely God has a favour for the people of these parts! He gives them so serious, zealous, lively preachers. By these and the Meth-odists together, the line is now laid, with no considerable interrup-tion, all along the north sea, from the eastern point of Cornwall to the Land's End.

John Wesley in his Journal for 8 September, 1760.[2]

13

Walker Opposes Separation from the Church of England (part 2)

During his correspondence with the Wesleys and others concerning lay preachers and the possible separation of Methodism from the Established Church, Walker kept a journal of his own spiritual experiences. It is a frank and humble account of his personal walk with God and of the care he took to watch over his own heart. The following are a few extracts that reveal his frame of mind during this most interesting period of his life:

> **Tuesday, June 15, 1756.** I know not how many evil tempers I have found working this day; particularly conceit when conversing with –. I have been kept from trials this day; so can say nothing what degrees of prevalence I am under of fear of men. I have come very short of that actual communion with God by meditation and ejaculation that I wish for.
>
> **Monday, June 28.** Sloth and business have prevented me the days past from continuing my journal, but I am sensible of the want of it. I cannot walk closely with God without daily watchfulness and examination. Yesterday's sermon related to a sense of the sinfulness of sin, as the great principle on which conversion stands contra-distinguished from servile fear. I cannot be so clear as I wish on this point.
>
> *In private exercises* I find a desire to serve God, and wish to see him glorified, but my heart I find exceedingly selfish *in the world.*

This day on the road to – I enjoyed useful meditation two hours; my heart much drawn up to God and approving his service and presence, but in the remainder of my journey I was confused and sometimes found myself carried away by carnal fears and proud reasonings. I resolved to be silent in the company I was to meet, if I might not be serviceable; and have found this evening the need and difficulty of being so. God grant me the spirit of meekness and charity.

Wednesday, June 30. I find it exceedingly difficult to hold communion with God, when not more immediately engaged in ministerial duties. *Conversation this day had been rather about religion than religious.* I want more of Christ's temper of meekness, having reason to suspect myself too solicitous when blamed unjustly. I see how vain it is to think of gaining Christ without forsaking all. Lord, make me more and more dead to the world!

Monday, July 5. I was striving much in prayer last night and this morning for a sense of the sinfulness of sin. My heart seems to have been quickened by it through the day, to keep a little close with God; yet how often have I forgotten him! O that I could love him more! I have been kept pretty much from fear respecting an approaching trial, being possessed with desire of professing Christ, with some confidence in his protection, and with compassion toward gainsayers. I have seen this day how needful it is to watch against a party spirit, and to love all who love Christ, leaving them to their own opinions, and to avoid love-destroying debates. I was rather affected, than piously devout in the prayers at a funeral.

I ought to guard against a sort of desponding thoughts from external circumstances, and from carnal proud reasonings in my own heart.

Wednesday, July 7... My comfort is, my salvation depends not on me, but Christ, the same yesterday, today and for ever, though I am so changeable.

Do I choose God for my portion? If so, why do I forget him so often, and think of him so coldly?

Monday, July 26. On reflection, I see my safest way is sitting down and abiding in the place I am called to. When absent from it, though in the way of duty, I do not so well retain the possession of my own mind.

This day I observed at waking, as I have often done, that the application of my heart to think on God was rather by force, it was not easy to keep him in view, though I had so many causes of thankfulness.

I have been engaged all this day in some needful service; yet find myself apt to seek my own pleasure even in doing God's work. I ought to be more sensible of the importance of my office, and to depend upon and pray more earnestly for the influences of God's Spirit on myself and labours. To be humble in the sense of my vileness and to believe the sufficiency of Christ, I find the two hardest things I have to attain.

Wednesday, August 11. Apt to wander in family prayer. My state is of very low advancement; more especially this appears by the infrequent applications of my heart to God; a true spirituality of temper I suspect I need for this reason; and that suspicion demands my strictest inquiry.

Last week when in trials, I seem to have been better than this when out of them. Let me inquire whether I am driven to Christ by necessity or drawn by love.

Monday, August 23. The devotions of this morning were shortened by the expectation of business. Somewhat like this often happens, and demands my greater attention.

Great experience this day of a corrupted heart; though not signally overcome, yet not watchful as I ought.

Tuesday, August 24. Public duty encroached on the morning private exercise.

Had this day for some hours a peculiar fear of falling away. I observed the actings of faith were weak, yet could not get them lively. Seemed, however, determined for God in Christ.

I am certainly influenced by a principle which makes me not unwatchful against sin, and not altogether unready to duty; but is it from the right motive, faith working by love?

Greatly wanting in thankfulness.[3]

Tuesday, March 22, 1757. I must be aware of sloth, worldly cares, formality, spiritual pride, and apostasy of heart; prepare my heart to meet God; and seek comfort; not merely for the sake of comfort, but of usefulness. I am greatly defective in actual communion (*out of* prayer, at least) and whether I seek God's face *in* prayer for *his glory*, is not quite clear; this is plain, I do not seek his face so importunately as I ought.[4]

Tuesday, March 29. When I see I am nothing, and do nothing right, I am most in a quiet frame. I have special need to be out of myself in prayer, to regard only my wants, and the promise of God. Methinks my exercises are rather meditations that warm the heart, than devout supplications. This evening the subject was reproof to *profit*; by which I must pray to get above conceit and prejudices.[5]

Tuesday, April 12. How many ways am I called upon to work in the Vineyard! Yet how forgetful! Might I not have done more at Mr A – 's *out of season*. Why should I not improve occasions more than I do? To keep the company under restraint, seemed the most I attempted while there.[6]

June 6. I am well satisfied the desire of esteem, of fear of men, has too much influence on my conduct. Lord, turn the fear of men's faces into a love of their souls.[7]

Throughout his ministerial career, and especially during his disagreement with Wesley, Walker was aware of the importance of conducting himself before all men with the meekness of Christ, of standing up for the truth in a way that would not engender a party spirit, of sensing the presence of Christ on the one hand and the sinfulness of sin on the other, and of guarding against any encroachment on his private devotions.

In a letter to Adam (2 September, 1756), he enclosed copies of the Wesley letters discussed in the previous chapter. He repeated to Adam his fears that Wesley's conference with his lay preachers – 'a very serious nature, and beyond what I fear they will be able to manage' – would 'end in a separation', unless they could be laid aside, a decision to which he could not see John Wesley agreeing. A separation, he thought, would end the usefulness of the Methodists and probably dampen the zeal of the regular clergy. He asked Adam's opinion and advice on the matter and expressed thanks that he had been 'directed to act in a regular way, as well as kept from their mistakes in

doctrinals. *I am perfectly satisfied we are members of a pure
Church of Christ'* in which he heartily desired to remain and to
promote its ends. Among his greatest joys was that 'God is
raising up here and there faithful men who speak and live the
gospel,' although most of them, according to Walker, were 'tinc-
tured with unscriptural notions, ministering gospel truths with a
dash more or less of Methodism, Mysticism or Moravianism'.[8]

He voiced concern that 'our friends in and near Bristol' were
'not so clear and distinct in their manner of setting out gospel
truths', and alluded to some correspondence with one of these
friends, which had given him the opportunity 'of laying before
them the substantial gospel as I understand it'. His friends in
Truro, having seen what he had written, wished it might be
corrected carefully so that it could be of more general service.
He asked Adam to review it and 'to make what corrections or
enlargements' he deemed necessary, and to tell him if, in his
judgement, it would be a help to young clergymen. At this point
he had not heard of the outcome of the Bristol conference.

Adam replied on 21 September, 1756. 'Methodism,' he
argued, 'as to its external forms, is such a deviation from the
rule and constitution of the Church of England, that all attempts
to render them consistent must be in vain.' He called lay preaching a 'manifest irregularity' that would 'not be endured in any
Christian society', and he could not accept Walker's proposal
to ordain the lay preachers. 'To what end would they be
ordained?' he asked. That they might continue to preach wherever they felt led? This would create a 'Church within a Church,
or more plainly, a Church against itself'. No. Either 'they set out
wrong, and must return wholly to the order of the Establishment ... or, they have acted hitherto, by superior direction of
the Spirit, and must not flinch from their leader... J. Wesley will
not, cannot give up the point of lay preaching, it will be giving
up all... But if he would, the generality of his followers will not.'
Furthermore, their preachers must offer themselves to be

ordained 'with a view to act irregularly, and take authority from
a Bishop to preach where they shall be lawfully appointed there-
unto, with a full resolution to act point blank against the tenor
of their commission, and preach where and how they please'.[9]

Nor did Adam agree with the idea of setting unordained
persons as 'inspectors over the societies and assistants to them'.
Such societies, disunited from their proper minister, would be
looked upon with suspicion by the incumbent and be regarded
as a 'separation and an inlet to confusion'. His judgement upon
the whole was that the lay preachers 'have embarrassed themselves past recovery, and must either go on in their present
form, or separate totally and openly'.[10]

Meanwhile, news arrived that the Bristol conference had
ended. The outcome was 'unexpectedly favourable'. Soon
after its conclusion John Wesley replied to Walker's August
letter. His letter is dated Kingswood, 3 September, 1756. He
opened by commenting that his only point in view was 'to
promote ... vital, practical religion; by the grace of God to
beget, preserve and increase the life of God in the souls of
men'. He then summarized how he came to allow several of his
brethren, whom he believed God had called and qualified for
the work,

> ... to comfort, exhort and instruct those who were athirst for
> God, or who walked in the light of his countenance. But, as
> the persons so qualified were few, and those who wanted
> their assistance very many, it followed that more of these
> were obliged to travel continually from place to place... So
> great a blessing has from the beginning attended the
> labours of these itinerants, that we have been more and
> more convinced every year of the more than lawfulness of
> this proceeding... Rarely two in one year, out of the whole
> number of preachers, have either separated themselves or
> been rejected by us. A great majority have all along
> behaved as becometh the Gospel of Christ, and I am clearly
> persuaded, still desire nothing more than to spend and be
> spent for their brethren.[11]

Wesley agreed with Walker's 'general advice' to follow his own conscience without any regard to consequences, and with most of his 'particular advices'. He claimed that 'All our preachers, as well as ourselves, purpose to continue in the Church of England. Nor did they ever before so freely and explicitly declare themselves on this subject.' Concerning Walker's last advice, 'that as many of our preachers as are fit for it, be ordained, and that the others be fixed to certain societies, not as preachers, but readers or inspectors', he replied:

If I mistake not, there are now in the county of Cornwall about four and thirty of these little societies, part of whom now experience the love of God; part are more or less earnestly seeking it. Four preachers, Peter Jaco, Thomas Johnson, W. Crabb and William Alwood, design the ensuing year, partly to call other sinners to repentance, but chiefly to feed and guide those few feeble sheep; to forward them, as of the ability which God giveth, in vital practical religion.

Now, suppose we can effect that Peter Jaco and Thomas Johnson be ordained, and settled in the curacies of Burrian and St Just; and suppose William Crabb and William Alwood fix at Launceston and Plymouth Dock, as readers and exhorters; will this answer the end which I have in view, so well as their travelling through the county?

It will not answer so well, even with regard to those societies with whom Peter Jaco and Thomas Johnson have settled. Be their talents ever so great, they will ere long grow dead themselves, and so will most of those that hear them. I know, were I myself to preach one whole year in one place, I should preach both myself and most of my congregation asleep.[12] Nor can I believe it was ever the will of our Lord that any congregation should have one teacher only. We have found by long and constant experience, that a frequent change of teachers is best. This preacher has one talent, that another. No one whom I ever yet knew has all the talents which are needful for beginning, continuing and perfecting the work of grace in a whole congregation.

But suppose this would better answer the end with regard to those two societies, would it answer in those where

W. Alwood and W. Crabb were settled as inspectors or readers? First, who shall feed them with the milk of the word? The ministers of their parishes? Alas, they cannot! They themselves neither know nor live nor teach the gospel. These readers? Can then either they or I or you always find something to read to our congregation, which will be as exactly adapted to their wants and as much blessed to them as our preaching? And here is another difficulty still: what authority have I to forbid their doing what I believe God has called them to do?...

Supposing these four societies to be better provided for than they were before, what becomes of the other thirty? Will they prosper as well when they are left as sheep without a shepherd? The experiment has been tried again and again, and always with the same event: even the strong in faith grew weak and faint; many of the weak made shipwreck of the faith; the awakened fell asleep; sinners, changed for a while, returned as a dog to the vomit, and so by our lack of service, many of the souls perish for whom Christ died...[13]

I cannot therefore see how any of those four preachers or any others in like circumstances can ever, while they have health and strength, ordained or unordained, fix in one place, without a grievous wound to their own conscience and damage to the general work of God.[14]

As promised Charles Wesley sent his account of the conference to Walker from Bristol on 6 September, 1756.[15] Almost all the Methodist itinerant preachers – between forty and fifty – had been present, as well as Henry Venn from Huddersfield. Charles quoted part of his brother's first account of the conference, in which the members 'spoke largely of keeping united to the Church, and there was no dissenting voice, but all were knit together in one mind and one judgement'. The Wesleys closed the conference 'with a strong declaration of our resolution to live and die in the communion of the Church of England. We all unanimously agreed, that whilst it was lawful or possible to continue in it, it was unlawful for us to leave it.' According to Charles, John 'seems farther from a separation than ever'. John had also undertaken to write a treatise to confirm the Methodists in the Church, entitled *Reasons Against a Separation from the Church of England*, which appeared in 1758. Charles concluded his letter by remarking that the 'awakening in this and in all places where the gospel comes, either through the Clergy or Methodists, increases'.[16]

Interestingly, the chief reason for Charles giving up his own itinerant ministry in 1756 was that he 'feared the course that Methodism would take and he felt that by promoting its interests he would actually be working against the Church of England'.[17] In a footnote to John's treatise, Charles wrote:

> I think myself bound in duty to add my testimony to my brother's. His twelve reasons against our ever separating from the Church of England are mine also. I subscribe to them with all my heart... My affection for the Church is as strong as ever: and I clearly see my calling, which is to live and die in her communion. This, therefore, I am determined to do, the Lord being my helper.[18]

A year later when John Wesley was again touring Cornwall, Walker, in a letter not preserved but agreed to by his friends, made the suggestion that 'the Methodist societies formed in Evangelical parishes should be handed over to the care of these enlightened incumbents'. This matter was evidently raised during Wesley's visit to St Agnes over the weekend of 3-4 September, 1757, when he had an hour's conversation with James Vowler, the curate, who subsequently proposed that a letter should be written to Wesley 'urging a greater measure of cooperation, and if possible the prohibition of Methodist societies in parishes with Evangelical incumbents'.[19] Walker, in his letter to Wesley, said:

> If you believed Mr Vowler to be a gracious person and a gospel minister, why did you not, in justice to your people, leave them to him?... Was there not inconsistency in your

visiting Mr Vowler as a gospel minister when you did not give up your people to him?... If that was not the design of your visit, you should not have visited him at all... Does not this conduct on the whole savour of a party spirit and show a desire to please Methodists as Methodists?... You spoke to Mr Vowler of your being as one man. Nothing is so desirable; but really, before it can be effected, something must be done on your part more than paying us visits, which, as far as I can see, can serve no other purpose in the present circumstances than to bring us under needless difficulties.[20]

Walker received a reply from Penryn, dated 19 September, 1757,[21] from which can be gleaned part of the contents of Walker's letter. Wesley assured Walker: 'I do "exert myself" so far as to separate from us those that separate from the Church.' At the same time he exercised as little authority as possible, 'because I am afraid of people depending upon me *too much*, and paying me more reverence than they ought'. Among the reasons he did not give up his people to Vowler were: 'No one mentioned or intimated any such thing, nor did it once enter into my thoughts;' he did not know if Vowler, whom he had heard 'preach the *true* though not the *whole* gospel', possessed the wisdom and experience to guide and govern a flock; nor did he know 'whether he could or would give that flock all the advantages for holiness which they now enjoy'. This is a surprising comment considering he wrote in his Journal for 3 September, 1757, that Vowler 'rejoices in the love of God, and both preaches and lives the gospel'.[22] He went on:

And with regard to the people: far from thinking that 'the withdrawing our preachers' from such a Society without their consent would 'prevent a separation from the Church', I think it would be the direct way to cause it. While we are with them, our advice has weight, and keeps them to the Church; but were we totally to withdraw, it would be of little or no weight. Nay, perhaps resentment of our unkindness (as it would probably appear to them) would prompt them to act in flat opposition to it.

> 'And will it not be the same at your death?' I believe not; for
> I believe there will be no resentment in this case; and the last
> advice of a dying friend is not likely to be so soon forgotten.[23]

On the contrary, 'the last advice of a dying friend' is very soon
forgotten, especially if that advice disagrees with the prevailing
view. In his letter he denied any consciousness of a 'party spirit'
and expressed his desire for 'a closer union with the clergy who
preach the truth', that is, the 'truth' according to his interpreta-
tion. He was prepared to do anything Walker suggested to
promote that end 'provided only that it consist with my keeping a conscience void of offence toward God and toward man'.
But was he not offending the Evangelical clergy by setting up
societies in their parishes? He then dealt 'very freely' with Walker's
objection that 'paying us visits can serve no other purpose than
to bring us under needless difficulties'.

> Can our conversing together serve no other purpose? You
> seem, then, not to have the least conception of *your own*
> wanting any such thing! But whether you do or not, I feel I
> do... I want more light, more strength, for my personal walking
> with God; and I know not but he may give it me through you.
> And (whether you do or no) I want more light and strength
> for guiding the flock committed to my charge. May not the
> Lord send this also by whom he will send? And by you as
> probably as any other? It is not improbable he may by you
> give me clearer light either as to doctrine or discipline. And
> even hereby, how much comfort and profit might redound to
> thousands of those for whom Christ has died! which, I
> apprehend, would fully compensate any difficulties that might
> arise from such conversation.[24]

There is no doubting Wesley's sincerity or his desire for 'more
light and strength', but it does appear strange that a man of his
experience was ignorant of the difficulties his lay preachers were
causing Evangelical clergymen. It is tempting to suggest that he
would not rather than *could* not see them. The only 'difficulties'
Wesley could envisage were 'the necessary consequence of your

sharing our reproach', which was 'no other than the reproach of Christ... And, indeed, you cannot avoid it any other wise than by departing from the work. You do not avoid it by standing aloof from us; which you call *Christian*, I *worldly*, prudence.' He closed his letter by asking, 'Are you sure God would add nothing to you by me beside what he might add to me by you?'[25] The question that Walker had put to Wesley was not so much about adding, but about taking the Methodists away from a gospel minister of the Church of England.

This was the last letter between the two men and it reveals a growing divergence in their relationship. Walker at this point realised that further correspondence would be fruitless. He had tried to set the Methodists on a firmer footing to strengthen the Establishment, but had concluded that to push his case further might be counter-productive. He at least had the knowledge that both Wesleys were doing all they could to stay within the Church of England, even if it seemed that John was unconsciously encouraging his preachers to look to him rather than to their mother Church. G.C.B. Davies remarked that at this stage in the problem of separation 'It was not by kindling in [the lay preachers] a natural affection to the Church as the mother of us all, but by their affection and obedience to himself as their particular father, that [Wesley] trusted to retain the Methodists within the English Church after his own death.'[26] However, the matter needed to be set on a regular and not a personal basis.

From this point, the two men, while retaining respect for each other and determining not to hinder the other, felt it wiser to work apart, an attitude that was reflected in the 'growing estrangement between the Methodists and Anglicans in the Evangelical parishes, though here the more ardent on both sides made matters more acute'.[27] Of Walker, Wesley graciously said, 'Gladly could I embrace my dear brother ... but I am content to let him work. I will pray for him wherever I go, and for the success of that work the Lord is making him an instrument to carry on.'[28]

If lay preachers had not been appointed, few problems would have arisen, but to retain such an organization within the Establishment proved impossible. The spiritual inertia and apathy of the clergy as a whole, motivated Wesley to continue his itinerancy, and, it was 'inevitable that an itinerant should desire to leave behind in each place some permanent organization, and here lay the root of separation'.[29]

It must be noted that to a certain degree Wesley kept to the Bristol declaration all his life.[30] He might have been a stronger advocate for adherence to the Church of England if his address to the Evangelical clergy in 1764, in which he attempted to effect a union between himself and them, 'without sacrifice of opinion' and 'binding themselves to no peculiar discipline', had been more enthusiastically received.[31] He appealed to between fifty and sixty clergymen, but only three responded to his circular, which caused him to exclaim peevishly, 'They are a rope of sand and such they will continue.' He immediately set about consolidating the union of his preachers.

The subject of lay preaching and separation from the Church of England has been dealt with at length, not only because of Walker's involvement and somewhat neglected views, but because it was one of the weightiest questions that had to be resolved by those connected with the Evangelical revival. That there was a divergence of opinion is confirmed by the fact that both Thomson and Bennet, two Cornish Evangelicals, followed Wesley's example of itinerating, and by the attitude of Walker's flock. Five years after the Truro curate had died 'the enmity in those who were called his people' was as real as ever. 'They still look upon us,' complained Wesley, 'as rank heretics, and will have no fellowship with us.'[32] Walker always stood his ground, and the uneasy difference of opinion remained without open rupture. However, after the death of the early Evangelical leaders, the attitude and actions of the lay preachers, resisted by the clergy, forced a wider gulf, and led eventually to an inevitable separation.

[Mr Walker] desired to be and was a Bible divine, one who wished to draw his religious principles entirely from the book of God, and who proved the real influence of those principles upon his heart, by the careful conformity of his life.

Ambrose Serle in a recommendatory preface to Walker's Christ the Purifier.[1]

In 'The Christian' we have Evangelical preaching at its best. It is pervaded by a positive tone, and there is an absence of those continual denunciations, often degenerating into mere scolding, which marred many sermons. The building up of the faithful is emphasized and there is no attempt unduly to stir the emotions. The language is Scriptural, and the Bible is constantly appealed to, but not apart from reason. In one sermon Walker says: 'I trust you have heard nothing which is not as consistent with reason as it is with scripture.' The sermons reveal clearly Walker's attitude and method, and make it all the more tragic that his comparatively early death should have robbed the movement of one who would have exercised great influence on its fruitful development.

L. E. Elliot-Binns.[2]

14

Ill Health, 'The Christian' and a Regiment of Soldiers

Samuel Walker's correspondence with the Wesleys and Adam added to his already heavy workload, which was exaggerated by his reluctance to hand over some of his responsibilities to other capable men within his congregation, and soon his fragile constitution broke down under the strain. As early as 8 September, 1755, in a letter written by a layman of 'excellent character', we read how 'Walker thrives, though his body decays visibly. It cannot long sustain the weight of his labours. He hastens, I believe, to his kingdom and crown. "Spare yourself" is a language he is unwilling to hear.' The writer, somewhat prematurely, lamented that 'so valuable a life should be cut short in the midst, when the church of Christ seems to thrive by its prolongation'.[3]

Others mentioned Walker's physical deterioration, but in most of his letters to friends, written in a firm hand and with his usual expressiveness, there were no obvious signs of weakness, nor did his congregation experience any lessening of his pastoral care. Nevertheless, he knew only too well that his health was poor and that he could only care for his flock a little longer. In a letter to Adam (2 October, 1755), a confidant to whom he had previously mentioned his state of health, he first described his workload, which, along with his weakness, had been the cause of a lack of 'literary correspondence with yourself [Adam] and other valuable friends':

My stated business (besides the Sunday duty, prayers
Wednesdays and Fridays, burials, baptisms and attendance
upon the sick in a parish where there are 1600 souls) is
Mondays, Wednesdays and Fridays to talk with such as
apply to me in private from six to ten in the evening; Tuesday
to attend the society and Thursday, a lecture at Church in
the evening; Saturday, and as much of Fridays as I can gain,
is bestowed in preparing the Sunday's sermon; to all of which
must be added what I may well call the care of the Church,
that is of above a hundred people, who upon one account
and another continually need my direction.[4]

He expressed no surprise that his strength did not prove equal
to these demands, that he found himself debilitated and 'under
necessity of making my time yet shorter by lying more in bed
than formerly'. He feared that what he was enduring was 'has-
tening my end, though there be no immediate danger'. He then
mentioned the conflict between his friends' advice to spare himself for the work's sake, and his own unwillingness to neglect
any present duty, whatever the consequences to himself.

[I] have dropped nothing. If I do wrong herein, God knows I
would gladly know his will in the matter, and beg your friendly
sentiments, whether I ought not in conscience to persist in
all such things as immediately require my assistance in the
ministerial capacity, though I feel and foresee a growing
decay by it? And whether I ought to have any regard to what
the consequences may possibly be with respect to the work
here, in case of my death? And, if I ought to drop anything,
what?[5]

There is no record of Adam's reply, but it is certain that he
received different advice from people, some encouraging him
to press on regardless, others exhorting him to continue only
with the bare essentials. Yet he carried on steadfastly until his
bodily weakness forced him to cut back. On 2 September, 1756,
he again wrote to Adam and said that if he could get time and
help, he would 'gladly make a long journey', even to

Wintringham. Such a journey, he admitted, would be particularly useful 'with regard to my health, of which I cannot boast,
although I have no more to complain of than a growing debility
and consequent inability to labour as usual'. He had decided
to abridge himself 'in some lesser particulars, though the public
Sunday duty seems now somewhat too hard upon me'. As far
as he could see, the issue was either to labour in Truro until he
could labour no more, or, if he could not procure an assistant,
to remove to another less demanding field of work. This is the
first time he had mentioned leaving Truro. He was only forty-one.

Nineteen days later (21 September, 1756) Adam, in his
reply, expressed concern to hear Walker 'mentioning again' his
'declining state of health and growing unfitness for service'. He
would be delighted to see him in Wintringham, if a long journey
was thought proper, and encouraged him to get an assistant
'some way or other for a time'. Walker replied on 7 October. A
long journey at this time was 'impracticable', but he hoped to
'attempt it another year' if his time and purse permitted and if
God spared his life. He again said that 'The Sunday's duty is
become too hard for me, yet I see no possibility of getting an
assistant, being myself but a curate under a neighbouring clergyman, whose natural defects and blameable timidity are such,
that he has never done the least thing since I have been here.'[6]

It appears from the correspondence between these two men
that Adam appealed to Lord Dartmouth on Walker's behalf in
an effort to get him a much needed assistant. Walker was obliged
for his friend's intervention, especially as his 'principal, the most
timid creature in the world', and with whom he could only 'live
on civil terms',

> was vastly fearful he might incur some general reproach by
> having any hand in procuring me an assistant, as it is a main
> object with him that the world may know he does not patronize
> my proceedings. However, if it might be done so that he
> should be no otherwise concerned in it than to give his
> consent, he would make no objection.[7]

During this time of fatigue he published a series of eleven practical sermons on the character of a Christian that he had delivered to his Truro congregation, and which, according to his
biographer, 'will long continue to be read with delight and profit
by those who value the grand fundamental doctrines of the
gospel'.[8] In his dedication of the book to the people of that
place, he warned, 'It is not indeed a character which will suit
the generality of those who call themselves by that name,' for
he hoped to awaken in those who had too high an opinion of
their religious conduct 'a holy disgust with themselves'.

The volume, which he entitled *The Christian*, was well
received, and its good sale gave Walker 'encouraging hopes
that my little attempt may not be altogether fruitless'. He was
not disappointed. Once he heard that someone in Dublin had
printed and given away a thousand copies of *The Christian*;
many Irish soldiers – 'and very serious ones they were' – had a
copy in their pockets at Plymouth, where they were stationed
on route from Ireland to America; and in a letter dated July,
1758, Adam told him that 'last summer' he saw the Bishop of
Cork at Scarborough and was informed that he always carried
Walker's *Christian* in his pocket. The second edition of five
hundred copies was printed in 1756 and a third edition
appeared three years later. After that it was re-issued again and
again until it reached a twelfth edition in 1879.

On 4 November, 1755, he wrote to Adam and thanked him
for his positive opinion of the work and 'the pains you have
used in making out inaccuracies', which he wanted his friend to
pass on to him that the second edition might be corrected. He
then asked a 'great favour': 'Will you write somewhat in the
way of a preface or otherwise, to be prefixed to this edition,
which I am persuaded will strengthen and recommend them.
As they are now going to the press, and will not take more than
six weeks in printing, this matter will admit of no delay.'[9] Adam
complied. His opening comments were:

As the following sermons are especially calculated to promote vital Christianity, by illustrating the means and necessity of a real *inward change*; or the recovery of man from his present state of gross insensibility under the fall, to a life of acquaintance and communion with God; it is hoped they will, with the divine blessing, answer the author's design, by rousing the stupid sinner, undeceiving the formalist, and animating the pious to higher attainments.[10]

In a letter to another friend – 'William' – that Walker wrote on 16 December of that year, he said that Adam had sent him 'a most judicious, smart and explicatory preface to my sermons, which will greatly assist them'.[11]

Walker's writings are distinguished by a methodical exactness and propriety in the arrangements of his thoughts, which are designed to strike the heart and conscience with conviction of sin and to enforce the necessity of fleeing to Christ for justification. J. C. Ryle, commenting on three of Walker's 'excellent' literary works: *Fifty-two Lectures on the Church Catechism, The Covenant of Grace in Nine Sermons* and *The Christian,* gave the following recommendation:

His sermons give me a most favourable impression of his powers as a preacher. For simplicity, directness, vivacity, and home appeals to the heart and conscience, I am disposed to assign them a very high rank among the sermons of [the eighteenth century]. It is my deliberate impression, that if he had been an itinerant like Whitefield, and had not confined himself to his pulpit in Truro, he would probably have been reckoned one of the best preachers of his day.[12]

Ambrose Serle, writing a preface to Walker's *Christ the Purifier* on 10 September, 1793, stated that, as with all his works, his 'earnest and continual drift was not to raise admirers for himself, but to win souls for his master'.[13] Charles Simeon, whose high opinion of Walker's sermons has been noted, commented in his introductory essay to the 1825 edition of *The Christian*: 'In his statements ... there is a surprising depth; so that he appears as if he were acquainted with every motion of the heart. We are not aware of any writer that equals him in this respect... For the attainment of self-knowledge, we cannot but recommend this book as of singular value.'[14]

Towards the end of 1756,[15] a new and important opportunity opened up for Walker, which he grasped with his usual earnestness. On 4 November three companies of soldiers (about 160 men) from the regiment of Colonel Anstruther at Plymouth were posted to Truro for the winter (nine weeks in all). Walker, valuing their immortal souls, immediately made them the objects of his pastoral care and before long wrote to Adam about the striking results of his labours among them:

> I endeavoured to lose no time with them from their first arrival, but without delay preached a sermon extraordinary on their account on the Sunday afternoon, called by the people here *The Soldiers' Sermon*. There was at first great difficulty to get their attendance to hear it; for though they were ordered to be at church in the morning, and brought thither by their officers, yet they used to turn off at the door. In this point I was helped by the zeal of my dear people of the society, who made it their business to speak to these poor creatures, giving them proper advice, and prevailing on a few of them to be at church as was wished.
>
> They soon became a larger number. And our labours were so blessed to them and us, that in less than three weeks, a full hundred of them came to my house, asking *what they must do* [to be saved]. This is what I aimed at, – an opportunity of personal and free conversation. The effects have been very striking. One or two of the whole only excepted, you would have seen their countenances changing, tears often bursting from their eyes, and confessions of their exceeding sinfulness and danger, breaking from their mouths. I have scarcely heard such a thing as self-excusing from one of them; while their desire to be instructed, and

uncommon thankfulness for the least pains used upon them by any of us, have been very remarkable. Such promising symptoms gave me great confidence it would come to something; and more so when I found that many of them were greatly stirred to pray.

Many of them, as was to be expected, soon went back. Nevertheless, thus far, both they and the others who never came near me in private, are plainly influenced, that a certain fear has restrained them from swearing and cursing, which, when they came hither, was universally their practice; has engaged them to attend public worship, and at least so far biassed their conduct, that military punishments are grown much less frequent among them. They are about twenty who have kept close to the means of grace, and concerning whom I have encouraging hope, that a *good work* is *begun* in them. Indeed, conviction of sin appears to have gone deep with them, and they are crying after Christ with such marks of *godly sorrow* as make me hope it is indeed *a sorrow which worketh repentance unto salvation*.

These I intend shall be united together, when they leave us, under the name of 'The Soldiers' Society', having already drawn up regulations for the purpose [and a special prayer for their use]. And while they are here, they make a part of our society, by the exercises of which, as well as by meetings I particularly appoint for their use, they seem to be much established. What such a society of soldiers may produce amongst that body of men, God only knows; yet I would comfort myself with the hope it may please the Lord it shall go farther.

It may be observed that seven of these, namely six Scotchmen, and one English Dissenter have enjoyed the benefit of religious knowledge in their youth; the rest, excepting two, I find totally ignorant of everything relating to Christ. And this, their total ignorance, has made me lament the superficial use or entire neglect of catechizing among the English clergy, by which, more than by any other thing, I am persuaded the kingdom of darkness and sin is established in England.[16]

In reference to the 'six Scotchmen', Walker could not but 'adore the mysteriousness of God's ways, in leading them from one end of the island [of Great Britain] quite to the other to do his work upon them'. He thought it was as if God had said: 'It shall not be done in Scotland, but Cornwall; [not] John Gillies nor John Porteous, but Samuel Walker shall be the instrument.' It was clear, however, that there is 'evident reasonableness in this procedure, for by some unaccustomed outbreakings since they have been in the army, they were more open to conviction'.[17]

Providentially, about a week before the soldiers arrived in Truro, Walker had been sent some books by *The Society for Promoting Religious Knowledge Among the Poor*, which he was able to put to good use immediately by giving each soldier a *Compassionate Address*, a tract he called 'for size, matter and address, the fittest in the world for their use'.[18]

At first Walker's efforts towards the regiment met with considerable opposition. The captain publicly forbade his men to go to him for private instruction, although over a period of time 250 disobeyed his order and visited the Truro curate for that very purpose. Walker thought that his office as a minister of the gospel had been insulted by this humiliating restriction, which evidently caused him great distress. After the soldiers' departure he examined his private attitude to what had happened. On one of these occasions, Monday 18 April, 1757, he praised God, saying, 'I have found little risings of resentment, if any; and do desire to pity the case of the blind officer; to forgive his advisers and to wait on God for opportunity to help his soldiers.'[19] The soldiers who embraced Christ were much derided at first, but they stood firm, and subsequently order prevailed in the regiment 'to a degree never before witnessed'. The officers acknowledged the good effects of Walker's exertions, and thanked him for the reformation he had produced in their behaviour.

When the soldiers left Truro in the first week of January, 1757, the scene was very moving. In the evening of their final day they assembled in the society's room to hear their minister for the last time. To a friend Walker said, 'Had you but seen their countenances, what thankfulness, love, sorrow and joy sat upon them; – they hoped they might bring forth some fruit; they hoped to meet us again at the right hand of Jesus in his illustrious day. Amen.' The hearts of some of the men were so touched that on leaving the room they grasped Walker's hand and then turned away without uttering a word. The following morning they began their march 'praising God for bringing them under the sound of his gospel; and as they slowly passed along, turned round to catch occasional glimpses of the town as it gradually receded from their sight, exclaiming, "God bless, Truro."'[20] They never saw Walker again on earth, but he received from Plymouth 'very agreeable accounts of them'.

Two letters, which gave Walker real joy and confirmed that his work among the soldiers had not been unproductive, were preserved by him as memorials. The first, dated 17 January, 1757, was written from Plymouth Dock by a grenadier Henry Robinson 'at a barick table with 14 men'. According to Walker, when Robinson came to Truro he 'knew little more of Christ than if he had lived in China'. The letter is addressed to 'DR. FATHER IN THE LORD' and is signed 'from your affectionate child in the Lord'. Robinson reported that since he left Truro he had suffered 'great trials ... but still I trust to Christ for to enable me to withstand them all'. Each day during the march to Plymouth 'religion was thrown in my teeth by calling me Methodist, and saying that I had made confession of all my sins to Mr Walker'. He answered these taunts by telling his mockers of that day when they must confess to one greater than Walker, the Lord Jesus, 'in whom I trust for help to withstand all the temptations of the devil, the flesh, and this wicked world, which

I have to war against'. He went on to share with Walker something of the workings of God in his own soul:

> Christ has promised to assist them that trust in him for aid, which is my great comfort, for I always pray to him, and hold him in view as my Saviour and Redeemer. And I hope the God of glory will be always with me, to enable me to fight on my good fight to salvation, and when the great and terrible day of the Lord shall come, I may be found acceptable in his sight, and be received into that heavenly kingdom which is purchased for me by the blood of Christ, and all poor condemned sinners; me the worst of all, deserving nothing but damnation and the heavy wrath of God for offending him, and breaking his commands, and making his sabbath a day of sport and drunkenness. Yet for all my great offences, transgression and sin, I do sincerely believe that Christ's righteousness is able to save me and nothing else, by still applying to him, and praying to him as a poor miserable condemned sinner, hoping he will wash away my sins through his blood, and by giving me a new heart, I may be made a child of God through Christ Jesus. Amen.
>
> I find my heart inclined greatly to the ways of the Lord, and ready to obey his commands; but when I left you I was under some dread of falling, but I find the contrary, thanks be to God. And although my parting was sorrowful, yet I hope we shall meet again with joy in the kingdom of heaven, never more to be parted, but to sit together singing praise to God and the Lamb, for ever and ever, Amen.
>
> And may the God of all glory bless you, and all my dear brethren, now and for ever, for, under God, you were the means of bringing me to salvation. I desire your prayers always, as mine are for you night and morning, weak as they are. Pray remember me to all my dear brethren... I hope in my next [letter] you shall have the news that we are met in our little society together. All my dear brethren desire to be remembered to you, and all these brethren in the Lord.[21]

The second letter, addressed to a member of the Truro society – 'my dear friend in the Lord' – is signed by two soldiers, John

Murd and Robert Moore. Murd, the writer, expressed his life-long gratitude to 'worthy Mr Walker', and the heartbreak he felt at his 'sudden removal' from Truro. Sergeant Moore 'for ever blesses the day that ever he saw Truro, and we both hope in the Almighty God to see it again, and to hear the glad tidings of salvation as formerly... For ever blessed be [God] that you were a means appointed to bring me to Mr Walker.' Murd promised to do all he could to help 'my brethren soldiers' and to exhort the second detachment in Truro not to neglect the means of grace. He concluded, with Sergeant Moore, 'with our kind compliments to worthy Mr Walker, our father in the Lord'.[22]

This second detachment of soldiers, referred to by Murd, arrived on the day the first detachment left (about 6 January, 1757), and Walker and his people were equally diligent towards them during their short stay. Some of them were still in Truro on Sunday 3 April as Walker wrote in his diary: 'I have laboured with the soldiers this evening; and my body would need be excused retired exercises. But I will exercise myself in them as well as I can.'[23] In a letter to Adam (9 March, 1757), he talked of the soldiers and admitted that 'At first I feared the bad influence such kind of people might have upon us,' but after reflection, he saw it as 'a dispensation of Providence, which demanded my attempting something for their service'. He then asked Adam for his opinion about writing to the Archbishop of Canterbury on account 'of the ignorance I have found them in, occasioned principally through a disuse of catechizing. They are of more than twenty different counties, and not one had the benefit of that instruction.' He also wanted to know whether regulations for their society, under which they were meeting weekly, should be drawn up; and he submitted for Adam's correction a catechism he had written for the soldiers' use, which needed Scripture proofs subjoined to every answer.[24]

On 29 March, 1757, the day after part of the second detach-ment of soldiers had left, Walker recorded in his diary: 'I have been enabled, in some measure, to labour for their souls, since their coming hither (4 November), [and] many of them seem to be awakened; not less than 250, in larger or smaller numbers, at my house. I desire to commit them to the Lord and to the power of his grace, which is able to build them up.' And two weeks later, on 12 April, after all the soldiers had returned to Plymouth: 'Another special matter of thankfulness is the news this day brought me that my dear soldiers still stand their ground at Dock.'[25]

In all his work with the soldiers there is again exemplified Walker's concern for the souls of men, even when it meant increasing his already onerous duties and further debilitating his fragile health. He not only superintended the flock under his care, training them to serve God and to minister to others, but was always ready to advise anyone who came to him from a neighbouring town, and to cultivate a spirit of religion among those who seemed to be accidentally thrown in his way. He

> ... never forgot to exhort persons of all conditions and occupations in life to apply themselves with diligence to the duties of their respective callings, telling them, as the strongest argument that could be urged, that the prosperity and tranquillity of their souls would be more effectually promoted by a careful and industrious attention to the business of their station, than by devoting themselves wholly to the study of religion, to the neglect of those employments, which the place that God had assigned them in the world required at their hands.[26]

Thus he never encouraged the soldiers to leave the army, but to be examples of godliness in their own regiment and so influence others of similar occupation.

This peculiarity of affection [between Walker and Adam] was probably founded in a similarity of mind, and the particular subject in religion which engaged their attention. They were both diligent students of the human heart. They who are deeply versed in this science are, in divinity, as scholars in a higher class, who, though they have a general respect for all friends of good learning, yet when they meet with one who is capable of entering into their deeper views, find a delight in conversation to which others are strangers, and they find a response to the observations of each other, which makes their intercourse very agreeable.

Possibly Joseph Milner of Hull, one of the editors of Adam's Posthumous Works.[1]

15

To Wintringham and Back

Soon after the soldiers had left and the excitement of their conversion had died down, Walker wrote to Adam (12 May, 1757),
and shared with him some of the difficulties and disappoint-
ments he was experiencing in his ministry among the
inhabitants of Truro, and the kind of people he had tried to
help.

> What a people! A quarter part of them never enter the church
> doors. Too many reject what they hear, not a few turning it
> into ridicule. The most go on their own way. When I beseech
> them by the mercies of God, they are unconcerned; when
> they are persuaded by the terrors of the Lord, they rail. Above
> all things it breaks my heart to attend their sick beds, where
> I too often find them secure and ignorant in the hardness of
> their hearts, it may be wishing to die merely to be rid of their
> present pains, or if a little awakened, yet so uninstructed as
> to leave me at a loss where to begin with them. There are
> now no less than three near death, and in a dreadful security,
> from which my attempts have not seemed in the least to
> move them.[2]

Through experience he had found that catechizing was the most
effective method 'for preventing such deplorable deaths in the
growing generation'. He was, however, still at a loss as to what
more he could do with those advanced in years, who were
'hardened, unteachable, sunk in cares and pleasures'. In his
desire to benefit the lost – when they searched out their sins,

they had no foundation through their ignorance of 'knowing the law in its spirituality' – he planned to draw up a simple explanation of the Ten Commandments, 'with some close applications respecting the curse of the law, and the necessity of faith in Christ'.

Adam responded by recommending a close examination of the Sermon on the Mount. 'Where can you have better direction, surer footing, or more sacred authority, than from Christ's own manner of opening them?' The design is 'in order to conviction, and not to practice till faith fits us for it and enables us to eye the commandments in their whole spiritual extent, both for serious endeavour, continual humiliation, and love of Christ the performer of them for his people'.[3]

As well as discouragements there were times of blessing and fruitfulness. One lady, writing to John Gillies on 30 April, 1757, referred to when she made 'half a year's visit to a brother in Truro, during which period a young person of that place, together with Mr Walker's ministry, in 1755, were the instruments of a gracious God to unrivet the scales and bring light to my eyes. You must allow I have cause to glorify God abundantly for his inestimable gift of free grace in Jesus Christ.'[4] In a letter to Darracott (15 December, 1757), Walker mentioned that 'There were many wet eyes last Sunday among the backsliders. This is encouragement. The Lord may please to bless us with one harvest more. I wish I had more heart to pray and labour for poor souls.'[5]

It may be that Walker would have travelled north anyway at this juncture, perhaps to discuss further with Adam his situation at Truro and how best to improve it, but it was for another reason that in the autumn of 1757 he visited friends in distant parts. A trip was certainly necessary for the sake of his precarious health, but he set out in order to see the bishop of the diocese. The occasion of this interview, as he explained in a letter to Adam, was that about a year previously (December, 1756) a 'gentleman [Robert Quarme] died, who had been unhappily profane, destroyed himself with drink, and went out of the world without any signs of repentance'. In the burial service Walker conducted, he could not, in all good conscience, use the words of the burial office concerning him: 'As our hope is this our brother doth.' This omission was reported to Bishop Lavington, who sharply reprimanded him for it. Polwhele, who viewed Walker as 'a stern Calvinist', swayed by his own bias, recounted: 'Mr W. was not disposed in charity to call him "Brother", or express "a sure and certain hope", etc. This was thought extremely harsh, and occasioned a great disturbance among many of Walker's flock. Mr Lemon took a decided part against Walker.'[6]

There the matter rested until Quarme's companion also died (about 7 October, 1757), called by Walker 'the worst of the two'. Walker was immediately presented with a dilemma, which he expressed in his letter to Adam (17 October, 1757):

I dared not read those words, yet thought I had no right to alter, and that on that head I had acted wrong in the former case. So, determined to make my mind easy at all events, I told his friends I could not bury him, and recommended to them the getting some other clergyman, which I thought it was not honest for me to do myself. Those who seek occasion against me, thought they had now found it, but it pleased God to make their impetuosity to do me hurt, the very means of preserving me from any damage; for they did not bring the corpse to the church stile, but hurried it away to a neighbouring church, which, indeed, they were forced in some sort to do, if they intended to make anything of it against me, because my brother Penrose was providentially come to town an hour before the time assigned for the funeral, and repeatedly sent word that he was ready to do the office [probably at Kenwyn]. What this may come to, besides a deal of noise, and indeed rage, I know not; but am told I have nothing to fear.[7]

This incident led Walker to consider the many others in Truro whose case was 'notoriously contrary to the design of the burial office'. He concluded that 'If I cannot bury them, I cannot stay at Truro. But will the matter be clear elsewhere?' To find out how the office could be applied to impenitent sinners who die, he read various authors on the subject, but they seemed 'to smooth it over in a way not satisfactory to me'. He even wrote to the bishop, and when he wrote to Adam from Exeter, he was on his way to Bath to consult him personally. It would have hurt him greatly to leave his people and the work at Truro. As recently as April, 1757, he had told Adam that he was

> ... desirous of continuing at Truro, unless a more enlarged sphere of usefulness should be thrown upon me. Be assured, my dear sir, that I tremble at the thought of appearing more publicly than I now do; and that were a removal proposed to me, the prospect of being more serviceable must be very clear indeed, before I would stir a foot. But I have not the least grounds to suppose I could be anywhere else so helpful as here.[8]

He then enthused to his friend how the 'work is spread abroad largely into the neighbourhood, and that very considerably, in no less than six different places besides Truro, while the direction of the whole seems to lie in a manner altogether on me'.[9]

Unless he could be 'made easy' in performing the burial service himself, or could get the matter devolved on an assistant, it would, according to his own reasoning, be impossible for him to continue at Truro. 'Indeed, if my doubts remain, I can serve nowhere, except as a principal, with an assistant under me (who may not have the same doubts that I have), or where I can be employed as a lecturer. It would be a dreadful thing to lay aside my ministry.'[10] There is no record of Adam's reply to this matter that so troubled Walker, but in a letter of 9 February the following year, the latter admitted following Adam's advice concerning the burial service, although he did not know the final outcome. 'If the worst should come,' he speculated, 'I am thinking that may turn out for the best, and my suffering inconvenience, be the means of relieving the consciences of many of our brethren.'[11] Again on 7 June that year he said he was following Adam's 'prudent advice about the burial office, and hearing no longer any murmurings about it'.[12]

Walker's concern not only unsettled his own ministry, but raised fears in the minds of his friends, who doubted his steady adherence to the Church of England. Knowing that Walker was on his way to see Adam, John Penrose wrote to the vicar of Wintringham from Penryn on 31 October, 1757. He only knew Adam through his *Lectures* and Walker's communication, but thought the matter serious enough to consult him. He mentioned the 'confusion that town [Truro] is in' as a consequence of Walker's action, and the report, credited by many of his friends, that he had 'expressed some thoughts of settling no more at Truro, nor of taking any other cure, but of prosecuting his ministry among the protestant Dissenters'. Penrose himself had no reason to suspect that Walker was about to desert the Church of England, but if he did a 'deep wound will be given to the cause of Christ thereby, at least throughout Cornwall'. His friends among the Dissenters, who he was planning to visit on his tour, 'would compass sea and land to gain such a proselyte'. 'I am satisfied,' said Penrose, 'he will pay the utmost deference to your advice, and, therefore, I take the liberty to hint the matter to you, that you may prevent by a seasonable statement, what afterwards it would be impossible to remedy.'[13]

Penrose's letter did not arrive at Wintringham until the 8 November, a few hours after Walker had left Adam. Adam replied on 11 November, 1757, and said that during his visit Walker, who he knew to be firmly attached to the Church of England, gave not the least hint of any defection to the Dissenters – 'I am persuaded the thought is far from his heart ... and dare be confident that he will never give such a blow to the interests of it, as his desertion would be.' He believed the report to be 'entirely groundless, and nothing but the *clamour* of his adversaries, who are wishing for such a handle to reproach him'. He was also confident, because of their close friendship, that he would never 'take such a step without giving me the earliest notice of it himself'.[14] When Walker returned to Truro after a tour of seven weeks and two days, he found the rumour of his defection to the Dissenters widespread. At first he was alarmed, then amused by all the fuss, and he shared a hearty laugh about it with his friend Penrose. Soon the whole affair was forgotten.

Walker had left Truro on 13 October, 1757. During his absence he made arrangements for his occasional duties to be taken at Truro by his brother James, vicar of Perranzabuloe, who first officiated on 16 October. Jonathan Peters, vicar of St Clement's, served during November. At Bath, Walker consulted his diocesan, who received him coldly. He then travelled on to Lord Dartmouth at Cheltenham, where he 'preached frequently with much acceptance'. He moved on to fellowship with James Hervey at Weston Favell, Northampton, who was deeply impressed by Walker:

> Mr Walker of Truro ... is indeed a most excellent man, much of a gentleman, and seems well to deserve the character he bears: there is something in him very engaging, yet very venerable. During our conversation, I felt a kind of reverential awe on my mind, blended with more than fraternal affection. How old is he? By his looks he appears to be past forty. What a reproach is it to our men in power, nay, to the nation itself, that so valuable a person should at this time of life be no more than a country curate? But he, good man! disregards the things of this world. That time which too many of his brethren spend, to the disgrace of their function, in worldly compliances, and hunting after church preferments, he employs as a faithful labourer in the vineyard of Christ; and pays all due obedience to the apostle's important injunction,

'Redeem time!' How would some of the primitive bishops have sought after a man of his exemplary piety, and have given him every mark of their real esteem![15]

On 2 November he was with Archdeacon Basset at Glentworth, and that evening, with his travelling companions Thomas Haweis, Joseph Jane and George Burnett, he arrived at Wintringham, where the two friends, correspondents for about four years, at last had the pleasure of meeting each other. The following day Walker wrote to George Conon and described both Basset and Adam, and more importantly, his intention of returning to Truro:

> They are both excellent men in their way: the former plain, open-hearted and tender; the latter sedate, hearty, solid, whom I could wish to talk a little more than he is inclined to do, not because I see anything blameable in his taciturnity, but that we might have more improvement from him... You will certainly believe I do not repent coming even all this way to get this satisfaction, which will bring me back to Truro with content, where you may be sure I wish earnestly to be, among other reasons, because I have seen nothing like Truro...
>
> I am not yet determined what course I shall steer from this place, nor when I shall set out from it, perhaps not till Monday. After all, I want to be at home in the more immediate exercise of my calling.[16]

Walker stayed at Wintringham for about a week. During his visit he met Adam's daughters and sister-in-law, as well as Mrs Adam, who was unwell, a condition she suffered from until her death in 1760. He left on 8 November and started the long trip home. It was probably on his return journey that he went to London and felt 'exceedingly pleased' with the fellowship he enjoyed with his friends. He hoped it was 'attended with an exchange of blessings' and that they were mutually helpful to each other. 'These serious interviews,' he reflected, 'between those who are cemented by the double ties of grace and friendship, are among the happiest seasons of this frail life; but yet they are short and changing. We meet only to part; blessed be God for the hope of meeting hereafter in a better place, upon better terms, and to part no more.'[17] When he arrived at Oxford he wrote to Adam. George Burnett accompanied him as far as Bristol, 'where a title for him reached us in the diocese of Canterbury'. Walker stayed in Bristol for two days, partly on Burnett's account. In a letter to Adam, written on 8 December, 1757, after his return to Truro, he gave further details of Burnett's struggle to be ordained:

> We judged it best he [Burnett] should return to London first, to try if our Bishop might be prevailed upon to authenticate his testimonial, so that he might get orders from the Bishop of Wells (now in London) and fix at Bath; but if that failed, then that he might apply to the Archbishop upon his title in Kent, and so obtain a hearing without the form of accusation. In the former it is now too plain he will not succeed, as Lady Coningsby, the principal person on whom we depended, says it will be in vain to apply. What friends it may please God to raise to him with the Archbishop, or how God may dispose *his* heart we know not. But if both fail, it will be a hard case with poor Mr Burnett, and some other employment must be found for him till his way be open into the ministry. We know nothing he can employ himself in but a school, for assisting in which he is peculiarly well qualified. Or think you a scheme might be fallen upon to support him at College till he could get orders? We must attempt something elsewhere for him, because, through the opposition made to us here, Mr Conon's school is reduced so low, that it neither needs nor will maintain an assistant.[18]

The other reason he stayed in Bristol was to talk at large with his brethren there, who were 'sensible of no other faith than John Wesley's, the mistake and unscriptural foundation of which,

I had frequent occasion to speak of. I hope in some sort to the clearing up of the matter in their minds.' He arrived at Bridgwater on Saturday, 26 November, where he met an old Oxford acquaintance, with whom he spent the following day 'being detained by the waters, which were swollen so as to render the roads dangerous'. In the morning he heard 'the most unchristian morality I ever met with', and in the afternoon he was asked to preach. With compassion for a poor, careless people, 'dead in sin and covered with Egyptian darkness', he addressed them as sinners and declared the wrath of God to be hanging over their heads. They listened carefully and afterwards 'a noted infidel' approached Walker to argue with him about what he had said. 'My conversation as well as my sermon put him quite off his bias and left him I think uneasy.'[19]

On Monday he visited Darracott, a Dissenting minister. 'He is an honest-hearted creature,' remarked Walker in his 8 December letter to Adam, 'and has been remarkably successful. We spent the evening with a considerable number of his humble, modest people. I have not seen much of the power of godliness among Dissenters, except here.'[20] After his visit to Wellington, Walker wrote to Darracott (15 December, 1757):

> I have been much reproved in my absence for the coldness of my heart, and a shameful lifelessness to call upon the Lord and to sinners. O how did the zeal of others reprove me! Well, I hope I got a little spark among you, and that something like zeal is enkindled in the coldest heart in the world. I have to thank God for his love to me at Wellington in a special manner, and desire to share always in the prayers of the good people I saw there... I have a high opinion of the work with you; and to be plain saw nothing like it in my long journey.[21]

The following Thursday, 1 December, he arrived at Miss – – –'s, a mutual acquaintance. 'She grows daily, and is indeed a great pattern of zeal and prudence. Her conscience is remarkably tender, and her constitutional temper low; so she wants evangelical means statedly, and is determined to have them in no long time.'[22]

He finally arrived home on Saturday 3 December, and discovered the rumours that had been circulating during his absence: 'I have been banished, silenced, preferred, married, as the whim of conjecture varied! But after all I do not find I am prosecuted.'[23] On 7 December a 'little compliment' (as he termed this act of spite) was paid him by the chancellor of the diocese, the bishop's son-in-law, 'who has lessened my income some pounds a year, by striking my name out of the list of surrogates that distribute licenses', which further exaggerated his financial straits. That evening he met with his 'dear people at the society', which he found 'greatly delightful and somewhat quickening'. In his letter he thanked Adam for his kindness and promised to pray for Mrs Adam,

> whose affliction I hope God has sanctified to you both, in making you more deeply sensible how much you deserve and need it, and thereby strengthening your faith and hope in God through Jesus Christ. What I recommend, it is my desire to practise, as troubles betide me; and am sensible (would God I were more so) that there is power of pride, worldly esteem, fear of men, and a self-will in my heart, which require the rod of affliction to suppress and mortify. Yet how thankful ought I to be on every account, and especially that with all my corruptions within, and trials without, I find an unwonted calmness resting on my spirit, and I would hope an increasing purpose of heart to cleave to duty.[24]

After his return home Walker drew up a summary of the lessons he had learned while away. He headed it: 'What have I brought home?' and on completion presented it to his society. It is dated Tuesday 6 December, 1757, and is an example of his willingness to use every opportunity and means to instruct his congregation.

1. *Matter of Thankfulness* that I am brought safely to you – for God's *patience* with me in forgetfulness of his presence, and the workings of unbelief concerning the issue of my journey – for his *grace*, keeping me in some sort from the fear of man, and desire of pleasing the godly; strengthening me against pride and conceit; enabling me to declare for the Truth, and delivering me from interesting doubts – for the success of the gospel, zeal of ministers, and their great concern for souls – for the plain proof I have seen that God has kept us in the truth of the gospel, between the two extremes of legalism and antinomianism, and in such prudent measures as he is using everywhere; particularly that he has provided us with means of establishment beyond others.

. ***Matter of Caution*** against itching ears – being puffed up for one against the other – resting in awakenings and frames – sinking into a worldly and formal state – unedifying general conversation among religious friends – a narrow spirit.

. ***Matter of Reproof*** because of the coldness of my heart and prayers, and endeavours towards those that are without, in public or otherwise – shame of the gospel among us – cowardice – despising the day of small things.

. ***Matter of Lamentation*** because of abounding wickedness – the few who oppose it – the dangerous errors of some even of those, and damnable errors of others.

Exhortation you have received much and should see Christ's love in it to fill you with zeal for his glory in bringing in others, which you should attempt by example, endeavour and prayer. So you will maintain life in your own souls.[25]

The journey to Wintringham and back revitalised Walker's spirit and health, and gave him a fresh impetus to work with all his might among his Truro flock, even if it meant further opposition. In a letter to Adam (9 February, 1758), he remarked: 'My dear sir, you need not tempt me with the thoughts of Wintringham. I know on whose side the loss falls. But we may not always dwell in the earthly paradise of converse with the well-beloved of God. It will rejoice your heart more that your house be full of those who inquire after salvation.'[26] On the same day he wrote to Mrs Adam and said: 'I think of Wintringham with much pleasure, and no small regret it is so far away.'[27] And at the end of the year (7 December) his visit was still fresh in his mind. He concluded a long letter to his friend by stating: 'The days I spent in the north I remember with great pleasure; the testimonies you all so kindly gave me of a Christian affection ought to be near my heart.'[28]

Adam too had appreciated and benefited from his friend's fellowship. In a letter dated May, 1758, he referred to the few days Walker had spent in Wintringham 'as a happy part of my life', heartily wished he had 'leisure for more such journeys', and noted: 'You leave a savour of yourself wherever you come, and should travel.' He thanked him for directing his wife to Christ, the sure foundation. She was better, but 'still lame and weak' with a 'feverish disorder lurking upon her'. Then he mentioned that some of the hard-hearted members of his congregation, who had heard Walker preach, thought him 'a stricter preacher than myself'. Since Walker's visit, and probably in accordance with his friend's advice, Adam had been reading a chapter of the Bible on Wednesday evenings to his congregation and had gone through Luke and was now in Ephesians. The encouraging result of his reading and preaching was an increase in the number of hearers from less than twenty to over a hundred. In previous years the numbers had always declined 'almost to nothing'. With the blessings that both men received, it was indeed a shame that Walker did not have 'leisure for more such journeys'.

The reciprocation of honest Christian counsel, when judiciously managed, is one of the few springs of pure refreshment to be met with in our pilgrimage through a desert world. A more delightful example of it can scarcely be found, than in the correspondence between Mr Walker and his esteemed friend Mr Adam...

[Walker's] letters were never hastily penned, but were always the result of deliberate reflection upon the topics to which they adverted, and their very appearance indicates the coolness and thoughtfulness of their author, by the neatness and evenness of the lines, and the rare alteration even of a single word. What is wanting in them of polished style, is made up for by soundness of matter; and generally, his words were the best that could be used for his object...

Mr Adam was not less careful than his Truro correspondent. He reflected well upon the points on which he wrote, and took copies of his letters.

Edwin Sidney.[1]

16

Walker Corresponds with his Best Friend

On his return from Wintringham he renewed his correspondence with Adam. In his letter dated 9 February, 1758, he opened
with news of George Burnett's struggle to be ordained. Both
Burnett and Haweis had been labelled from the outset as Methodists, which caused problems as far as their ordinations were
concerned. When Adam had written in June the previous year
he mentioned that Burnett's case was at a standstill. Walker
told his friend that the Bishop of Worcester declared that he
could not pass him if there were an opening in his diocese. For
the time being Burnett was 'engaged with a master of an acad-
emy in London, where he is to teach the languages'. In Walker's
judgement, that had 'a better aspect on his future obtaining
orders than going to Oxford'.

Walker went on to confirm his strong attachment to the
Church of England, thereby distancing himself further from
Penrose's suspicions, which had arisen from Walker's own family:
'I am as well pleased with the church as any one that belongs to
it; but take more pains than some would have me to revive the
doctrines of it; and this in the eyes of high church people is to
pull down and be disaffected to the church.'[2] He then made
some personal remarks:

> I have every way cause of thankfulness, but come sadly
> short in that grace. I suppose spiritual sloth is most in my
> way, which hinders me from adverting sufficiently to my vile-
> ness, and God's mercies. How hard am I forced to struggle,

that I may get anything near God in prayer. And then, how
soon am I weighed down again? Nevertheless, a better righteousness supports and keeps me in peace (I sometimes
fear it is security), and then in the views of a reconciled God
I can a little loathe myself.[3]

There had been 'some little stirrings again among the careless
ones. I had a comfortable evening of it last night amidst eight
or ten under awakenings.'[4]

With this letter he enclosed a word of consolation to Mrs
Adam, who was suffering a long and painful illness. It is a typical
example of the counsel he offered to the needy.

That it has pleased God to restore you in some degree, dear
Mr Adam informs me now, and be assured I rejoice in it. I
hope, too, he has blessed his correction to you, lifting up his
reconciled face upon you, and causing you to be glad in the
fulness of his salvation. These were the sentiments it gave
me much pleasure to hear you express your alone confidence in; and I am promising myself God has prepared your
heart under your late long disorder to receive them more
abundantly in all their fulness and consolation.[5]

He urged her not to turn to herself but to the merits of her
Redeemer, for then she would experience the peace that passes
understanding. When poor sinners looked to Christ

... that love which they see in the life, death and resurrection
of Jesus for them, God bears to them, spreads itself over
their whole souls, draws up their desires after God, subdues
their stubborn wills, making them easy with his dispensations, whatever they be, and causes them to long
earnestly for spiritual liberty, that they may serve God in
holiness; while also the fears of death abate and the hope of
glory taken possession of by Christ for us glows with vigour,
we long, we thirst, for the living God, and the cool deliberate
choice and wish of our souls is: 'When shall I come to
appear before the presence of God?' Surely, happy are the

people that are in such a case. I hope you can say so for yourself, and now more than ever. The Lord increase your faith a thousand fold, and give you plenteously of that joy, wherewith a stranger to Jesus cannot meddle... The way to peace is to walk believingly; and the only way to that is to walk humbly, lying low in the sight of our sins, past and present.[6]

Walker did not receive a reply until May, when Adam mentioned that the 'papers say, "Mr Walker has got a living in Cornwall." If it should be the man of Truro, I wish it may be agreeable to him. I know you have but one view in life.'[7] In fact, the reference was to Samuel's eldest brother.

Walker replied to Adam's letter on 7 June and expressed dissatisfaction at Adam's hesitancy over publishing his sermons. 'The gifts we have are not our own,' remarked Walker, and should be exercised for the benefit of the Church. After making the comment that what is 'fittest to preach is not to be read', he urged Adam 'to sit down and write a sermon with a design of publishing. Whether part of a scheme or not, it might be published immediately. A second might be added as you had opportunity, and when as many as would make a volume were gone out, your preface would be prefixed to the whole.' Walker himself, in view of 'the present abounding ignorance and the confusedness in stating gospel truths under which our zealous brethren lie', had set about writing some sermons on the scheme of religious conversation. While working on these he had received a paper from Henry Venn, which he enclosed for Adam's correction.

He complained again about the 'remaining lamentable ignorance of many of my people, witnessed in their last hours, and for the more lamentable licentiousness of more, daily growing worse. The leading people are against me and countenance the rest.' He then passed on some good news:

Browne, Bishop of Cork, lately preached the gospel so freely at Bath, that as it is reported to us from London, he was at last refused the pulpit. He is certainly an evangelical man. The aid-de-camp to the present expedition was so shaken by a sermon of Romaine's, as to become a bold professor. Tom Haweis has good speed at Oxford. There are pretty many already coming to him in private, and he hopes very well of a few of them. Christ rides prosperously at St Agnes. Brother Vowler tells me, he has there, who meet among themselves in little parties weekly for free conversation, no less than seventy persons; and the number is as large of those who apply to him, but are not gone so far. His patience and prudence will I believe overcome the strange opposition made against him by the Methodists. In their eye, both he and I are *well-meaning legalists*. Mr Philp acquaints me that the alarm increases in his parish and neighbourhood in the north of Devon.[8]

Adam replied in the July of 1758 and said that George Burnett had transcribed for him Walker's *Helps to the Better Knowing our own Hearts*, 'a searching piece, and [it] may be of excellent use to those who are in earnest, and willing to know themselves. I cannot stand before it... I could wish to have it published for general benefit.'[9] Mrs Adam was a little better and appreciated her friend's advice and prayers.

About this time Walker's financial position was far from secure, which may have tempted him to look for another field in which to work. In an effort to forestall Walker's move from Truro, at least for the time being, Adam in another letter said: 'I am persuaded it would be almost a heart-breaking to you to leave your present large sphere of action, where you are so well employed, and have been so remarkably blessed. As to a maintenance, *Deus providebit*.' He went on: 'You have already had some earnest and experience of this, and if you can be content to work with him by the day, will not find him a forgetful master.' Adam then asked, 'Does not Mr E. [Walker's rector] want to get rid of you? In that case I think you would do well to disappoint him at any rate, till another scene of as great usefulness presents itself. The Lord counsel, support and comfort you.'[10]

At the end of July, 1758, Walker's friend and fellow servant in Christ, James Vowler, died. He had been curate of St Agnes and almost certainly a member of the Clerical Club. Vowler's death was deeply felt in his parish, where many attended the funeral. The address was given by Walker, who used the opportunity to stress the fragility of this life and the need for assurance of salvation. In a letter to two friends (Truro, 6 August, 1758), Walker described his friend's final hours:

I called the society together last night and spoke to them from Vowler's death... Monday, July 29th, 1758, at two o'clock, he was suddenly brought into the nearest views of death, concerning which he told me when I came to him (by which time he was revived) that he had found it an awful thing to go into eternity; that the thought at first shook him, but that he was soon supported. I asked by what. His answer in substance was 'the righteousness of Christ'. I spoke a good deal from Scripture on that head and then asked if he had anything on his conscience. He told me shortly, with an evident content on that head, he had nothing. We had frequent short discourses during the day, wherein he appeared to be quite composed, joining in prayer with calmness.

Next morning at two, I was called to him and found him near his end, but tolerably in his senses. His head was hurried, yet he employed his last use of reason in a solemn surrender of himself into the hands of Christ, in the deepest expressions of his own vileness and the most importunate requests for mercy. He ended thus in David's words, as the whole in a manner had been, 'Why art thou so heavy, O my soul, and why art thou so disquieted within me? Put thy trust in God; for I will yet give him thanks who is the help of my countenance and my God.' There was an inexpressible force in his manner of saying *my God*. After this he panted and then fell into an act of thanksgiving, as the other, in Scripture phrase. I suggested a Scripture or two; but he was too far gone to give attention. This I believe was his last use of reason: he said he would compose himself, but soon fell into a delirium, in which he continued either raving or speechless (but when he raved, always evangelically), till half an hour after nine that morning, when he expired.[11]

When Walker wrote to Adam on 7 December, 1758, he mentioned his 'dear friend and most indefatigable fellow-labourer' James Vowler and how at the funeral 'Faith appeared so awful in its operations, humility so deep, the vastness of eternity so greatly impressed on the mind, that I thought I had all to learn of the act of dying, and was so far left behind, that I could presume only to hint a question and a Scripture. It was a season never to be forgotten.' He expressed concern that 'such prostration of spirit, such cleaving to Christ, such importunate humble prayer and praise' had 'so little effect on me'. 'Methought I was a stranger to all.'

I have very serious complaints against myself on this head... I am examining with some care, I hope, the state of my soul, and searching after [the causes] that I find little of vital change. The carnal enmity against God stands, I think, principally in my way, opposing the constant and lively sight of God in the face of Christ and so leaving me without anything, I am ready to fear, of that delight in God, reverential fear, trust and desire to please God, which constitute the hidden man of the heart. And while I am so exceedingly wanting here, I am principally condemned, that, through spiritual sloth, I am no more animated to seek and long after the renewings of the Holy Spirit. I would not be content with a negative religion, ceasing from evil, were that possible, without positively learning to do well; yet we are apt to sit down too easy when conscience has no great thing to say against us. In such views of myself, I am forced to make Christ all my righteousness, in spite of pride.[12]

On 25 September of that year, he wrote to George Burnett, who had eventually been ordained, an appointment Walker had long desired and promoted. He assured his friend of his prayers and the Lord's assistance in increasing a 'ministerial temper'. 'We cannot,' he continued, 'be in our ministrations what we are not in ourselves.' He then shared, with his usual honesty, some of his own ministerial experiences. First, seven lamentations:

1. The workings of conceit, especially in talking or hearing of what was done by me, which has cost me a deal of self-condemnation and needed much fear and watchfulness to oppose. In the beginning I saw little of it and less of its evil; and though now it is but rarely I experience what I call a sensible conceit, the pleasing tickling of the heart, yet I have cause to fear a worse thing: a more settled self-opinion, which would receive commendation as its due and expect submission in others.

2. A most abominable fear of men's faces, especially in personal conference. I have been forced to fight every inch of my way against this, and not without repeated advantage on its part and a perpetual consciousness of not having acted up to duty. I have hardly courage to this day in that private way, to act on the offensive. This was evidently from a love of esteem, supported by a constitutional timidity.

3. Love of ease, wishing to be quiet, and hoping to be so when this and that trial should be over, and often making myself so at Christ's expense. This is a most pernicious, anti-ministerial sin, wonderfully repressing zeal, and diligence and charity.

4. Sloth, which has often invaded duties, and being joined by bodily indisposition, sheltered under it. I have special cause to be on my guard here, lest insensibly it eat out all, and bring my state and conduct into a consumption.

5. Resting on means and distrusting grace. The latter has brought me many needless *fears*, the former as many needless *labours*.

6. Much self-will, in expecting that all things should be ordered to my mind and liking, not approving the ways of the Spirit, nor waiting his time.

7. Not enough committing my work to God by prayer: this is a capital fault![13]

On the other hand, he had been supported:

> **1.** By views of God's dishonour in the sins of men, begetting a desire to retrieve his glory.
> **2.** By frequent deep impressions of compassion over sinners.
> **3.** By a strong confidence Christ would be with me in my work according to his promise, and that he would not suffer me to be tempted above what I am able. This confidence regarding the success of my work is not sensible on my heart as formerly, and seems rather hid from me.
> **4.** By much comfort in those God has given me.
> **5.** By a great jealousy over myself on their account, lest I should be an offence to them. This has helped me out in many a pinch.
> **6.** By conscience also I have been often supported, when afterwards I could not see there had been much, if anything, evangelical in the motive.[14]

He closed by saying that he had often been discouraged and diverted from seeking the practical influences of faith by 'looking too much for sensible impressions'. He desired the Spirit of God to work on him in these ways:

'**1.** That by a divine illumination, he may present to me the certainty, greatness and importance of spiritual things.

'**2.** That hereby and herewith, he may bring my will to a more resolute, determined, free, absolute, and abiding agreement with them. Let me see this done and manifested to be so by my conduct, and I am easy.'[15]

In Walker's 7th of December letter to Adam he mentioned that two months before there had been a 'strong push against friend Conon ... to turn him out of his school, but it came to nothing'. In the church on Sunday evenings he had begun to expound the Sermon on the Mount, probably in accordance with Adam's earlier advice, 'setting out Christ as magnifying the law, especially in opposition to Pharisaism'. He was encouraged to start this new exercise by the increasing numbers that attended his Catechetical Lectures, which had ended in October. His remarks to Adam about Christ preaching the law reminded him of an incident that took place some four years ago at the archdeacon's visitation:

> When the clergy were met, the preacher was not found, and I was then for decency's sake desired to supply his place, which I did by preaching the sermon my people had heard the Sunday before. More than one of the clergy were astonished at hearing me accuse every one present of having broken every commandment, and two of them to my knowledge expressed much resentment and ridicule on the occasion. And now it is but a week ago, that being in conversation with a very sensible, aged and in some respects well read clergyman, he charged me with the same as a thing absurd, and contended that himself was blameless of some of them, instancing the second commandment. I doubt not since the Arminian doctrines have had their full swing, this may be very common among our order. What a pitiable case, considered in its consequences![16]

He exhorted Adam to complete a few sermons for publication, perhaps a spiritual explanation of the law if it suited him, and to go beyond convicting his people of sin by opening up 'the fruits of faith and gospel holiness'. He then referred back to a conversation that took place during his Wintringham visit:

> It seems to me ... that you were rather rough with that man who was shaving me in the kitchen. What you said was so close at once to his case that he could not bear it and grew afraid of you. Suppose we were to talk a little with such in general; to begin, hint only at the person obliquely, and so remove fear of us and gain further opportunity? Somehow or other, I would needs have your people converse with you. You say they do not; I am fishing for some reason for it in yourself.[17]

He noted his satisfaction with the *Conversation Scheme*, a series of religious subjects illustrated in a practical and experimental manner. About eighty of my people 'meet weekly among themselves in little parties to converse upon these subjects alternately by the week, with an inquiry how they have behaved and a communication of what they have seen or suspected or heard to be amiss in one or other'. The profiting from this exercise 'has abundantly appeared – I think beyond any other we have taken up'. He again complained about the state of his heart, which 'has all the pride of an Eastern monarch'. He was ready to revise and enlarge his work *Helps to the Better Knowing of our own Hearts*, while *Practical Christianity* had been finished and sent to London for publication. He had laid aside *Advice to Young Ministers* in accordance with Adam's opinion, and was content to let the catechism *Operations of the Spirit* answer its purpose. At the close of his letter he passed on the encouraging news that two or three individuals had made particular application to Burnett, and Haweis, whose parish was 'very hopeful', had three or four students joined with him.

In the summer of 1759 Walker wrote again to Adam and thanked him for 'stirring me up to the exercise of faith in Christ as the Lord my righteousness'. He was soon to finish his *Conversation Scheme* of which Adam approved, and had laid a plan for enlarging *Helps to Self-knowledge*, a tract found in his *Practical Christianity*. He encouraged Adam to publish without further delay what he designed on the commandments as 'nothing is more wanting'. He also wanted him to publish his lectures on the Scriptures: 'They are very striking and drive me, every word of them, to the fountain opened for sin. It is there great recommendation that they are short, yet they are abundantly full, and give much insight into the mind of the Spirit in the Scriptures.'[18] He then mentioned his financial problems and their providential benefits:

There is a third edition of *The Christian* now in the press at the joint expense and profit of Dilly and myself. You know the depth of my purse, and that I cannot run the hazard of thirty pounds, which, it seems, will be the cost of the impression. Yet I was never more above water in that respect than now; and that by a strange turn of Providence, which has turned me out of doors as a housekeeper, sent me to lodgings, and will probably take away the half of my income. Yet it has lessened my expenses, and by putting the current money, which was wont to go out in the family, into my pocket made me rich for at least half a year.

You will know, sir, that before I came here, it was agreed between Mr – – and me, that I should serve the cure, and have one half of the income for my maintenance. No sooner did I come here and saw the circumstances of the living, than I found our agreement would not go down with the people; and as the income rises in a manner all together from voluntary donations, must be to our mutual detriment. I therefore proposed paying my principal a certain annual sum, instead of his half. This was consented to, but with reservation of liberty to return to the original agreement, when he might see fit. This reserved right was insisted on at Christmas last; by which means my income is not only considerably lessened, but rendered quite precarious.

We have had several conversations on this head. I insist on a certainty, as fit for me to do at this time of life, and under my infirmities. Anything but this Mr – – is willing to do; but not this, because it would, he says, put the living out of his power. But 'what will be the issue?' you ask. 'Will you have a maintenance?' These are questions I cannot answer. All relative to me in this regard is uncertain. But how have I borne, and do I bear this? I wish you were nearer to sift me. I am, and have been, as one unconcerned. It seldom comes into my thoughts. I do not find either resentment against him, or anxiety about myself. Can this be right? Is it not rather stupidity? The Lord have mercy upon me, my heart is very deceitful.

What perhaps I may say, only has given me trouble, is an old and very fond sister, who has kept house for me, and is now in advanced years, obliged to seek another habitation, which we (for we are three brothers) have provided for her in this place. Poor thing! She was brought up in formality, knew nothing of her heart till lately, and I wish she now knew it in a more humbling manner. This business, I believe, has made her see more of herself; but she is not yet brought enough low. Will you think that this affair of mine should be carried all the way to London, and I suppose represented in a light which Mr – –'s conduct does not deserve? And will you think too, that Lord D[artmouth], about six weeks ago, sent a bill of twenty-five pounds, with a letter which gave me a great deal more comfort than the money? What shall I say to these things? I was never more confounded, than by such an instance of God's care and love.[19]

In an undated letter of around this time he again urged Adam to print his literary works instead of making excuses: 'Mediocrity (if that were the case, which nevertheless no one will think so but yourself) is no excuse for keeping at home when you may be useful abroad.' He referred back to the time when Conon first proposed printing to him: 'What I in print! I am not fit.' 'No, but these sermons may be of use,' replied he, 'and you must be content to be accounted a fool.' Besides, remarked Walker, 'To us here, you are wonderfully intelligible in your brevity. Our consciences make us understand you. Whoever have the unction cannot miss your aim.'[20] While writing this letter a young shoemaker, 'a good youth', entered the room. Walker read to him Ephesians chapter 2, with Adam's remarks, and, as if to prove a point, he related to Adam, 'perfectly without the least difficulty, he understood you at once'. He then spoke of his resolution to remain at Truro:

These years past, it has been my determination to stick by the work here, unless God should plainly call me from it. There is not much likelihood that the present difficulty shall drive me [away]. While I have food and raiment it ought not, and by grace shall not. We are not however nearer an accommodation. Indeed, it would search me to leave Truro.

My children are very near me. And besides, God is making use of me to others besides those in this place. Over and above this, my strength seems hardly sufficient to endure going over again what I have done here.[21]

At the time of writing Burnett was struggling with his health and Henry Venn had been presented to Huddersfield. The latter had requested Burnett's help. The main stumbling block was that Burnett would be obliged to have the care of a school. But, said Walker, as Venn 'proposes to lay him under no restraint, and he may continue only as he sees fit, I fancy he will determine to be in your neighbourhood'.[22]

In his next letter to Adam (25 July, 1759), Walker surprisingly used the same excuse that, in his previous letter, he had rebuked Adam for using. Adam had asked him to write a preface for the expositions he was about to print – Adam had already written a preface for Walker's *Christian* – but Walker replied: 'I am in no way fitted to write a preface to your book. What I could say, would be so flat as to be far from a recommendation.' Instead he suggested Talbot of Kineton (Warwickshire) and enclosed Haweis's account of his character. He named his friend Alexander Cruden as an 'experienced corrector of the press', who would be willing to help him prepare his work for printing. In reference to Adam's 'decaying state of health', he made these comments:

You have a tender conscience and Satan will be busy. Are you past the fear of death, and longing in submission to the divine will to be with Christ? This I have been labouring after with some diligence and at times encouragement. The grand adversaries are unbelief and consequent aptness to cleave to life, partly through want of full assurance of faith, and partly through present attachment. But I doubt not your faith is steadfast, and your victory over the world clear. In which view I can cordially rejoice over you, and commend you to the Lord with comfort and confidence.

It has pleased God to take from my head some helpers nearer home, particularly Petrie and Vowler. I beseech him in mercy to us, myself in particular, spare you. Yet methinks, I am more importunate that you may be enabled to adorn the gospel by a Christ-like temper under every afflictive dispensation.[23]

The warmth, intimacy and openness of these letters is very evident. Walker and Adam were ministerial best friends, urging and exhorting one another, in every way possible, to live up to their high calling, and always encouraging a closer and more practical walk with God. *The Christian Observer* called them 'clergymen of uncommon sagacity, and inferior to none of their contemporaries in real godliness ... two holy and exemplary men ... true sons of the church'.[24] Their motto of communication could be summed up in the words of Adam: 'Think free, and speak plain,' and both men used this liberty to good effect, without giving or taking offence. In his July, 1758, letter, Adam remarked, 'All your admonitions are friendly, seasonable and welcome, and need no apology. Spare them not, and I can assure you they shall never be so far lost as to be ill taken'[25] – an attitude of humility that marked both ministers in their correspondence with each other.

[There is a] wide difference between awakenings and humiliations, between a fear of God's wrath and a deep true conviction, between a sight of sin and a sense of its sinfulness... A clear and distinct sense of the evil of sin, not merely as we are, but as God is affected by it, is the main thing; which not obtained and maintained, there is no saving work done in the soul.

Walker on the evidences of a genuine conviction of sin.[1]

The contrivance of the devil is evidently ... to drive from the means [of faith] by terror, and thereby to lead into carelessness, debauch, &c. The counterplot of his device is this: to select some two or three chosen promises, such as, 'The blood of Christ cleanseth from all sin,' &c. wherein the word of promise is evidently without deduction, and seen as soon as attended to; then to press home in a peremptory way, such as, 'You dare not say, you will not have the boldness, the confidence to say God cannot, is not willing to forgive you; I rest it with your own conscience; speak, dare you say so?'

Walker on Satan's devices to destroy faith.[2]

17

A Wise Counsellor

Throughout his ministerial career Walker was ready to advise anyone who approached him for help on such topics as Christian doctrine, experience and duty. With patience and insight he unveiled the heart of the issue and drove home to the conscience the essential points necessary to inspire, console or rebuke his hearers. Rightly did Thomas Jackson, in his biography of Charles Wesley, call Walker 'a wise and holy man'.[3] One friend, who had received his counsel, enthused, 'O how profitable and full of comfort was the advice he gave me, when I first made known to him the impressions I had received under his ministry! I cannot well express my love to him.' The first book Walker gave this grateful recipient was Doddridge's *The Rise and Progress of Religion in the Soul*, with the words: 'You must not, my dear friend, be prejudiced at this book, when I tell you it was written by a Dissenter, for believe me it is the best book, next to the Bible, in print.'[4]

On a different occasion he urged a young Christian just entering university, who was 'constitutionally warm and lively', to let holiness 'fix itself into temper and habit, before we adventure upon hazardous trials, and I must honestly assure you that the university will afford you abundance of them'. He went on: 'Keep yourself out of debates; they hurt the mind; and labour not to be disturbed about names given to you and others by unthinking men.'[5] He wrote to another young man, whose parents opposed his Christian beliefs: 'The honour due to parents is not implicit and blind; it means submission to this purpose – that children may be made the better children of God.' If 'parental injunctions' go against this rule, 'disobedience does not dishonour them; nay, parents ought to be unattended to, even in much younger persons than one of twenty-six'. He warned him to be 'actuated by a meek and filial disposition, showing a more peculiar tenderness in all your expressions and carriage'; and 'to be aware of impatience and resentment under the opposition', not allowing 'the contention of others [to] drive you to an over hastiness to expedite that which demands much cool thought and attention'.[6]

He urged a convert, whose faith was shaken by reproach, to 'stand fast in the Lord... Stand still and you shall see the salvation of God. Leave all your matters to him.' To a zealous but much opposed young Christian, he said, 'The various oppositions you meet with ought not to discourage you; rather, knowing from what quarter it comes, to make you comfort yourself that it is proof of some shock given to the kingdom of darkness. Blessed are they who are instruments in this cause.' Indeed, God's blessing so attends their labours 'that even opposition is made to further their undertakings'.[7]

He wrote a word of caution to an active layman, advising him not to preach and to confine his meetings to 'reading, prayer and psalm-singing'. In this way he would protect himself from the 'imputation lying on the Methodists, that they set up lay-preachers'. 'While we go on regularly,' he counselled, 'we shall be able to vindicate ourselves, and what is more desirable, leave it still in the power of clergymen to countenance us whenever they may be disposed to it.'[8] To a young man about to take orders, he encouraged to grasp 'a right sense of the importance of your office – as it regards Christ, who honours you with so distinguished a station in his church, and commits to you ... the care of his gospel, which will be abundantly disgraced, or as you may reasonably hope, be glorified through

you, as you are faithful or otherwise';[9] and a 'due consideration of what your conduct must be [with regard to preaching
and example], if you will be a faithful minister'.[10] He spent no
little time advising the young man along these two headings
before asking him to 'try your heart, whether, God helping you,
you are desirous to engage in [the ministerial office]'.

Walker congratulated a friend on the birth of his child, but
warned him to beware of the arguments of the world: 'There is
a new idol to engage the affection, and a new care to solicit
anxiety. Strive hard ... to keep your heart unspotted from the
world.'[11] To 'my dear William', who complained of a 'defective
frame of mind', he wrote: 'The fault is in your heart ... in the
unbelief, murmuring and unthankfulness that seem to have too
much place in you.' He then urged him to be satisfied with and
to trust in the perfect righteousness and atonement of Christ,
and to be persuaded that 'Christ is able to keep you ... in whatever frame you are.' In this way, you are 'always and only fit for
service and improvement'.[12]

Once a woman applied to Thomas Adam for comfort and
direction. She was under great mental agitation, convinced that
her 'day of grace was passed'. Sometimes she was seized with
fits of laughter, which were followed by a propensity to utter the
most terrible blasphemies. She shed 'thousands of tears', prayed
in vain and persuaded herself that there was no relief from the
power of what she believed to be an evil spirit. At last she opened
her secret feelings to Adam, that he might advise her and pray
for her deliverance. Adam not only wrote to her himself, but
laid the matter before Walker, who, at his friend's request,
offered his opinion. Walker had met many similar cases and
always pursued the same method, which, without exception,
had brought relief to the sufferer. His method was:

1. To convince the conscience that the person into whose
mind these horrible thoughts are injected by the Devil, is
guilty of no sin by means of such suggestions...

2. To direct to a right temper of mind under such temptations, which is by no means a restless desire of deliverance, but submission and patient waiting upon the will of the Lord. [13]

From a subsequent letter of Adam's, it is clear that the afflicted woman made a complete recovery.

Walker wrote to William Rawlings, whose wife lay seriously ill: 'Endeavour to help the exercise of her faith in God through Jesus, by dropping a seasonable Scripture. If she has any doubts because of a low frame, or inability to pray or fix her thoughts, make her sensible that faith is deeper than these, and that in such a case it is the very office of faith to support her under and against them.' [14] To another, who was saddened by the death of a friend, he said:

> I cannot but look upon it as a rare act of a gracious Providence, that your friend should die here in your arms, and desire you not only to make the serious reflections which so awakening a circumstance demands, but to bring them as near as possible to the present state of your soul; and, that it may not slip you, to commit to writing the purposes you now find possessing you. These are excellent days of grace when properly improved; and may God give the due influence of such a warning to your own heart, and direct you in applying it to others! [15]

On 21 June, 1759, after the death of her husband Risdon, he wrote a letter of condolence to Mrs Darracott, which afforded her much consolation. It is a fine example of Walker's ability to impart Biblical advice sensitively and to promote a thankful rather than a resentful spirit, regardless of the circumstances. He directed the reader to put her confidence in God, to submit unconditionally to his will, and to prepare for and resist, with all her might, the devil and his accusations. Part of the letter reads:

The loss of so kind a partner is sensibly affecting. But time will contribute to reconcile you to that. Your greater loss is that of a near faithful and excellent friend, example and helper. Your loss on this side it is probable will be increasingly felt, as time and change of circumstances and ministers advance upon you. Permit me therefore to say, that it is here you need to be on your guard, that you may always patiently submit to the perfect will of your heavenly Father. May you be enabled to say in every case, and peculiarly in the want of so quickening a guide, 'Even this, O Lord, I needed also, to make me more entirely seek my all in thee.' In the sense of what you have lost, it will be very natural for you to reflect on yourself that you did not more value and more profit by the blessing, while it was in your possession. Possibly in such reviews Satan may be attempting to cast in his accusations, and to discourage you in the thought of your unprofitableness. I beseech you, yield nothing to him, nor give up the least jot of your confidence in God through the merits of Jesus, which is what he waits for. Unprofitableness is a just cause for humiliation in the people of God, but never of doubting: rather should we be thankful for anything received under whatever means, since the measure as well as the means is the gift of God. I am much mistaken in you, if you are not enabled to adorn, and will not do so, the gospel of God our Saviour in your meek and cheerful submission.[16]

Walker's advice was sought not only by friends and ordinary people, but also by the leaders of the Evangelical revival. John Wesley, as noted, applied to him for counsel, and on a separate occasion he was asked to attend a meeting to discuss the itinerancy of John Berridge, vicar of Everton. Berridge had started to preach outside his parish in June, 1758. Up to that time he had been troubled in his mind over the itinerant ministry and had consulted friends for their advice, 'but received unsatisfactory or discouraging answers. Then I saw [Berridge said], if I meant to itinerate, I must not confer with flesh and blood but cast myself wholly on the Lord. By his help, I did so, and made a surrender of myself to Jesus, expecting to be deprived, not only of my fellowship and vicarage, but also my liberty.' On 22 June he noted in the flyleaf of his Bible that 1 Chronicles 17:1-2 had been given to him 'when I began to itinerate'. From then on he started to preach in barns, cottages and farmhouses in the immediate vicinity and further afield.[17]

The question considered at the meeting was whether or not the vicar of Everton should continue his irregular practices. Whitefield was present and as expected advised that he should continue. Berridge stated what he believed to be the Scriptural grounds for the course he pursued. He pointed to Nathan's reply to David in 1 Chronicles 17:2, about his design to build the temple, 'do all that is in thine heart, for the Lord is with thee', and used it to support his argument, stressing how it had moved him to adopt his present conduct. 'This,' said Walker in his account of the interview, 'appeared to poor Berridge a strong warrant to go on with his object, though the context showed that it was the contrary in the case of King David.' A long discussion ensued, which Whitefield cut short by enlarging on his own ministry and the success that attended it. According to Walker, 'nothing was concluded' and Berridge continued with his itinerancies.

In August and September of 1759 Walker welcomed both William Talbot and William Romaine to Truro. On 11 October he wrote to Adam and after some comments on the state of a believer's mind in the dying hour told him why they had come and the enjoyment their visits afforded him. Talbot stayed a month and they talked a great deal about 'a determination to keep close to the discipline of mother Church', much to Walker's satisfaction. Talbot expressed certain apprehensions about others leaving the Church, so Walker proposed a scheme he had thought about for some time 'which might possibly contribute to our greater establishment and usefulness in this day of small things'. He called it *Hints for a Scheme more Effectually to Carry on the Work of Reformation at this Time Begun in Divers Parts of the Kingdom, Under Regular Ministers of the Church of England;* and its main design was to 'preserve regularity; thereby to promote union and gain weight to the cause; to remove needless objections, and open a way to others to engage in concert for the interests of religion'.[18]

Romaine arrived unexpectedly, a day or two after Talbot had left, to discuss his 'very critical circumstances at St Dunstan's'. In 1749 Romaine, a contemporary of Walker's at Oxford, had been elected lecturer of St Dunstan's, Fleet Street, London – an appointment that brought upon him some of the fiercest opposition of his ministerial career. The rector of St Dunstan's refused to accept Romaine's right to the pulpit, and in order to deny it to him, occupied it himself during the time of prayers. At length the dispute was brought before the Court of King's Bench and Lord Mansfield confirmed Romaine's legal right to the lectureship, and appointed seven o'clock in the evening as the time for him to preach the lecture.

However, this decision did not satisfy Romaine's persecutors. The church wardens refused to open the doors until exactly seven o'clock, which meant the congregation was left waiting in the street. This caused congestion and no little inconvenience to passers-by. Nor did the wardens light the church when necessary, leaving Romaine to read prayers and preach while holding a candle in his hand. The situation was only resolved when the Bishop of London, Dr Terrick, who had once held the lectureship himself, happened to walk down Fleet Street one evening when the congregation was assembled outside St Dunstan's. When he discovered the reason they were locked out of the church, he spoke to the rector and the church wardens on their behalf, 'expressed great respect for the lecturer, and obtained for him and his hearers that the service should begin at six, that the doors should be opened in proper time, and that lights should be provided in the winter season'.[19]

Coupled with the years of frustration at St Dunstan's, Romaine experienced great difficulty in obtaining a stated position as the incumbent of a parish. Several solutions were suggested to him: Lord Dartmouth offered him a living in the country, Whitefield advised him to take charge of a large church in Philadelphia, and a group of his friends wanted to build him a chapel, where he could carry on as an independent preacher. All this made his enemies predict that he would leave the Church of England and become a regular Dissenter. But Romaine was deeply attached to the Establishment and he refused to leave. It was at this point that he travelled to discuss the matter with Walker, and as a result was 'greatly strengthened in his determination' to stick with the church in which he had been ordained, and to be patient and wait for the right opportunity.

> When Romaine came [remarked Walker in his 11 October letter to Adam], I thought, or rather found it necessary to communicate what we had been proposing to him [Talbot]. The design of his visit ... unthought of by him till the day before his setting out, was to consult upon his present very critical circumstances at St Dunstan's. While his opposers, the vicar and vestry, probably with a view of going farther, have actually prevented him from preaching there during the long vacation, upon the words of White's will, who gave the lecture, his too hot friends have been, he says to a man, pressing him to come out, engaging to build a chapel. Between the both his trial was not small; and the rather, because none in London will permit him to preach in their pulpits. Hence, he was almost ready to conclude that were he turned out of St Dunstan's, he should get no employment in the Establishment. In these uncomfortable circumstances, he told his friends he would come down and consult me, because he knew I was in his opinion for sticking to the Church. (I feel a twinge of pride this moment.) We talked over the matter fully. He is determined to stick fast, and to wait. He sees his friends are in a bad spirit. He will not engage in a lawsuit against the vicar and vestry; if his friends will, they may.[20]

Romaine stayed two days in Truro and returned home in 'pretty good spirits', with a copy of Walker's *Scheme* in his pocket. The *Scheme* was also sent to Adam for his consideration and via Burnett to Henry Venn, as well as shown to a neighbouring clergyman, who 'approved the thing'. Adam wanted his friend to advise Romaine to stand fast: 'His road is waiting and patient suffering; and desertion of the Church, of which he has otherwise a good opinion, on account of hardships, will be nothing but resentment, and can never have a good issue, or give him comfort on cool reflection.'[21] In fact, Romaine had to wait five years before his appointment as rector of St Andrew-by-the-Wardrobe with St Ann's, Blackfriars, and even then, because of 'a hotly contested election, a poll, a scrutiny and an appeal to the Court of Chancery', his position was not secured until February 1766. Thus he became the first Evangelical incumbent in London.

G. C. B. Davies, commenting on Romaine's visit to Walker, reckoned that for

> ... the most eminent Evangelical of his generation, [to] undertake the long journey to Cornwall for a stay of only two days in order to consult his [Walker's] opinion ... was probably the highest compliment ever paid him, but the effort of the journey and the effect of Walker's judgement and persuasion were of incalculable value to the whole cause of enlightenment within the Church of England. Had Romaine seceded at this stage, it is not too much to say that the result might have been disastrous to the Evangelical movement.[22]

On 22 October, 1759, Walker again wrote to his Wintringham friend. He spoke of Haweis's success in his Oxford parish, and with some of the younger members of the university, and how in Truro

> ... about twenty young persons have within these six months been brought under a serious concern for their souls; of

> several of them I have very encouraging hopes. Otherwise I
> think we lie under a sad security, and are not so much as
> angry at whatever is said. This is terrible. But the effect in
> regard of us is peace, and that is peculiarly dangerous on
> our side.[23]

For his own part he had experienced 'some quickening' during
the last few months. 'I find it very difficult and very desirable to
walk closely with God,' he said. 'Pride has been hunting me
grievously at times, and forced me to many a *miserere*. I
suspect indulging it, but am sure I do not hate it, nor am
humbled for it as I ought.' The possibility of a French invasion
at this juncture was very real, but he was not afraid and hoped
that 'God may be glorified by it being made a means of our
reformation, if it takes place.' He thought the invasion appeared
'both practicable and probable', and 'I do not think we are a jot
more safe for our fleets and armies;' but what alarmed him
most was 'that I see none alarmed by the threatening to think
of their sins'.[24]

The *Scheme* that Walker had proposed to Talbot and given
to Romaine, aimed to encourage 'as many clergymen as are
willing' to agree with and determine to proceed upon, three
resolutions: 'that the Church of England, both in her doctrines
and discipline, is such as they are satisfied with ministering
therein, with a quiet conscience'; that they would preach the
Church's doctrines; and avoid all irregularities in their ministrations, 'confining themselves within the limits set them by the
discipline of the Church'. Walker wanted to make clear the
position of the Evangelicals within the Church and to take away
the suspicions of other 'regular' clergy. Adam in his reply strongly
disagreed with the proposal.

> In my opinion, it will be considered as an open declaration
> of war, increase and strengthen the opposition, and in a word
> set all in a flame without any good effect that I can perceive

to counterbalance the great clamour that will be raised upon the occasion. We are not wanting in bringing our testimony, and the difference is sufficiently observed, so things may very well rest as they are without injury to the conscience, or cowardice in the cause of our Master. If our preaching and conduct do not witness for us that under him we are true members and ministers of the Established Church, no declarations or protestations of ours will be available; and if the contrary imputation is cast upon us, it is better to leave the issue quietly to him under a sense of having done our duty, than needlessly to provoke more reproach and contempt, which I apprehend would be the consequence of the proposed subscription...

It seems to me that a much greater handle will be given by such a combination, to traduce some as Separatists and Dissenters, than has been given yet, or I hope ever will. It is a principal part of your design to confirm those who may be feared to be wavering, but what reason have you to think that such a tie, as you suppose, will hold them faster than *present engagements*? And besides, would not this in some measure be allowing the suppositions already conceived of them, to be well grounded? Think again.[25]

Adam sent Walker's paper to Archdeacon Basset, who could not approve of the *Scheme*, 'either as to the propriety of it, or the consequences which might attend it, were it to be put in execution. I cannot see that a *private* subscription would bind the consciences of the clergy more than a *public* one.'[26]

In Walker's desire for union among the Evangelical clergy, as the only means to ensure their usefulness and comfort, he had proposed his *Scheme*, the outcome of which he had not fully realised, and which may have led to a wider breach among the Evangelicals in the Church of England, thus weakening their position. Thankfully the arguments of his friends prevailed and nothing came of the *Scheme*. In all this, we see that Walker was not only prepared to give advice, but to act upon the wise counsel of his friends.

Alas, alas, my dear friends! How shall many of us appear before the judgement seat of Christ? For what have we to appear in? Where is our faith in Jesus Christ? What fellowship is there between him and our souls? Where are the works of faith, love to him and to his people? Have we none of these to show? No owning of Christ, no following his words, no renouncing the ways of men for his sake, no love of his people, no giving so much as a cup of water to any because they are his? What! In no kind, in no degree, such works as he will own?

And yet shall we receive according to our works? But what can we think of it then, if instead of owning Christ, we have been opposing him; instead of loving his people, we have been hating them for being so; instead of having any good works to show for ourselves, Christ will find an endless number of evil works to show against us? What can we think of it, if nothing shall appear to have been done by us but what is evil continually; ceaseless, number-less works of darkness, in thought, word or deed, as many as the days, hours and minutes of our lives have been?

What! My dear friends, will any one of us be hardy enough to appear under these circumstances before Christ's judgement seat, where nothing can be hid, and all will be laid open? Yet remember there we must all come, whether we will or no. God will have it so, and who can prevent it?

From Samuel Walker's last sermon at Truro.[1]

18

Heading to the Journey's End

Walker's constant labour and many anxieties so weakened his constitution that for some time before his death he found himself giving way under the daily strain. At times he felt so weakened and unable to continue his round of duties, that he considered a temporary rest from them, but was urged to continue in the work by some over-zealous friends, who should have advised him otherwise.

On 27 April, 1760, he preached what proved to be his last sermon before his Truro congregation. It was his twenty-fifth sermon on *The Church Catechism*. Though unaware that it was his final discourse, there was in his 'manner of address an unusual degree of emotion, and he seemed filled with joyful anticipations of his own rest from all trials, and with even more than ordinary longing for the souls of his people'. The previous Sunday he had preached on the exaltation of Christ to God's right hand. On this his last Sunday he chose a most fitting theme: the second coming of Christ to judge the living and the dead. 'He described with all the feeling of one prepared to meet his God, those triumphant expectations of the Lord's coming ... and accompanied these declarations of a hope full of immortality, with most solemn warnings and exhortations to the careless and impenitent.'[2] It is an excellent example of his style and, as James Stillingfleet commented, it afforded him 'an opportunity of speaking to them [his congregation] in such a manner, that if he had been actually apprised that it should be his last sermon, he could not have taken his leave of them more properly'.[3]

Can I think of this day [of Christ] so honourable to him whom my soul loveth, without longing and wishing for its appearance?... Surely I would rejoice to see and be for ever with the Lord; to behold his beauty as the express image of his Father's person; to contemplate with endless and insatiable transport, the glory which the Father hath given him; to make my acknowledgement, in the praises of heaven, among the multitude which no man can number, as saved, for ever saved, by his love and care, his power and grace. What! When the least beam of his glory let in upon my soul turns my earth into heaven, and makes me cry out with Peter, *'it is good for us to be here,'* can I wish to delay his coming?

When remaining in this vale of misery I groan under corruption, and am burdened with a corruptible body, can I say, this is better than to be fashioned in soul and body like unto the Lord? When I find here nothing but vanity and vexation of spirit, shall I be averse to the Lord's coming to change my sorrows into joy unspeakable and full of glory? Here, beset as I am with enemies, would I not long for that blessed day when I shall see them again no more for ever? And would I not be glad to be taken from a world lying in wickedness, into the new heaven and earth wherein dwelleth righteousness?... I have humble confidence that he will own me among the children; and shall I ... cleave to this base life as my all for happiness and not wait and wish and long for the day of my Master's glorious appearance?[4]

Towards the close of the sermon he turned his attention to many in his congregation for whom he was grieved in heart as he thought of how they would make their appearance before Christ's judgement seat:

You have no works to speak there for your belonging to Christ; I can see none. I see works of various kinds that prove you do not belong to him. If a life of pleasure, idleness, indulgence, drunkenness, pride, covetousness, would recommend you to the favour of the judge, few would be better received than numbers of you. In the name of God, my friends, when you know this moment in your own consciences, that if, as you have been and are, you should be called to judgement, you would be as surely cast into hell, as if you were already scorching in those dreadful flames, why will you live at such a rate?

Well, we shall be all before the judgement seat of Christ together! There the controversy between me, persuading you by the terrors of the Lord, and you determined to abide in your sins, will be decided. There it will appear whether your blood will be upon your own heads for your obstinate impenitence, or upon mine for not giving you warning. Christ will certainly either acquit or condemn me on this account; and if I should be acquitted herein, what will become of you? I tremble to think how so many words of mine will be brought up against you on that day. What will you say? What will you answer? How will you excuse yourselves? O sirs, if you will not be prevailed upon, you will with eternal self-reproach curse the day that you knew me, or heard one word from my mouth. Why, why will you die with so aggravated a destruction? Oh, think of the judgement! Think of it, and you will not be able to hold it out against your own souls. May the Lord incline you to do so; may he cause this word to sink deep into your hearts; may he show you all your danger; and with an outstretched arm, bring you out of the hands of the devil, and translate you into the glorious kingdom of his dear Son, to his own glory and your unspeakable happiness in the day of the appearance of our Lord and Saviour Jesus Christ! Even so, most mighty God and most merciful Father, for the same Jesus Christ's sake. Amen.[5]

These were his final words to a congregation among whom he had ministered for so long with such godly zeal, and for whom he had spared no pains in his efforts to promote the glory of God.

Soon after this urgent appeal Walker was attacked by a violent fever, which confined him to his room for several weeks. He recovered somewhat, but its effects had seriously weakened him and his friends feared the worst. On 17 May, 1760, from Blackheath, Lord Dartmouth wrote to William Rawlings, who had been keeping him in touch with Walker's condition. He expressed his deep and sincere concern for Walker, whom he described as 'that holy man of God, our valuable friend',

and for the prospect 'of the continuance of his useful labours'.
He added:

> My prayers were sometimes faintly offered up for him. Had
> they not been addressed to him who searches the heart and
> tries the reins, whose all-piercing eyes discern the very
> thoughts and intents of the heart, they must have been lost
> in the multitude of strong cries and earnest supplications
> that have been offered up at Truro and elsewhere. These I
> trust have prevailed to the prolonging a life, which is to be
> made yet farther instrumental in promoting the Redeemer's
> glory, and the salvation of redeemed souls.[6]

Lord Dartmouth thought that Walker's fever was similar to an
illness that many in and about London had suffered from in the
spring, but with one main difference: 'that in these parts, it has
usually been attended with an eruption, which the physicians
have endeavoured to promote as much as possible... They have
... supported their patients with cordials.'[7]

On the 26th of the following month Lord Dartmouth again
wrote to William Rawlings and rejoiced, albeit prematurely, that
Walker had been restored to 'life and usefulness'. He hoped his
latter days would be greatly blessed and that 'many souls yet
be added to his crown of rejoicing in the day of the Lord
Jesus'. The next day, Thomas Adam, who knew nothing about
his friend's health problems, complained in a letter to George
Burnett, 'What is become of the clergyman of Truro (the Rev
Samuel Walker)? I have not heard from him for several months,
though my last letter to him was of an interesting nature.'[8]
Either Walker had been too ill to write, or he had not wanted to
alarm Adam unnecessarily by mentioning his fever.

By the end of June he had mostly recovered, although he
was still afflicted with a violent cough, and in August he was
advised by his doctor to visit Bristol hot wells, which he thought
might help his condition. He saw the necessity of withdrawing
from his flock for a while in order to regain strength. Just before

he left Truro he received the sad news of Mrs Adam's death, and, though he wrote with difficulty, 'compassion constrained' him to pen a long letter to his bereaved friend. It is dated 20 August, 1760. As expected he expressed not only his sympathy at his friend's loss, but offered wise counsel as to whether his resignation to God's will was 'real':

> I cannot but feel with you for the loss of a wife, and therein a friend, who had been the long-accustomed partaker of your joys and sorrows, and whose absence is therefore the more to be regretted because of your advancing years. I doubt not but our covenant God will every way make this up to you. All his dispensations are mercy and truth to such as keep his covenant and testimonies...
>
> You know resignation implies loss, and evidently a feeling of it too, without which under such losses, I see not how there could be any exercise of that Christian grace. Go into your inner man. Can you there in your coolest judgement justify God in what he has done, abhorring the thought of asking him, 'What doest thou?' Can you there find also that you are acknowledging there is wisdom, mercy, love, as well as justice in the stroke, and that both because you assuredly know who has done it, and because you see this goodness of God therein in many instances? And as the upshot of both, are you determined never so to hearken to the pleadings of flesh and blood, as to admit any suspicion to be harboured in you of either God's justice or mercy in this affliction, but on the contrary to give God the glory of being a righteous and gracious Father in this as in everything else? Withal, so far from being disgusted with the work he has for you to do, that you are better pleased with and more resolved upon it? Is not this resignation?
>
> And as you find this to be your happy case, disquiet not yourself about the measure or continuance of your grief. In respect of that, be content to be a man; and if you imagine your grief excessive, impute that imagined excess to the peculiarity of your circumstances and constitution. In truth, my dear sir, had I heard you had been capable of losing such a wife without feeling, it would not have raised my opinion of you.[9]

Regarding himself, he felt he was overly concerned about 'making provision' for his journey to the Bristol waters, which he was to embark on the following Monday in a post chaise. He intended to stay there two months. His friend Talbot had invited him to Warwickshire, where he was willing to stay for a week, if well enough. The previous year he had told Talbot that if he ever visited Kineton, he would want to meet Adam there. Had he not been sick, he would probably have gone to Kineton about this time anyway. He closed his letter with the comment: 'Let us be of good cheer, my friend, we shall be soon home. May our hearts be increasingly above, and our lives testify that we are taken out of the world, and have our conversation in heaven.'[10]

On 18 September, 1760, he wrote to his congregation in Truro from the Bristol hot wells. It is clear from the sentiments expressed in this letter how dear his people were to him: 'What a blessing, comfort and refreshment the thought of you has been to my soul always.' And again: 'While ... you are so near my heart, my comfort and happiness having so much dependence upon you, it is impossible that I should either forget you, or forbear to pray and praise God for you, [and to] contribute what I may in my present circumstances to your establishment, progress and joy.'[11] He urged them to yield to God's will and 'not to indulge an untimely, unsubmitting wish' of seeing him again.

He thought he was very slowly recovering from his sickness, which had brought him to but a 'step off' from the eternal world. 'Views of the riches of Christ,' he said, 'and prospects of the glory that shall be revealed, have been and still are, blessed be God, my best cordials.' He also admitted some struggles:

I have found much opposition from the quarter of unbelief, and that to be strong in the faith of our Lord Jesus Christ, when everything of my own is, and is evidently seen to be against me, when grace is so imperfect, when this life appears to be closing up, and all the false confidence

> derived from the esteem and supports of most pious and
> endeared friends is stripped away, is an attainment indeed
> which I long after myself, and earnestly wish may be vouch-
> safed to you also in life, as well as in death.[12]

His only relief in these circumstances was in the truths of the
word of God illuminated to his mind by the Holy Spirit. He
exhorted his congregation, with his usual penetration and
fervour, 'to a more diligent use of the Scriptures, in much prayer
for the light of the Spirit that the glory of the Lord may shine
more abundantly into your hearts, and produce in you a more
lively desire of seeing him as he is, with an increasing transformation of your whole man into his likeness'.[13] He highly valued
their prayers and desired to be speedily with them, but God's
will was concealed from him in this matter, 'for although I grow
better, I have no strength to do anything.'

Ten days after Walker's letter, on 28 September, John Wesley
wrote to his brother Charles: 'If possible you should see Mr
Walker. He has been near a month at the Hot Wells. He is
absolutely a Scot in his opinions, but of an excellent spirit.'[14] A
month later John recorded in his Journal: 'I had the pleasure of
spending a little time with that venerable man, Mr Walker of
Truro [at Bristol]. I fear his physicians do not understand his
case. If he recovers, it must be through an almighty Physician.'[15]

Walker spent about two months at Bristol but derived no
benefit from the waters. He moved to Kineton in Warwickshire,
with a view to spending some time with his friend Talbot, but
the weather was so bad that it was thought best for him to
return to Bristol. From there he wrote to Jonah Milford at Truro,
a member of his society and manager of a tin-smelting works,
asking him to search for and send him his papers on or relating
to *The Corruptions of the Heart, The Illustrations of the Familiar
Catechism* and the *Directions Relating to Marriage*. The
general plan under which he intended to methodize *The
Corruptions of the Heart* was written in a few lines on a scrap
of paper, which he had left in the desk in his study. He already

had *The Corruptions* themselves. The hints concerning *Marriage* were 'somewhere or other in the study'. He wanted to make use of his 'idle' time to finish these works. He closed his letter by saying, 'I find the thought of my dear people at Truro a trying one. I could wish to see you all. But God gives me herein a measure of submission. I can say in some sort, his will be done.'[16]

The last letter he wrote to William Rawlings was from Bristol on 11 November, 1760, and it gave hope of improved health:

> The complaint on my lungs is in a manner, I may say entirely, gone; neither have I any cough that gives me trouble. I sleep well enough, the colour of my face is better, and within about ten days I have eaten with some appetite... In short, all is much better than I could expect, and in my judgement it will, if I can rub through the winter at this rate.[17]

However, he was not putting on any weight or gaining strength, and was 'continually getting cold', though every effort was made to keep him warm. He had no thought of leaving his dear flock at Truro 'unless driven to it by being unable to labour any longer among them'. He then mentioned the growing health of his soul:

> I have found of late a more happy concurrence of self abasing, and Christ glorifying views than ever before in my life. Never before could I say such bad things of myself, or good ones of him. I have been led to justify the Lord in taking me from my people, and in stopping my mouth; yes even should he never allow me to open it more, and lay me quite aside as a vessel in which he has no pleasure. Views of this kind have, I believe, wrought more resignation in my spirit to God's way with me; but I desire to remember, that if he hides his face I shall be troubled. Yet why should I think he will? He could never see anything in me worthy of his least regard; yet he has never forsaken me from the day that he first caused me to know him, and in the perilous time. Oh, blessed be God![18]

Four days later he wrote again to Jonah Milford. He acknowledged receipt of some of his papers and asked his friend to search again for the scrap of paper 'whereon is methodized the scheme in which I last determined to publish *The Corruptions of the Heart* ', which he had not been sent. Everyone said he looked better and in many respects he thought himself better, but he was still not gaining strength and therefore was unable to work. He concluded by saying, 'It will give me unspeakable comfort to return to my dear charge at Truro, if God will; and as I do not grow worse, but rather better, there is reason to suppose it is his will I shall so do, but not quickly. Was I now at Truro, I must keep within doors unless carried abroad.'[19]

In his conversations with various people at Bristol he was 'eminently useful', but about a month after his last letter to Jonah Milford, near to mid-December, he was advised to move to London so he could benefit from the drier and healthier air. He accepted the invitation of Lord Dartmouth to visit him at Blackheath, where he arrived a few days before Christmas and where he was attended by the best doctors. On 21 December, Henry Venn wrote from Huddersfield to Mrs Knipe, the sister of John Thornton of Clapham: 'I hope you see dear Mr Walker as often as you can now he is at Blackheath. I could wish Mr Thornton was with him; he is one of the jewels which is highly polished before it is made up in heaven. Humbleness and spirituality of mind, with extraordinary degrees of wisdom and judgement distinguish him.'[20] In a letter to a friend, written from Blackheath on 30 December, Lord Dartmouth gave an account of Walker's health.

He appears to be better than he was a week ago. You may possibly have learned that he caught cold upon the road, which brought on a return of his cough and of the oppression upon his lungs, and made so much alteration as gave some of his friends, who had seen him not long before, much uneasiness; but within a few days, the case appears to be much altered with him; he now coughs not at all, breathes with more freedom, and the lameness which the cold had settled in his limbs, has almost entirely left him; his appetite is not very good, but by means of asses' milk, broth, and other things between meals, he receives a sufficient quantity of nourishment in the day. The opinion of an eminent physician in London, whom he has consulted, is that there is no unsoundness at present within him, and consequently no immediate danger; that his disorder proceeds from malignant matter which, in his late fever, he had not strength enough to throw out upon the skin; that if this should form upon his lungs, there will then be great danger.[21]

During his stay with Lord Dartmouth he suffered severely from 'a pulmonary consumption'. In this miserable condition the care and kindness of Lord Dartmouth and his wife were without limit and the doctors, who were aware of their patient's tight financial position, which had been aggravated by his long illness, offered their services cheerfully and free of charge. His flock at Truro, as an expression of their love for him and in recognition that he had impoverished himself for their sakes, were continually sending him money, and other friends came forward to help supply his needs.

During his illness he retained full possession of his mental faculties and visitors were struck by the calm dignity and peaceful resignation of his manner. In conversation he was 'as capable as ever of guiding the inquirer, consoling the desponding and rebuking ignorant pretenders'. On one occasion while at Blackheath a presumptuous young man came to him, not to receive spiritual advice as Walker first thought, but to set him straight on points of doctrine peculiar to his own denomination. Walker received him very courteously, thanked him for his kind intentions, and then asked him a few questions:

'Pray, Sir, what is your age?'
    'About three and twenty, Sir.'

'Well, Sir, and how old do you suppose I am?'

'I should imagine, Sir, past fifty.'

'May I ask the nature of your occupation, Sir?'

'A journeyman cabinet-maker.'

'I suppose you know mine?'

'Yes, Sir, you are a minister.'

'How long should you think I have been one?'

'Why, Sir, I have heard you have been a very zealous clergyman for some years.'

'Which of us should you imagine possessed the most learning?'

'You of course, Sir.'

'But which of us, do you think, has studied the Scriptures most attentively?'

'Sir, you have had the most opportunities of doing so.'

'Now, Sir, which should you conceive has prayed the most?'

'Very probably you may, Sir.'

'Which do you suppose has enjoyed the most advantages for improvement and experience?'

'Of course, Mr Walker, you, Sir, in your situation.'

'Well, young man, I have only one more thing to say to you. What do you think of the self-conceit that could induce you to come here to instruct a person who, according to your admission, had been eminently useful in the church, and was certainly your superior in age, length of religious experience, learning and study of Scripture? Now allow me to return you the kindness you designed for me, by instructing you in the pride and vanity of your own heart.'[22]

This rebuke, doubtless delivered with Walker's usual mixture of force and tenderness, and with the solemnity of one who was on the verge of the eternal world, produced a profound effect on the mind of the young man.

With all the helpers about him, busying themselves to do whatever they could to make his stay in London more comfortable, and with friends near and far praying for him, Samuel Walker was ready for the last great battle that stood between him and the celestial city.

The dying hour is an awful one; unbelief, however, gives it the terror... The joyful frame of the heart at that time is not the criterion, and [I] wish to have my daily testimony with me in a life of faith, while I am able to serve the interests of Christ... That I am a sinner, I certainly know; that there is no hope for me but in the Redeemer, I am perfectly satisfied; but I want to have the grounds of his salvation as they lie in the Scriptures made plain to me, and its great truths confirmed more abundantly in my heart.

From Walker's letter to Adam dated 11 October, 1759.[1]

How greatly am I obliged to you for the particular account you have sent me of the temper of this happy man [Samuel Walker] in his late trying circumstances! My earnest wish for myself, for you, for all who I love, is, that whenever we are brought to the borders of the grave, we may be possessed of the same calm and steadfast confidence in the loving promises of our redeeming God and Father, and taste of that peace which passes all understanding, which Christ did bequeath as his dying legacy to his beloved disciples, and in them to all that believe on and love him to the end of the world. If we would thus die the death of the righteous, we must of all necessity die daily to the world, to sin and self; the Lord help us so to do.

A letter from Lord Dartmouth to William Rawlings.[2]

19

'God is Love, all Live to Him'

On 9 February, 1761, Walker wrote to Adam: 'All is against me,' he said, 'all dark, uncertain, dreadful, but ... the Lamb slain from the foundation of the world opens God's loving heart to me, and ministers ... at seasons a glance of future things, which warms my spirit.' He went on: 'While I can keep steady in that view only of a Redeemer's righteousness, I find a calm, settled peace which nothing can discompose,' a peace he had often enjoyed since the beginning of his sickness, 'and such effects from it, as I know to be beyond all power of my own'.[3]

He told Adam that he had been tempted to love life too strongly, so that the 'thought of recovery seems to be too pleasing and not to be resolved into a pleasing acquiescence with the divine will, if such should not be the case. But do not think that these things distress me; they rather endear Christ, and cause me in spirit to rejoice that a day is coming when they will be all done away.' He was thankful that he could 'write more at a time without that exceeding pain, which the posture I am obliged to use in writing was used immediately to occasion'. Since 20 January, when he began using James's powders, his disorder, which had been hurrying to end his life, had received a check, and in several respects he was 'unquestionably better, mending, I think, every day, though slowly'.[4]

He had been refreshed by news from Conon in Truro that his society people were walking in the truth. He was also pleased that, though he could not speak in public, he had been used in private conversation. At Bristol and Blackheath he had talked with the Wesleys, Whitefield, Madan and Berridge. 'In regard of these,' he wrote, 'there has not been much gained on either part, except only in the case of Mr Madan. The rest have spread, whether such a spirit of licentiousness as to all order, or through the leaven of Moravianism, such a spirit of enthusiasm, as I fear will not be soon extinguished.' He had enjoyed 'sweet counsel' with two or three other clergymen and a group of young gentlemen from Oxford, who would soon be clergymen. Some of these men had been tutored by the Hutchinsonians, so Walker in his feeble state wrote a paper for their guidance which, unfortunately, was not preserved. After further comments about various publications he had to close his letter as 'my back has been long crying stop'.

In the summer of 1761 Walker's health deteriorated. He had a burning fever during the day and at night perspirations and a persistent cough kept him awake, but in all his suffering he was upheld. On 30 June, at Walker's request, Thomas Haweis, who had travelled to London to watch over his 'dear friend and father in Christ' and to pay his final respects, but who probably returned to Oxford before Walker's 'last hour', addressed the following letter to Adam. It was Walker's last communication to his Wintringham friend:

> Mr Walker, who seems drawing near the verge of eternity, desires me to present to you his best regards, with thanks for all the light he hath received from you, and the edification you have, through grace, been the means of communicating. He tells me his outward man perishes, but that his inward man is renewed day by day. Much lower he cannot be till he breathes no more. He professes entire satisfiedness in the blood of the covenant; and though without the least measure of sensible delight, enjoys a serenity and peace in believing, which everlasting promises received by faith into the heart minister. This probably will be, dear Sir, to you his last farewell. May you stand fast, and be partaker with those

who 'through faith and patience inherit the promises'. This is *his* ardent wish, nor less, believe me, dear Sir, that of his amanuensis.[5]

At the end of the letter Walker wrote in a trembling hand: *'I would say much of my hope. Blessed be God, we shall soon be in heaven. Then we shall see all the loving-kindness of the Lord. Adieu! Adieu!'* He could write no more as is apparent from his signature.

At times during his final weeks he complained of 'great deadness of spiritual affections, and of the absence of all sensible impressions of joy and delight in the contemplation of the exceeding love of God towards him, and of his approaching happy change',[6] which is hardly surprising considering his physical weakness. At times, when the powers of nature failed him most, he would say,

What a miserable creature should I be in my present situation, if I could not look upon God as my covenant God, my reconciled Father in Christ! The weakness of my body and of my spirits deprives me of all joyous sensations; but my faith in God's promises, I bless the Lord, is firm and unshaken. What though my loss of strength and spirits robs me of all comfortable communion with God, the promises are not therefore made void. Abraham believed and it was counted to him for righteousness. I believe God is faithful and true in all his declarations of mercy, which I have fought for, though I cannot now feel the impressions of his love.[7]

When he considered the doctrines he had taught he was convinced that they would stand the test of the last day. 'Conviction of sin,' he argued, 'original as well as actual, is the grand inlet to all saving knowledge; where this is wanting, the superstructure will not stand; but if this foundation be deeply laid, the heart will then welcome the glad tidings of salvation.' He blessed God for the many symptoms of the power of genuine grace on his heart, and when he closely reviewed his life over the last ten years he could 'see evident marks of my having lived with a single eye to the glory of God, in opposition to the selfishness of my nature'.[8]

Whenever he felt better he immediately looked forward to continuing his ministry among his people at Truro, 'of whom he never spoke without evident tokens of singular pleasure and satisfaction in them; sometimes not without tears of affection and tender concern for the welfare of their souls'. But when the symptoms of the disease reappeared he calmly turned his thoughts 'to the awful scene that called for his more immediate attention, and spoke with equal delight of the joys reserved beyond the grave for the faithful servants of the living God'.[9] Seeing his response to these fluctuations in the state of his health, a friend wrote afterwards, 'It could never be discovered that he desired to live or wished to die.' He was content to submit all to the will of God. Occasionally he felt apprehensive that he might wish for a release from suffering sooner than God had purposed. If he said something that seemed to express fretfulness or impatience, he would immediately check and rebuke himself, although nothing of this nature happened for some time before his death.

On 2 July, Lord Dartmouth wrote to Sir Richard Hill and made the following reference to Walker:

Poor, or rather happy Mr Walker is so much altered since you saw him, and grows weak so fast, that there is no prospect of his continuing many days. He enjoys the most delightful satisfaction in the approach of that hour which will put an end to the sufferings of his body, and give his soul an entrance into the regions of everlasting bliss. His greatest fear is that he should long for it with too much impatience. His extreme weakness makes him incapable of fixing his attention upon things unseen for many minutes, but he has a calm and unshaken reliance on the truth of God's word and promises, and as ever, steadfast confidence in his mercy

towards him. I cannot wish for myself a more solid assurance of hope than he is possessed of, though without those
lively sensations which his weak body is now incapable of.[10]

The very next day Lord Dartmouth wrote to a correspondent
in Cornwall and spoke of Walker's desire for prayer that he
might not 'dishonour Christ in this last scene of his life'. He also
mentioned his 'calm and peaceful resignation' and 'steadfast
faith and exemplary patience' as ornaments to his profession.
'He has an unshaken reliance on the faithfulness and truth of
his redeeming God, a firm dependence on his word of promise,
without any support from pleasing frames or animating views,
which the extreme weakness of his body, and great depression
of spirits, utterly deprive him of.' Although his guest was growing
weaker by the day, he still had enough strength to sit up and
Lord Dartmouth thought it possible that he would 'continue
yet for some weeks'. He was about to try a medicine of Dr
Ward's. In all Walker's afflictions Lord Dartmouth was so
impressed with his friend's faith that he desired 'to die the death
of this righteous man'.

On 4 July, Walker was strong enough to pen a few lines to
his 'dearest' and 'most faithful friend' Conon:

My disorder, though by no means affording to myself the
least prospect of recovery, yet seems to affect me at present
more with weakness, than with that violent heat, which
rendered me incapable of all thought. I can now, blessed be
God, think a little; and with what comfort do I both receive
your thoughts and communicate mine to you!

Oh, my dear friend, what do we owe to the Lord for one
another! more than I could have conceived, had not God
sent me to die elsewhere. We shall have time to praise the
Lord, when we meet in the other world. I stand and look
upon that blessed world with an established heart: I see the
way prepared, opened and assured to me in Jesus Christ;
and for ever blessed be the name of God, that I can look
upon death, that introduces that glorious scene, without any

kind of fear. I find my grand duty still is submission as to time and circumstances. Why should not I say to you, that I find nothing comes so near my heart, as the fear lest my will should thwart God's in any circumstances? Here I think I am enabled to watch and pray in some poor measure.

Well, my dear friend, I am but stepping a little before you. You will soon also get your release, and then we shall triumph for ever in the name, love and power of the Lamb. Adieu! Yours in the Lord Jesus Christ for ever. Amen.[11]

Walker sank slowly and with much suffering to the grave, but those who witnessed his final days said that his mind was at perfect peace. George Burnett, who arrived at Blackheath on 11 July, wrote to a friend:

There I saw the dear, dear man lying upon his bed of sickness, pining away in the last stage of a consumption, burnt up with raging fever, and wasted almost to a skeleton. He was perfectly sensible, and so was able to express himself much to our satisfaction.

The first things that struck me exceedingly was his patient submission under God's hand, and his thankful, tender concern for all those who were near to him. So little was his mind engaged with things which pertained to himself merely, that in the smallest things concerning my own convenience and comfort, he behaved as if I had been the sick person.

He said he had been uneasy in the beginning of his sickness at the want of sensible frames, but was relieved by that Scripture – 'they that worship God must worship him in Spirit' – with the nobler powers of the soul; and that now he found experimentally the worship of God's Spirit on his heart in a degree with which he was never before acquainted.

'I am now enabled,' said he at another time, 'to see when it was that the Lord Jesus first laid effectual hold on my heart, which I was never able to discover before, and bore down all opposition. I have a perfect satisfaction in the principles I have preached, and the methods I have taken in general. I have no doubt respecting my state in Christ, or respecting my future glory. Behold, I am going down to the gates of the grave and holy angels wait for me. Why do you trouble yourselves and weep? Cannot you rejoice with me? I am going to heaven. Christ died; my Lord! O had I strength to express myself, I could tell you enough to make your hearts leap for joy! God is all love to me, and my trials are very slight.'[12]

Two days after the above letter (13 July) Burnett wrote to George Conon and described Walker's physical state:

He is at present reduced to the lowest degree of weakness, of which I suppose human nature is capable; sometimes almost fainting away, and at the same time burnt up with a scorching fever, attended by profuse sweating, &c. I left him last night; I expected not, neither did there appear the least probability, that I should see him again in the morning; but he is alive still, and, what is far more, alive unto God through Christ Jesus, beyond whatever I have hitherto seen him.[13]

Burnett went on to say how at this time Walker perceived 'more evidently the constant workings of God's spirit upon his soul than ever aforetime'. 'Thou, Lord Jesus, has shown me,' said Walker, 'the truth of that Scripture *unless a man forsake all that he has, he cannot be my disciple.*' To Burnett, who was weeping, he said, 'Do you not rejoice with me?' 'Yes,' replied Burnett and Walker clapped his hand. How impressed Burnett was with Walker's submissive and yet resolute spirit is evident from the further remarks he made in his letter to Conon:

I have never heard one impatient or complaining word come out of his mouth; but when I see the smallest particulars which pertain to his friend's comfort, I am low on the comparison of how it was with me in similar, but better, circumstances. Would you believe it, that being in the condition he is, he has more than once given directions about my diet?... On mentioning to Mr Walker I was writing to you, he repeated your name with tokens of endearment, and desired me to tell you, that you might soon expect to hear of his release; that he died confidently in the principles he had preached; that, as to a shepherd to his people, he was not much troubled; for that the work belonged to Christ, the Great Shepherd of the sheep, and to Christ he committed them; in particular, that he remembered you, sir, at times as he was able.[14]

In a final letter to Conon, which Walker dictated five days before his death – at that time he was not able to hold a pen – he assured his friend that 'with great confusion of thought, I have no doubts, great confidence, great submission, no complaining. The great thing, which I always feared is, I believe, coming upon me; that I am coming into a diarrhoea, confined to my bed and have no strength.' He expressed a steadfast belief in Christ and then said: 'What I have found in myself for months, both as to the review of time past, and the present working of the Spirit, has left me without all doubt of my union with Christ.'[15]

Shortly after his letter to Conon it became apparent that death was fast approaching. 'His throat rattled, a cold clammy sweat ran down his cheeks, and the muscles of his arms and face appeared to be convulsed with frequent spasms and contractions.'[16] In the midst of his suffering he experienced an awful sensation in his heart, which, he said, seemed 'to be tied round with thongs', but he remained prayerful and composed, and begged his friends about him to pray that he would remain patient to the end. When someone sitting on his bedside observed what a blessing he enjoyed in his present situation and that his soul was ripe for heaven and eternity, he interrupted and said, 'No, my dear friend, the body of sin is not yet done away. I shall continue a sinner to the last gasp. Pray for me as such.'[17]

In the evening of the same day, Tuesday 14 July, Joseph Jane, who had been called to his side at Blackheath, wrote to

William Rawlings. Walker, on hearing from Jane that Rawlings begged his prayers, told Jane to write, 'I cannot pray for him, I am unable to pray for myself ... God bless him and keep him unspotted from the world. That I can say for him with all my heart, and perhaps that short prayer is better than a multitude of words.'[18] To Jane's letter, which was not immediately sent, Walker added: 'Thursday noon. *Two days nearer heaven* is the great comfort of the departing spirit of his surviving friend.'[19] On that day, Thursday 16 July, Walker awoke from a doze and seized the hand of his nurse, who was sitting near him, and cried, 'I have been upon the wings of the cherubim, heaven has in a manner been opened to me; I shall be soon there myself, and am only sorry I cannot take you with me.'[20]

In all his sufferings he was not forgotten by John Wesley. Writing to James Roquet earlier in the year (30 March, 1761), he had remarked:

> The grand breach is now between the irregular and regular clergy. The latter say: 'Stand by yourselves; we are better than you!' And a good man is continually exhorting them so to do, whose steady advice is so very *civil* to the Methodists. But we have nothing to do with them. And this man of war is a dying man – it is poor, honest Mr Walker.[21]

And on 16 July, he wrote to Blackwell: 'I hear poor Mr Walker is near death. It seems strange that when there is so great a want of faithful labourers, such as he should be removed.'[22]

The following day, Friday 17 July, Walker lifted up his eyes in a manner that spoke of a joy that words could not utter and remarked to George Burnett, who was standing by his bedside, 'O! my friend, had I strength to speak, I could tell you such news as would rejoice your very soul: I have had such views of heaven – but I am not able to say more.'[23] On the same day Lord Dartmouth wrote to Rawlings and described Walker's state:

Dear Mr Walker is still alive, but so near the confines of the grave, that the only wish we have left is for his speedy release; the extreme weakness to which he is reduced, so as to be scarce able to speak, must be a state of great suffering, but it excites in him no murmur or complaint, nor the most distant expression of impatience. His chief concern while he had any strength left, was that he might not dishonour his master in the last stages of his disorder, by any fretfulness or impatience, whatever he might have to undergo; his prayer has been heard, and he is now silent and submissive, so that it is scarcely to be known from himself that he is not perfectly at ease. He opens not his mouth, but to utter some useful admonition and advice to those about him, or to declare his sense of the loving-kindness of the Lord, and his steadfast confidence in God his Saviour. 'I know,' said he to me yesterday, 'that when this earthly tabernacle shall be dissolved, I shall have a building of God, an house not made with hands, eternal in the heavens.'...

No, my dear friend, he shall not come back to us – may we be happy enough to go to him. He has more than once expressed his delight in the prospect of finding many of his dear Truro friends in those blessed regions to which he is going, and of seeing others come after him to the same happy place...

I trust a lively and grateful sense of the great blessing that has been bestowed upon Truro, will be fixed upon the hearts of those who have been partakers of it, and that the want of their pastor and father, will keep them watchful and humble. He has often thankfully rejoiced in reflecting, that they have been brought on in such a way, as if they continue in it, the devil himself shall never prevail against them.[24]

The next day Walker appeared to be at the last extremity and Lord Dartmouth said, 'He will hardly live till tomorrow.' James Stillingfleet, another witness, agreed: 'His voice faltered exceedingly and his head seemed rather to ramble. We scarce imagined he could have lived out the day,'[25] but he did. That night he passed in extreme weakness. On a previous occasion, noticing the distress of his watching friends, he had said to his servant, 'I would I might slip away when nobody but you should be present.' And so it happened. On Sunday 19 July, 1761, at about nine o'clock in the morning, just after everyone except his servant had left the room not realising he was so near the end, he turned his head aside on the pillow, gave a long and deep sigh, and made that short journey from earth to heaven. He was only forty-six. His last words are a fitting memorial: 'God is love, all live to him.'[26]

Burnett described his end: 'He was on the Friday seized with a stupor with delirium, till on Sunday morning, at a quarter past nine, he expired without a groan.'[27] The following day he wrote an account of Walker's death to Rawlings:

I was not present; Mr Jane and Mrs Randall had withdrawn for a moment, and the next moment, word was brought that he was gone. We cannot judge distinctly how or in what manner he was engaged previous to his dissolution; he seemed to be in prayer, and was heard to say 'Lord Jesus'; but for a day and night before at times his faculties were much benumbed... Remember what he has said to me more than once, 'Why are you sorry, &c. I go to heaven, Christ my Lord died;' and 'Christ, my dear friend, will speedily return again.'[28]

According to his own wish, that he should be buried in whatever parish he died, he was interred in the churchyard at Lewisham in Kent. (Shortly before his death he had been moved, for his own comfort, to a lodging not far from Lord Dartmouth's home.) The grief of his friend Adam was very real and deep: 'I think such men so much better than myself that I could almost worship them.' He had 'felt little less at his death than at the loss of another wife'.[29]

After his funeral Lord Dartmouth wrote to his friend Sir Richard Hill and told him of Walker's behaviour and faith during the last stages of his illness: 'As his suffering increased, his faith and patience increased also. Indeed, as the outward man decayed, the inward man appeared to be renewed and strengthened day by day.' For near a week before his death he had been so weak that he could only speak with pain and difficulty, and so said little; yet he praised the Lord for his mercies and expressed his entire confidence in his faithfulness and truth. After his death his countenance was 'full of sweet composure and peace'. Lord Dartmouth also mentioned that the three pieces lately revised by him, *Conviction of Sin, The Corruption of the Heart,* and *The Sacraments,* 'are now in the press and will be published as soon as possible. It is proposed that his friends should contribute to take off among them, such a number as will defray the expense of the publication.' He then made a personal comment:

> I look upon it as a blessing and peculiar privilege, for which I have cause to be abundantly thankful, that I have had the opportunity of seeing so much of Mr Walker's behaviour, observing the temper of his mind, and hearing his wise and instructive conversation. I hope the remembrance of what I have seen and heard from him, will open, warm and quicken my slothful soul.[30]

To use the words of Burnett, Walker, a faithful servant of Christ, was 'as eminent and remarkable in his death, as he had been in his life – a witness of the truth and faithfulness of the Lord our God, who manifests himself to his faithful people, when flesh and strength fail'.[31]

A few years after Walker's death, the clerical secretary of The British and Foreign Bible Society, being a deputation for Cornwall, asked W. M. (the writer of the narrative in *The Cornish Banner,* 1846)

> ... if there were any relics of Mr Walker's ministry still living. He was told there was one: he was however an unpolished Cornish jewel. He begged to be taken to him. He was introduced and said, 'My friend, I understand you knew Mr Walker.'

'Yes, sir,' he replied, 'he used to call me his boy, and so I have known him; but, sir, you are too young.'

'Yes,' said the secretary, 'but "he being dead, yet speaketh", and his works have been blessed to me.'

They wept together. The secretary then turned and said to the writer, 'I felt so strong an attachment to his memory that I determined to visit his tomb. I went, and, after a lengthened research in the churchyard of Lewisham, in the county of Kent, deep concealed beneath the long grass, I found at length a small slab with the simple inscription, "Sacred to the memory of Rev. Samuel Walker, of Truro." But,' he added, 'if no marble monument recorded his worth, this heart, our friend's heart, and many more, will record it in eternity.'[32]

****

Walker's successor at Truro was Charles Pye (1761-1803), a man of very different character and doctrines, who was opposed to any form of 'Methodism' in religion. He was instituted as rector of St Mary's on 9 July, 1761, where he remained until his death in 1803. Polwhele referred to him as an 'odd character';[33] Miles Brown said he was 'universally disliked' and called him 'a Latitudinarian of flippant speech', which is borne out by Polwhele: 'Probably, indeed, Mr Pye, the rector, would have frightened away many from the Church by levities which all must have condemned.' In a reference to Walker's ministry, Pye complained, 'My pulpit so stinks of Calvinism that not a century will purge it.'[34] Walker was unashamedly a Calvinist, but at the same time 'gentle to all men' and far removed in both doctrine and conduct from the 'rigid, rancorous Calvinism of his time'. Pye obviously tried to 'purge' Walker's pulpit himself, for it was not long before Walker's people, unhappy at the lack of gospel preaching and with the frivolity of their new minister, tried to make up for his inadequacies by meeting more frequently as a society during the week.

After several years in this uncomfortable state, and 'after many deliberations, consultations and prayers for divine direction, and with much dissuasion from some of their pious friends',[35] about forty of them formed themselves into a separate church, where they could enjoy religious services and obtain a stated ministry.[36] They purchased the lease of a house, which for more than half a century had been used for cock-fighting, a sport abandoned during Walker's ministry, and quickly transformed it into a chapel. In March 1769 it was opened for divine worship. Their opponents, knowing the history of the building, nicknamed them Cockpittarians or Walkerites. This group formed the nucleus of a new independent society, out of which arose the Congregational Church in Truro. At first they were supplied by a rotation of ministers, until in May 1770 Peter Sampson was ordained to serve them.

Six years later, the congregation having increased, a new meeting house, Bethesda Chapel, was erected, where Sampson continued his ministry until he died in 1785. He was succeeded by several others, preaching in probation, until Mr Parish, who had itinerated in Cornwall under the patronage of Lady Huntingdon, was chosen to be pastor. His ministry was 'generally acceptable' and he stayed for three years. He was followed by William Paddon, 'a man of unquestionable piety, although not of commanding talents'. He died in 1815 and was succeeded by William Moore. Thomas Jackson, one of Charles Wesley's biographers, stated that Walker's congregation became 'perhaps the most powerful Dissenting body of the kind in the entire county of Cornwall'.[37]

Most of Walker's congregation, while remaining members of the Church of England, could not sit under Pye's ministry; nor could they be prevailed upon to become Dissenters, so they held separate meetings in *the room*, as it was called, on the Lord's Day and Friday evenings, as they had done during Walker's lifetime. On Fridays their Dissenting brethren often joined them. Occasionally they were addressed by Thomas Haweis or Thomas Wills, both of whom were well known in

Truro. Eventually the Truro theatre was purchased by Lady Huntingdon and converted into a chapel, and the remainder of Walker's congregation moved there to worship.[38] For many years they were supplied by the students, like the other chapels in the Connexion. Thus two independent churches were founded in Truro from the members of Walker's society.

To see his beloved flock broken in two by the liberalism and trifling behaviour of his successor would have saddened Walker, whose ministry was not to uphold the tenets of Calvinism, as Pye intimated, but to preach Christ and him crucified, as the following extract from Walker's twentieth sermon on *The Church Catechism* indicates. It is an appropriate summary of and conclusion to his life and work:

> I see my Lord hanging victoriously on the cross, and conquering every adversity. Here I see that *law of ordinances*, whose multiplicity, strictness and expense were so burdensome a yoke, which none were able to bear, abolished in the fulfilment of all its design. When Jesus died, *the veil of the temple was rent from top to bottom*. Here I see the *moral law*, as a law of works for righteousness, fulfilled in every tittle of its demands, and executed in every tittle of its curse, and as no longer therefore breathing out threatenings against transgression of its precept, now impracticable by us, but changed into a pleasing rule of delightful obedience.
>
> Here I see the sting taken out of the hand of *Death*. How horrible was his countenance wont to be! I heard the thunders of Sinai when he approached me. I saw the flashes of everlasting fire breaking out behind his back. I was dismayed. I cried for mercy. I looked upon the cross. I considered who hung there. My spirit revived within me. Turning to Death, I said, 'Where is thy sting?' I saw and was astonished. The scene was changed. His dart terrified no more. His countenance was smoothed. He smiled and seemed to say, 'I am thy friend.'
>
> Here I see *hell* disappointed. Hell was waiting for all the race of mankind. The sentence was gone forth, and the place was prepared. The whole world was guilty without exception,

and justice demanded recompense. Jesus would make atonement, and the stroke fell upon him. He died, and believers cannot perish.

Here I see *the devil* dethroned. What can the accuser do, when God is reconciled; when the law condemns no more; when its penalty is executed to the full; when justice appears on the side of the sinner? See, Satan, the issue of thy rage and malice! in persecuting the Son of God to the death, thou hast been thy own destroyer. That very death has disarmed thee of all thy might, and even such a babe in Christ as I am is able to put thee to flight.

Here I see *sin* receiving its deadly blow. It was laid upon him that had done no sin. He bore it to the cross. There it was crucified, brought to public shame, and the power of it taken away...

Here, finally, I see *the world* subdued, the world in all its strength. Jesus had before defeated the attempts of worldly glory, pomp, wealth and ease; and now on the cross he stands the shock of worldly shame and suffering; this he endured, that he despised. The ingratitude of friends, the being forsaken of all men, the being singly exposed in the hands of implacable enemies to all that malice set on fire of hell could invent or cruelly execute, made no impression upon him. 'Be of good cheer,' thou hadst said, 'I have overcome the world.' Truth, Lord, I see it to be a vanquished enemy. Thus, looking on the cross, I see all my adversaries put to confusion.[39]

Samuel Walker's pulpit in St Mary's,
now part of the present day Truro Cathedral

You cannot form a full idea of Mr Walker's many labours without being on the spot. The principal of which are his real and solicitous care of no inconsiderable town, in his public ministrations, prayers, preaching and lectures, which, through God's blessing, have been attended with abundant usefulness, all this in the church...

He carries with him into all company an easy, polite affability of temper, always cheerful, yet grave, never shows any resentment but at sin, which he never suffers in his presence to pass unreproved. He speaks of common things with an air of pleasantness, but of religion with that solemnity which becomes an ambassador of Christ. He avoids all disputes where the glory of Christ is not immediately concerned, and then he readily speaks and acts for him. He tenderly loves all mankind but especially the household of faith of whatever denomination...

His ready submission to the yoke of Christ in being counted little and low like his great Master, and those many condescensions to which a proud heart could never stoop; his extensive charity in every sense of that word both to the souls and bodies of men, these and many more compose the amiable character of that truly pious and excellent man.

One of Walker's young converts.[1]

20

'That Excellent Man, Mr Walker'

Although Samuel Walker was 'no more than a country curate' in a small town at the extremity of England, he still attracted the attention of his pious and well known contemporaries, many of whom commented on his character. John Wesley, for instance, spoke of him as a better man than himself and, if differences had not pulled them apart, would have happily worked with him. Risdon Darracott called him a 'worthy and amiable man', while Henry Venn, writing to his son, listed him among those who possessed so much grace 'that everyone who comes near [them] is enlivened and edified in his own soul'.[2]

Sydney Carter, in *The English Church in the Eighteenth Century*, referred to Walker as a man 'whose wonderful life and personality entirely changed the character of his parish';[3] Boggis said of him that men were 'attracted by his loving nature, and, while he boldly rebuked vice, he was gentle in dealing with sinners, and withal was felt to be a wise guide of souls';[4] Colonel Richard Pownall, in a letter dated 20 December, 1786, to Rev Robert Storry, vicar of St Peter's, Colchester, wrote, 'Mr Walker of Truro possessed a most benevolent mind, directed by Christian principles, and went about doing good; he was as amiable in his manners as he was pure in his morals;'[5] and Elizabeth Smith, in her work *Life Review'd* (1780), called George Conon and Samuel Walker 'two bright luminaries of Christianity ... through whose unwearied assiduity and stead-fast perseverance in the promotion of religion and virtue, it is

no way to be doubted but thousands of souls in the last day will
be added to the number of the blessed'.[6]

In appearance Walker was graceful, with a good presence
and a piercing but pleasant eye. James Stillingfleet gave this
forceful description of him:

> As to his person, he was tall in stature, his features were
> strong and comely, and his deportment such as commanded
> respect. An air of authority, which was natural to him,
> usually struck an impression of awe, at the first interview,
> upon those that conversed with him; but he conducted him-
> self in such a manner, that whilst with a becoming dignity he
> extorted even from the forward and petulant a respect due
> to the ministerial character, by his affability and readiness
> either in communicating his own thoughts, or attending to
> what was said by others, he rendered himself an agreeable
> companion to those who were willing either to impart or to
> receive instruction.[7]

Throughout his pastorate in Truro it is said that a thousand
souls sought his counsel, which was marked by sound sense
and solidity of judgement. Many were ready to listen and weigh
carefully his knowledgeable and wise advice and opinion, even
if they did not always agree with everything he said. His natural
sagacity and penetration carried him deep into a subject and
gave him, not only an accurate knowledge of the company
before him, but an insight into their troubles. Although many
were strangers, by asking a few questions relating to the experience of their minds, he was able to tell them what had passed
within their hearts before they acknowledged it with their lips.
He was a strong reasoner and a skilful physician, who could
discern how a prevailing corruption or temptation would affect
an individual's conduct. 'His practice was to examine the
disposition of the heart to the bottom, that he might be the
better enabled to advise how to counteract the growing malady
of any disorder and to direct to the proper means of recovery.'[8]

Charles Simeon said that Walker's forte was 'probing deeply into the human heart, taking close, heart-searching views'.[9]

A deep work of divine grace in his own heart enabled him to direct others, with peculiar skill, in the way of salvation. In his last letter to William Rawlings, which he wrote from Bristol on 11 November, 1760, with a lifetime of experience behind him, he advised his friend how to lead a despairing soul to Christ, by beginning with a conviction of sin:

> Your method I conceive, should be, not to press him to the application of particular promises, so much as to lay out the scheme of redemption from the very fall, insisting on the person and transactions of Christ, and then observing the fulness and freedom of the promises issuing from it. By such a channel it is that you probably will be able to lead him to see the evil of sin. I would talk this over and over to him, and never without this, speak of the justice, majesty and holiness of God, explaining these as they are illustrated in the life of Christ. It may be very proper by and by also to open the corruption of nature. The Lord be with you in this work.[10]

In the advice he gave he was always particular to instruct the recipient not to accept what he told them simply because he said it, but to search the Scriptures that their faith and confidence might not be founded on man's authority but only on divine testimony.

Walker was a man who practised rigorous self-examination. He watched over the reasonings of his mind and compared all its conclusions with the plain sense of the word of God. In this way he guarded against the delusions of a lively imagination. Nor was he overly influenced by the opinion of others, even when he held them in high regard. His rule of faith and practice was to lay all open before the Scriptures. His insight into the idols of the human heart and the many false motives that are hidden therein, was the result of a diligent and careful search of his heart. His biographer Edwin Sidney said,

He marked all the uncharitable feelings, all the forward, peevish, and impatient workings of his mind; he battled with the pride of his heart, seeking the enemy diligently, that he might overcome him; he noticed and guarded against his wanderings in family prayer, and his [lack of] devotion in public worship – in short, there was not an action of his life which he did not examine for the purpose of improvement, caring not how deep and painful the probe, if it did but reach the bottom of the wound, and extract the poison of the sting of sin.[11]

One of the ways he searched his soul was constantly to recall the days of fruitlessness, with a view to humiliation before God and to motivate himself to a more zealous and selfless exertion in his service of God. He told Thomas Adam that there were times that he 'could never think of without great abhorrence'. He felt ashamed of the 'conceit and interest' that had guided him to Truro; that

... by his worldly-mindedness and ignorance of vital religion, the service of Christ was prostituted, the souls committed to him starved, and he feared, many of them perished; and that he had sought his own glory in the very pulpit where he was placed to proclaim the Redeemer! 'I know not,' he says, 'how to endure the reflection: mourning over this scene I shall go to the grave. It is not a lost case indeed; we have an advocate with the Father; but I can never undo the wrong I have done to God and man.'[12]

These reflections were of great benefit to him. 'The remembrance of my unfaithfulness humbles me,' he said, 'though not as it ought; and as I desire, stirs me up to diligence and to labour more abundantly; and what I chiefly rejoice in, serves in some measure to repress that conceit, wherein my desperately wicked heart would needs swell one thing upon another.'[13] In a letter to two friends, written from Truro on 6 August, 1758, he complained, with his usual honesty and straightforwardness, of a 'very bad heart, overcome with selfishness, which contends for indulgence ... and I am ready to gratify it'. He went on to lament that my 'conduct is too much on the defensive, and wants abundantly that zeal which seeks and uses every opportunity'.[14]

His diary is full of self-reproach for short-comings and earnest longings after a deeper communion with God. For Friday 25 March, 1757, he wrote: 'A lowness of spirits returned after dinner, which subjected me to a sort of slothfulness, and that to a disposition towards peevishness. I was not so ready to bear the bad tempers of the people as I ought.' On Sunday 3 April of the same year, at ten o'clock at night, he said, 'I need to see the necessity and excellency of walking (that is, of keeping, in opposition to all difficulties) more close with God, than I have usually seen it.' A week later, Monday 11 April, he rebuked himself: 'I have been like one dead, nor could fix my attention in public. This is very heartless and disheartening... Surely I am not influenced, as I ought, by zeal for God.' Three days later: 'Delight in God is a lesson I have much to learn;' and on Friday 25 April, he complained, 'I wrote nothing last evening, being rather disposed to cry unto God, because of the coldness and wandering of my heart from him.'[15]

He knew the importance of humility in the life of a Christian and continually stressed it to his congregation. The most solid foundation for humbling the heart, he thought, was through a sense of the sinfulness, guilt and impotence of man's fallen nature. He exposed the corruption of the human heart in order to push pride in the dust and to cover it with shame and abasement. An acquaintance with our fallen state, he said, leads to 'the right manner of our seeking pardon and acceptance with God'. In a letter to William Rawlings he answered the question 'What do I find within me?' by stating:

Principles most unreasonable, neither directing me to God, nor consequently to happiness. Principles which have debased my understanding to an aptitude only for the mean regards of the world. Principles which tend alone to gratify something in me I call *self*, a monster that ungods God, and will have the whole of creation at its command; a haughty monster, big with self-sufficiency; a monster that knows neither pity nor gratitude, pregnant with envy, rage, revenge, that bears intent of murder to every opposing man or woman, a lazy monster which would have all nature sacrifice to its indulgence. Principles, atheistical because self-idolatrous; which deny the blessed God to have either justice, mercy, holiness, wisdom or truth; which confront his superintendence and government with the most determined hatred; which demand an eternal separation from everything that is called God, because they cannot endure submission, and the thought of parting from the present scene.[16]

To his religious society he said:

Let us consider that all our undertakings, though never so good, will fail and come to nought, unless we be truly and deeply humble. Indeed, it cannot be otherwise; because the proud person quits his reliance on God to rest in himself, which is to exchange a rock for a reed.

Alas! What are we poor empty things! Yea, what is worse, we are condemned perishing sinners!... We may have some attainments in grace, but spiritual pride will wither all, and soon reduce us to a very profligate and wretched estate...

You that are young in years and younger in grace are in danger of self-conceit, and of being puffed up, which is a quicksand in which thousands have been swallowed up and perished...

By pride the angels fell from heaven and if we are ever to climb up to those blessed seats from which they are fallen, it must be by the gracious steps of humility and lowliness of mind... Let us walk humbly with our God and ever have lowly thoughts of our vile selves and of our poor attainments and of our defective performances, and with Paul ... let us always say, 'I am nothing.'[17]

These were not simply pious words, but the outworking of his own experience. One visitor to Truro exclaimed: 'The remarkable meekness and love of God's servant at Truro, confounds or overrules all prejudices.'[18] Another, writing in *The Religious Tract Society*, noted how he walked 'humbly before God, with a tenderness of conscience that is far from common, [and] was ever as ready to attribute any failure in his ministry to some error in himself, as to the hardness of the hearts of others'.[19] Thomas Adam, in a letter of June, 1757, said to him: 'You want nothing from the world, and are one of the happy men who can be hurt by nothing but your own conscience.'[20]

On numerous occasions he complained of 'desiring man's esteem', which would sometimes make it difficult for him to confront those who might oppose him. One of many examples from his diary will suffice. 'I ought to be thankful,' he wrote on Monday 4 April, 1757, 'for some clearer discoveries of my desire after esteem; and of the difficulty, as well as necessity, of breaking with the world more than ever.'[21] However, he managed to overcome this weakness by 'the mighty influence of the Spirit of God', and was given the grace to continue 'in the discharge of his duty in opposition to this secret enemy'. He also wanted to experience an honest indignation against sin which did not excite his temper or injure his peace of mind. With this end in view, he cultivated the grace of compassion for the offender, not excusing or ignoring his sin, but acting in the manner of Jesus, when he 'looked upon them with indignation, being grieved at the hardness of their hearts' (Mark 3:5). In 1756, when he reviewed his ministry, he could only remember two instances when he had 'been angry, without plainly seeing sin'.

Whenever Walker noted his own spiritual experiences, a sense of the presence of sin was usually prominent. This acted as a check upon his feelings in times of success. 'I have most zeal,' he remarked, 'and least wildfire, when I am most humbled in

the sense of my sins.' In a prayer he exclaimed, 'Lord, for thy
mercies sake, make me vile in my own eyes.' In one of his
journals he stated, 'I was striving much in prayer last night and
this morning for a sense of the sinfulness of sin. My heart seems
to have been quickened by it through the day, to keep a little
close with God.'[22] He knew better than most the battles a Christian fights against sin and self, the need for a close walk with
God, and of looking to Christ for all things. In one of his letters
he unveiled, in an honest and fervent manner, the desires and
difficulties of his own experience:

> Oh what an important thing it is to walk with God! What a
> comprehensive phrase – what a lovely part both of our duty
> and privilege! But alas! How many difficulties and obstruc-
> tions do the enemies of our souls lay in the way. Unbelief
> draws a veil before our eyes – sin builds a wall across the
> road – the world spreads a thousand snares to entangle our
> feet – the devil attacks us with his fiery darts, and self,
> wretched self, joins issue with them all, and either gives or
> takes occasion with us continually. When I reflect how many
> they are that rise up against me, how weak my best
> defences are, and what a treacherous party I have, as it
> were, within the walls, how many things there are that amaze
> me! I am surprised to think that I am upheld, that a spark of
> divine grace is still preserved in me unquenched, amidst an
> ocean of sins, snares, temptations; yet I am alive, and trust
> to live for ever – for he who is the truth hath said, *because I
> live ye shall live also*.
>
> Oh blessed be God for Jesus Christ! When I look to
> myself, what do I see but sin and misery? – but in him I have
> righteousness and strength; in him I have life and peace. O
> my friend, let us daily learn to go out of ourselves, and look
> unto him, lean upon him, live upon him. *All fulness* is there;
> emptiness, yea worse than emptiness is here. In short, with
> respect to myself, I find both comfort and crosses, feasting
> and fighting, in the experience of every day. A body of sin
> and death constrains me to cry, *Oh, wretched man!* The
> knowledge of a better righteousness enables me to sing,

I thank God through Jesus Christ my Lord. Oh, what a mine of comfort is comprised in that last verse of Jeremiah, *I have loved thee with an everlasting love!*[23]

Walker was a man of constant prayer. 'In short,' said one of his converts, 'he prays over and lives what he preaches.'[24] He knew that God's gracious presence was with him night and day, and that any time, in adversity or prosperity, he could unburden his soul to him. 'It is equally good and pleasant for me to be in Gethsemane's garden, or Mount Tabor, or tossed up and down by the storms of this world, so I can but see his countenance and hear his voice saying, *It is I; be not afraid.*' In the same letter as that quoted above he gave thanks for the throne of grace, which is always accessible to poor sinners, and then remarked:

Secret prayer is the one great thing in experimental religion, the mainspring (if I may so say) which if not kept in order, the whole movement of vital, heart religion must grow faint and languid. On the contrary, shut me in a dungeon, or fix me on a mountain, let me see neither men nor books (if such a situation was my lot, not my choice), provided my heart were enlarged to call upon the Lord, I should be no loser. On the other, if I spent every day in reading the best books, in hearing the best preachers, in conversing with the best men, if secret prayer was not carefully kept up, and every other means watered and improved by this, my soul would starve in the midst of plenty. Union and communion with Jesus is the greatest mercy on this side of eternity, and that perfected is the heaven of heavens.[25]

As this letter shows his heart was much drawn to God. He carefully examined his emotions in prayer, and on one occasion, when conscious of greater fervency during a week of trial than he was after the trial, he asked himself, 'Am I driven to Christ by necessity, or drawn by love?' His prayerful exercises were, he feared, 'rather meditations that warmed his heart, than devout supplication'. At another time he said, 'I get a glimpse of God in prayer, and lose sight of him again as soon as prayer is ended.' Once he lamented, 'I scarcely ever keep him in view through my devotions.'

In spite of these complaints Walker enjoyed much intimate communion with God, and often experienced a practical sense of divine love on his heart. Although he was not always conscious of God's presence, he could remark, 'while I seem to have no sensible delight in God, I am not however without some evidences; particularly I would improve opportunities of serving Christ in the conversion of sinners'. When he did not experience sensible assurances, he drew comfort from the tendency of his desires and actions. On the sacrament Sunday for 3 April, 1757, after he had left the Lord's table, he observed, 'I am not returned rejoicing. My frame has been some-what disordered; yet I think I have not been careless. Sure, I deserve no favours; so I will endeavour to be thankful for, and to improve what I have received – a composed purpose of heart to serve the Lord, in opposition to the desire of my heart of men's esteem.'[26]

It is interesting to note Walker's attitude to the Lord's Supper, the nature and purpose of which he meticulously explained to his communicants at Truro. He himself carefully prepared for it, looked forward to celebrating it, and afterwards inquired into its effects on his religious comfort and progress. It became to him a rich covenant blessing. On Friday 1 April, 1757, he remarked, 'Complaint of want of communion. Sunday next is sacrament Sunday. My thoughts have been somewhat drawn this way by the exercises of the week. I am much called on to lament my little profiting by the last supper, and little desire after this. What a tendency has my heart to pass over duties in a customary manner!'[27] From these comments it is apparent there were times when he did not always receive the comfort and happiness he desired, but he rarely returned from the table without some consolation. On 29 May, 1757, he wrote:

> Just returned from the sacrament where I met an unwanted rebuke; the enemy had great advantage of me, taking occasion of the fewness of the people present, especially of the society, to raise up reasoning mixed with resentment, when it was suggested whether the society people did not dislike coming with others, and were influenced by pride. I could get no deliverance from these thoughts, though they were earnestly prayed and contended against, till the last people were receiving, and was in a manner prevented from the exercise of every grace. *Yet in the midst, I could see the Lord gracious*, and thought I could justify him. I have been confessing my sins and seeking the cause; but see no special reason, being in everything sinful.[28]

The curate of Truro was not always so tried, but on many occasions returned from the Lord's Table rejoicing. On one of these happy occasions, Sunday 4 March, 1753, he declared:

> By the endurance and goodness of God, I am alive this day, and have been enabled, without disturbance, to renew my covenant of grace. Praise be to God, my mind was clear, my conscience quiet, and with due deliberation, and without distraction, I was before the Lord. I must bless him also that the ordinance was with comfort. Faith seemed in exercise more than usual, to see, receive and in some measure to appropriate Christ to me in communicating. Though always I have cause to complain of the hardness of my heart, yet now I could in some sort mourn and love. I found heartiness in my purpose of serving the glory and interest of God in Christ, and was forward to make full surrender of myself, depending upon divine grace. It has been a day with me signally marked with divine favour. Notwithstanding the insensibility and unbelief of my heart, I am returned rejoicing.[29]

After this enjoyment of the divine presence, being unwilling to rest in what he had received, he said, 'What now shall I render unto the Lord? It may be, some greater trial than ordinary is at hand. Let me be mindful therefore of the vows I have this day made.'[30]

One night Walker was struck down by a sudden illness. His response and submission to God during this trial are proofs of his piety and humility. These are the lessons he learned: the importance of making the most of every hour; the day of health is the time for the work of religion, not the dying bed; the necessity of not allowing the things of this life to overshadow eternal interests. In a letter to Adam in the summer of 1759, he mentioned the trials of Archdeacon Bassett, calling them 'the parents of true comfort'. 'Christ sits as the refiner,' he continued. 'If his corrections do not break us, they cannot purge us.' The one great use of affliction, wrote Walker, 'is to make us know ourselves better. Whoever thought himself so proud, self-sufficient, unbelieving, unsubmissive, as he found himself to be when put into the furnace? It is a great thing to be undeceived here. That which mortifies self, is the thing we need.'[31]

To a person afflicted by the death of a friend, he wrote a word of personal testimony, which may refer to the above 'sudden illness': 'O my friend, I was near the borders of death but a week ago; suddenly seized, in danger of a hasty summons. God has lengthened my days, but how unequal am I to fulfil his good purposes of various sorts herein! He that bade me live, says, "My grace is sufficient for thee." Here will I hope.'[32]

The uncertainty of life was constantly before him. In another letter to a distressed young man, after reminding him of the certainty of death and of how our natures try to convince us that death shall not come near us, he wrote:

O my friend, could I but live in that expectation of death, which both the certainty and uncertainty of its coming demand, and consequently in the immediate view of an eternal judgement, what manner of man should I be! How above and dead to the world; how diligent and active in my Master's work; how undisturbed by a thousand things which now disorder me; how quiet under all afflictions; how content in my station, &c. &c.! Surely to learn to die is a lesson hard, yet most needful to be learnt, else God would not so discipline us in it; and who will say he has got this lesson so perfectly as to need no further teaching?... Comfort us, you say – think of death and what lies behind. By the grace of God, bring yourselves near the departing hour. It will show you what you are and should be, and will suggest the plainest way in the world of improving your present heavy trial.[33]

Walker was kindly disposed towards all men, regardless of their opinion of him. When he discovered their imperfections, he prayed over them and forgave them; if anyone opposed him, he asked God to fill the offenders with the spirit of loving- kindness and patience. His penetrating eye and analytical approach could usually discern a hypocrite, yet this did not cause men to shy away from him, rather it awed them into a fear of doing wrong. He asked God for 'a charitable temper to endure with meekness' the outrages of the violent, 'the prejudiced mistakings' of the ignorant, and the calumnies of slanderers; and one of his favourite prayers was: 'O God, give me all needful direction, that I may speak boldly and prudently among them, without pride or resentment.'[34]

In conversation he had an uncommon depth of thought and an incisive understanding, which, coupled with his quick apprehension and retentive memory, enabled him to express himself clearly on most subjects. He was very careful over the tone, manner and topics of his conversations. On one visit he said, 'I resolved to be silent in the company I was to meet, if I might not be serviceable; and have found this evening the need and difficulty of being so... God grant me the spirit of meekness and charity.' When the conversations turned to the things of God, he noted its real tendency and found it sometimes to be 'rather about religion than religious'. He also described some discussions that take place between serious people as 'love destroying debates'. His mind was very sensitive and he became easily disturbed by fruitless conversations. Even after talking to his sister about unimportant matters, he found it to be injurious to his spirituality. On addressing his people, he described himself as 'carried away from my attempts to say much to purpose, by the insignificance of conversation'.

The great labours of Walker caused him to have a nervous temperament, which occasionally destroyed his comfort. He guarded the impatience it engendered with the utmost care, and when he did say something rashly or in the wrong spirit, he mourned over it in private and prayed for the grace to overcome such tendencies. When opposed by his enemies, there were times when he remained at ease; at other times, he prayed, 'Lord, turn the fear of men's faces into a love of their souls.'

Although he obtained a high degree of self-knowledge and a deep conviction of his own unworthiness, he did not allow these to obscure his faith in the atonement of Christ. He noted: 'To be humble in the sense of my vileness, and to believe the sufficiency of Christ, I find the two hardest things I have to attain.' And again, 'God has removed some trials I have been under, yet I would remember that Christ is our peace,' and that 'My salvation depends not on myself but *Christ, the same yesterday, today and for ever*, though I am myself so changeable.'[35] The private thoughts he entertained of his own heart, invariably turned his mind to his great Redeemer. The pages of his diary are filled with careful and accurate notes on the changes in a Christian's experience, designed, as he observed, to check undue enthusiasm, to stir up a slothful state and to move the soul towards its Saviour. When in need, his habit was to apply directly to Christ, and his experiences and emotions, his public duties and private devotions, were all tested by the standards of the word of God.

There were times when Walker was assailed with doubts. Occasionally he found it hard to agree fully with the Biblical sentence declared against sin, and he hesitated as to the perfect goodness of God, but these doubts and hesitations, laid before the Lord, ultimately led him to right views of divine things and to a deeper and more established faith. When tested in this manner, he would say, 'I must seek more light,' and soon light came to restore spiritual health to him. His reflections led him to discover the impossibility of reasoning on the divine perfections, and to a more secure and settled faith. 'Were I incapable,' he observed, 'of answering ten thousand objections which do not affect the main doctrines of Scripture, I should not doubt the truth of them.' His faith was further strengthened by seeing 'such discoveries of God respecting him to *me*, as just that very Being I would desire him to be'.[36]

In his ministry a deep desire for the salvation of souls activated him. He was not satisfied with producing excitement in others, but laboured in helping his converts distinguish between emotion and the true workings of God's Spirit. He was able to gain the ascendancy over the minds of others, but never used it for selfish purposes, but for their spiritual benefit.

As 'one of the greatest of Evangelical preachers',[37] he was master of the plain and vigorous style, which never degenerated into the grotesque. He spoke from a full heart, moved by compassion and zeal for perishing souls, and prepared at all times to proclaim, in a forceful and uncompromising fashion, the essential doctrines of the Christian faith.

> Having in view the glory of God and the salvation of the souls committed to his charge, as the great end of his preaching, he studied not so much to please the ear, as to inform the mind and amend the heart. To this end he applied with closeness and energy the spirituality of God's law, together with the curses denounced against the transgressor, to the careless sinner, in order to beget in him a conviction of his lost estate, and to awaken him to a sense of his danger.

> The more decent formalist ... he flattered not on account
> of his fair outside, but faithfully represented to him the folly
> and absurdity of resting in *a form of godliness void of the
> power thereof.*
>
> To the serious Christian, who was already made sensible
> of the corruption of his nature, and desired to serve God in
> spirit and in truth in the way of his appointed ordinances, he
> laid open the plan of the Gospel in its various parts, as a
> scheme devised by infinite Wisdom for the recovery of
> sinful fallen creatures; to such as, by the renunciation of
> their own wisdom, righteousness and strength, were prepared
> to receive a proffered salvation, he preached Christ Jesus...
> He taught the true believer to behold his sins expiated in *the
> blood of the Lamb of God, which taketh away the sin of the
> world*; to see his person accepted in the righteousness of his
> Redeemer, and to rest in nothing short of a real and universal
> change in heart and life... Nor is it to be forgotten that ... he
> strenuously enforced ... the necessity of observing the rela-
> tive and social duties in civil life.[38]

With these truths of the gospel burning on his lips, he awakened a careless town out of its lethargy and urged its inhabitants to flee the wrath to come, putting all their confidence for
salvation in Christ. 'He applied the axe to the root of
self-righteousness; he thundered with thrilling energy in his
appeal to the consciences of sinners; he soothed the
broken-hearted, and with patient care cherished the work of
piety in the heart.'[39] The result was astonishing. Eight hundred
persons were converted in seven years, an effect in such a
parish as Truro that caused Bishop Ryle to remark that his ministry 'must have been one of singular power, and singularly
blessed of God'.[40] Many from neighbouring towns came to hear
him and carried away the message of truth, and through it places
of worship were erected at St Columb and Tregony.

In conclusion, the words of his first main biographer are a
suitable tribute:

He sought no other reward than success in his ministry, and he resigned his benefice and the prospect of a rich alliance, that nothing might obstruct him in his one pursuit; nor was he ever heard to express a desire to exchange a scene of retirement and poverty, honoured by the especial blessing of God, for a more productive or more prominent situation. He was content to cultivate the portion of the vineyard assigned him by his heavenly Master, and had no anxiety but to dress it into health and fruitfulness, and to excite his fellow labourers to similar diligence. He owed nothing to this world, and tasted chiefly of its bitters; all his enjoyments descended from above, borne to him on the stream of that river which makes glad the city of our God, of whose waters his soul is now drinking at their source before the throne.[41]

It was qualities such as those mentioned above that moved one admirer to write: 'I have heard much of that excellent man, Mr Walker. He goes on gloriously; may our Lord help him more and more.'[42]

Perhaps these two apostolic directions, 'Do all to the glory of God' and 'Let all your things be done in charity', may more easily be reduced to practice, and serve as a discriminating rule. Whatever has not a tendency to glorify God and profit man must be avoided; for it cannot be our duty. And again, it implies, that we must labour to do our duty, so as to glorify God and benefit our brother.

Part of a letter from Walker to Adam dated 7 October, 1756.[1]

Your 'Conversation Scheme', as might be expected, is a searching piece and contains a fund of precious knowledge... Suppose something like this should be added to your preliminary advices: 'Lastly, let me advise and caution you, with regard to the following marks of trial (or heads of conversation), not to be forward and assuming on the one hand, in thinking and speaking more highly of yourself than you ought, which will effectually hinder all farther improvements; nor, on the other, to be too much dejected if you find, as probably you will, that you do not come up to some of them; but first grounding yourself wholly on the Lord Jesus Christ, for salvation, to be thankful for the measure of grace which is given you, carefully to improve it, and in all faithfulness and love to your Redeemer, pressing on to higher degrees of perfection.'

Some of Adam's comments on Walker's Conversation Scheme.[2]

21

'My Dear Friends'

Walker's most intimate friend and a kindred spirit, with whom he enjoyed an honest and lengthy correspondence, was Thomas Adam of Wintringham, 'regarded as a sort of oracle by his fellow Evangelicals'.[3] Skevington Wood remarked that he 'lived to be the doyen of the Evangelical party'.[4] Adam was born on 25 February, 1701, at Leeds, where he began his education at the local grammar school under the pious Thomas Barnard, before moving to Wakefield. He proceeded to Christ's College, Cambridge, where his tutor was Matthew Hutton, who became archbishop of both York and Canterbury. After two years he transferred to Hart Hall (later Hertford College), Oxford, which was under the principalship of Dr Richard Newton. In 1723 he took his BA degree and as early as the following year was offered the living of Wintringham, Lincolnshire, which he entered in 1726 being then of canonical age. He remained there for fifty-nine years until his death on 31 March, 1784.

His own more personal account, which he gave to Walker in June, 1757, and which includes his refusal to accept preferment, is given below:

> After a youth of levity and frolic more than study, I came hither [to Wintringham] in the year twenty-six, to a living of £200 per annum, which was ready for me at twenty-four, with some repute for learning, a tolerably smooth outside sense of decorum, and not without some qualms. Though I

had swallowed a camel on taking orders with some expectations to the articles, and more for the sake of worldly advantage than anything else, yet from the very first I strained at
the gnats of plurality and non-residence, though with a
deceitful heart at the bottom, insomuch that an uncle in high
reputation in the law, who had set his heart upon advancing
me, and could have commanded anything for me,
pronounced me mad. These qualms by degrees brought on
others, and ripened me into your friend and acquaintance,
The Catechist.[5]

In 1730 he married Susanna Coke, the daughter of the vicar of
Roxby, who, after a long illness, died in August, 1760, only a
short time before Walker's death. About 1745 he read William
Law's *Serious Call* and felt so humbled and ashamed that for
months he dared not enter the pulpit. 'His health was impaired,
and his parishioners saw, with concern, their minister weeping
and trembling during the public services on the sabbath days.'[6]
For several years he struggled in a state of uncertainty, and was
'greatly harassed in his mind and conscience', until one morning
he went to his study,

as he had often done before, under feelings of great
distress... He fell down upon his knees before God in prayer
– spread his case before him – implored him to pity his
distress – and to guide him by his Holy Spirit into the right
understanding of his holy word. When he arose from his
supplications, he took the Greek Testament, and sat down
to read the first six chapters of ... Romans. He was sincerely
desirous to be taught of God, and to receive, with the
simplicity of a little child, the word of his revelation; when,
as he read, to his unspeakable joy, his difficulties vanished;
– the subject appeared in a clear and satisfactory light. He
saw the doctrine of justification by Christ alone, through faith
in him, to be the great subject of the gospel, the highest
display of the divine perfections – the happiest relief for his
burdened conscience – and the most powerful principle of
constant and unfeigned holiness of heart and life. He was
exceedingly joyful, and found peace and comfort spring up

in his mind. His conscience was purged from dead works, and from the guilt of sin through the atoning blood of Christ, and his heart was set at liberty, to run the way of God's commandments without fear, in a spirit of filial love and holy delight. From this period he endeavoured to preach salvation 'through faith in Jesus Christ alone'... Mr Adam was made happy; God was glorified by his servant; and those around him began to receive benefit.[7]

When Adam had first arrived at Wintringham the parish was in a very low state – it was the scene of riots and blasphemy, of wrestling, fighting, and drunkenness; but after his conversion there was, according to James Hervey, an 'amazing reformation amongst the people in his neighbourhood'. He drew 'large congregations ... not only from his own parish but from round about'.[8] But if truth be told, his ministry at Wintringham was not overly successful. As early in his relationship with Walker as November, 1754, he admitted, that although he had for years insisted upon 'the great evangelical points of repentance, faith, and renovation by the power of the Holy Ghost ... I cannot say that much impression has yet been made upon my own parish'. Nevertheless, neighbouring parishes had been 'either awakened or confirmed' by his preaching, 'and the influences of it reached more or less to no inconsiderable distance'.[9]

By June, 1757, there was little change, as he related to Walker: 'I can make very little impression seemingly in my own parish, though I am not altogether idle and unconcerned.' At that time he catechised the children on Wednesdays, both children and young persons separately on Sundays, as well as lecturing to the whole congregation, and he had just finished going through the Gospel of Matthew with a very small group one evening a week. A few of his parishioners were helped by a school he started, but most continued in their godless ways. Henry Venn, who listed Walker as one of his 'very dear friends', in a letter to his son John Venn, written from Yelling, 21 April, 1784, was near the truth when he said: 'Dear Mr Adam finished his course at Wintringham, three weeks ago, after being fifty-nine years rector of that parish. Exceedingly small was his success amongst his people, after preaching the gospel thirty years!'[10]

Walker's acquaintance with Adam began when he read his *Lectures on the Church Catechism* (1753), which exercised an influence far beyond Adam's own parish boundaries, and moved men from all over the country to seek his advice. John Thornton travelled all the way from Clapham to consult him; Lord Dartmouth received his counsel on 'how to live a Christian life and yet take part in affairs and society'; Wesley desired his opinion on 'a formal separation of the Methodists from the Church of England'; and Venn was indebted to him for his critical comments on his most popular work, *Complete Duty of Man*: 'If it were not for dear Mr Adam's encouraging approbation, I should faint in my book.'[11] Walker wrote to Adam in October, 1754, and received a reply the following month. From that time an intimate and prolific correspondence began between the two men, which brought them together for the first time in the autumn of 1757 when Walker visited Wintringham. Walker so respected Adam's counsel that before any important ministerial undertaking, he usually consulted him.

Many extracts from the correspondence of these 'true sons of the Church', as William Richardson of York called them, have already been presented and reveal their honest, straightforward and affectionate dealings with each other, and the varied topics they discussed. Both men were ready to advise, encourage and, where necessary, disagree with the other, as is exemplified in Adam's opposition to Walker's *Scheme* for union among the Evangelical clergy. In Walker's 7 June, 1758, letter, he said to Adam that he thought he was held 'by a constitutional reservedness, which would be apt to keep your people at a distance when you talk with them'. Adam's response was typical of the humility that existed in their relationship:

> The reservedness so apparent in me, and which you call
> constitutional, is really so in a high degree, and hard to over-
> come. But I do not excuse it to myself in that manner, calling
> it timidity, and fearing that a superior principle of zeal for the
> glory of God, is not strong enough in me to counterwork it.
> Ply me with advice and exhortation, and do you go on exert-
> ing your advantages of nature and grace. I should be sorry
> to say a word that might administer the least food to pride,
> and when anything of that kind drops from me, be upon your
> guard.[12]

Earlier in the year (9 February, 1758), Walker had commented
on Adam's preaching, an opinion that was based on 'friend
Jane's and George's observation chiefly': 'Your style is nervous,
your sentences long, and I fancy your elocution rather swift. Do
your people understand you?'[13] Again Adam received this criticism graciously: 'There is truth in what you observe.' In
another letter, written in the summer of 1759, Walker admitted,
'You provoke me to say all the ill I can of you. I thought I had
said all already.'[14] 'Go on increasing in humility,' exhorted Adam
to his friend, 'as well as labour and success, and like Paul, be
less than the least of all littleness.'[15] Frank exchanges such as
these, always delivered in a Christian spirit, not only endeared
the two men to each other, but, as iron sharpens iron, strengthened them both in their ministerial labours.

The two men had been writing to each other for several
years before Walker asked his friend for any personal particulars.
Walker knew Adam's heart well, but for the rest he imagined
him to be

> ... a man upward of fifty, unmarried, your stature not of the
> sons of Anak like mine, your frame slender, your complexion
> dark, rather tending to the colour of your book, having
> contracted somewhat of its whiteness by much acquaint-
> ance. I fancy you are constitutionally cheerful and some-
> what warm. You do not talk overmuch in company, perhaps
> rather reserved. You know the world, and are well received.

With such a person I sometimes hold an imaginary conversation and call him my friend Mr Adam.[16]

Walker's imaginary sketch, which he sent to Adam in a letter
dated 12 May, 1757, was not far off the mark in some particulars, as Adam mentioned in his June reply:

You are sadly out in the article of marriage. I have been in
that state between twenty and thirty years, but have no children living [their only daughter died when she was young].
My wife is, and I have reason to be thankful for it...
    My stature is little; my frame slender, so that a small
degree of labour brings on lassitude. My complexion is pale,
but a little bronzed with fifty-five. I am tolerably cheerful and
more than somewhat warm. I do not talk much, and wish I
talked less. The world takes me for an honest man, and as
such I am pretty well received; but the greater part of my
acquaintance, who are pleased to say I was once all air,
smartness and repartee, do not think I have made good
exchange for my present reserve, which by the bye, is most
natural to me – for I had a very uncommon settled gravity in
my countenance from a child, which those who are inclined
to take things by the worst handle, now call austerity.[17]

It was typical of their open relationship that Adam, after the
above sketch, seriously requested Walker to furnish him with
'hints for my improvement' and defied him to 'chagrin me with
any liberties'.

While Walker is chiefly remembered for his ministry, Adam
is remembered more for his writings: 'There is a force and weight
in what falls from the pen of Mr Adam,' wrote Colonel Pownall
to Robert Storry, 'that the more you reflect upon what he says,
the more you are impressed with the solidity of his evangelical
sentiments: they mark a heart deeply experienced in all the
great and essential truths of the gospel.'[18] His most famous work
is *Private Thoughts on Religion*, a series of aphorisms and
pious reflections from his diary, which Overton compares to the
Confessions of St Augustine and *The Imitation of Christ* by

Thomas à Kempis, 'after the Evangelical pattern'. This 'choice little book', published posthumously, was originally written for his eyes only, and shows him to be a man 'of no common power of analytic and speculative thought. With an intrepidity and integrity of self-scrutiny perhaps unexampled, he writes down problems started and questionings raised, and conflicts gone through; whilst his ordinarily flaccid style grows pungent and strong.'[19] The language is somewhat penitential and morbid, but the general tone is lit up by many striking and memorable aphorisms: 'Hell is truth seen too late.' 'Heaven is wherever God is: in my heart if I desire it.' 'I see the devil's hook, and yet I cannot help nibbling at his bait.'[20] It was widely read and appreciated not only by Evangelicals, but by men of very different views. Coleridge, Bishop Heber, Thomas Chalmers and John Stuart Mill were influenced by it, and it has been translated into Welsh and several European and Eastern languages.

There are some glowing accounts of Adam's character. George Burnett called him 'a good master, a steady friend and a kind neighbour'. Henry Venn, in a letter to James Stillingfleet, likened him to a 'truly wise Christian', in the sense that he spoke 'very little of himself'. Westoby said he 'ever bore a strictly virtuous and moral character... His mind was resolutely opposed to vice, and to whatever militated against conduct proper to a gentleman and a believer in the truth of Christianity.'[21] And Colonel Pownall, already quoted, wrote, Adam's 'character approaches nearer to an apostolical one, than any one I ever yet met with; the simplicity of his life, and the eminent piety of his writings, place him, I think, in the first class of Christians'.[22]

George Burnett and his friend Thomas Haweis, Walker's 'two particular protégés', prepared for the ministry under the tuition of Walker and Conon at Truro. As well as studies in Latin,

> they were put through an intensive course of homiletics. Serious attention was paid to the important but often

neglected craft of sermon construction. Each week they were given a text of Scripture to divide into suitable heads, together with the inference and application. Sometimes these outlines were to be filled in at length, sometimes they were left as skeletons. Always they were carefully reviewed by Walker and Conon, and improvements suggested. Walker bitterly regretted that in his early training he had not acquired the art of extemporaneous speech, and he therefore determined to exercise his two pupils in this particular from the start. Not only were they set to study rhetoric but encouraged in the actual practice of extempore preaching. One afternoon each week they were called upon to make the attempt before a small congregation consisting of the members of Walker's household.[23]

Skevington Wood said that by this means Haweis was 'equipped to become one of the most effective extemporaneous preachers of the Evangelical movement'.[24]

After Truro both Burnett and Haweis went to Christ Church, Oxford, in December, 1755. They are first placed together (as George and Tom) by Walker in one of his letters, probably to William Rawlings of St Columb. The letter is dated 16 December, 1755.

We have continually letters from T. and G. which gives us a good deal of content. They are in a barren land [Oxford University] and will need your prayers. Poor young men, it is well for them they are together, and especially for your favourites that George is with them. Nothing [can be] more providential, he is so suited [to him]; I know no other so fit for him. They are lovely youths. I have the greatest hopes for them. If they stand their ground, they will both be diligent and useful. They have both their temptations, and both their excellences. Tom will be in danger of over-rashness, and George of over-caution. George will make the greater figure, and Tom will be the most liked. Should they be associates in a cure, nothing would be more desirable. Well, you never forget them. Their well doing is a matter of great importance to the world, for I am either so fond or so foolish as to think they have not many equals.[25]

Both men returned to Cornwall in the spring of 1756. The main problem they faced was not their education or training but their ordination. Truro was then in the diocese of Exeter, and Bishop Lavington, suspicious of any Evangelical, was not about to help, and many other diocese were equally unhopeful. However, from a letter of Walker's to Adam (9 March, 1757), the Truro curate stated that this particular difficulty was solved fairly easily for Haweis, but not for Burnett.

> I mentioned a while ago a young gentleman to you [Haweis], who had turned his thoughts to the ministry. Mr Jane has taken him with him to Oxford to assist him in his parish there, and the bishop of Oxford has promised to ordain him.
>
> But we have another, Mr Burnett, his friend and companion last year at Christ Church. For, to say the truth, he is all I could wish him, and I doubt not will be eminently diligent in the ministry. His getting into orders will we suppose be attended with no difficulty, as he is a Master of Arts in the University of Aberdeen, being one of that place, and brought hither by my father and his countryman Mr Conon [Burnett's godfather], to assist him in the school. We cannot get him a title in this country for evident reasons. Can you serve him in yours? I venture to answer for him in every respect; and we shall be glad if he may be near you, since we cannot keep him near us. Young men always need advice; and I assure you he would be glad to take it.[26]

It appears that in Adam's reply he thought that there were better prospects for Burnett in the north, for Walker wrote again in April 1757, stating:

> I heartily wish you may succeed for George Burnett. Nothing will please father Conon and me better than having him near you. As for the country, George is a Scotchman; and for the pecuniary conditions, he will take what you may agree to in his behalf; so should the thing offer, do not let it slip through your hands while you are writing to us. Nothing will hinder George's acceptance but a pre-engagement, of which at

present, he has no immediate prospect. I am sure you will like him mightily.[27]

This letter sounds upbeat and hopeful, but seven months later, on 3 November, Walker reported to Conon: 'George Burnett has great opportunities of improvement, but, as yet, no way is opened for his getting into orders.' Eventually, however, a way did open and he was ordained, although there are few details as to how or where. It must have been before 25 September, 1758, because that was the date when Walker wrote to Burnett and remarked, 'I was hoping to write you previous to your ordination, but could not effect it.' He assured Burnett of his prayers and then said, 'I have the greatest confidence that the blessed God, who has kept you hitherto, will not leave you now that you are entrusted with so vast a charge by him and for him; and that as the spirituality, zeal and diligence of your ministrations will depend upon the dispositions of your heart, he will abundantly increase a ministerial temper.'[28]

On 22 October, 1759, Walker wrote to Adam and told him that Burnett 'intended setting out for Huddersfield about this day [to work with Henry Venn]. He will need your counsel, and will come over to consult you when he has taken a little time to look about on the state of things there, which I fancy are such as will demand a good deal of prudence.'[29] Venn held a high opinion of his colleague, as his testimony to Lord Dartmouth shows:

> I am greatly relieved and comforted by the presence and help of my dear fellow labourer in the kingdom and patience of Christ, Mr Burnett; a man made to reprove the lightness of my mind, quick to discern, and bold to admonish, of unseemly carriage, yet with such unaffected humility and visible tenderness, as to make his reproofs like a polished shaft. I have great reason to adore the Providence which has brought us together, and if I do not pervert the grace of God, his joining me will further much the prosperity of my soul.[30]

Owing to various health problems Burnett spent only two years in Huddersfield. Towards the end of his stay Venn wrote to Mrs Knipe (20 June, 1760):

> I am about to have a severe trial, I fear, in parting with Mr Burnett. His friends in Cornwall advise him entirely to leave Yorkshire, under a notion that he has too much duty laid upon him. I am apprehensive he will be persuaded; and where shall I get an assistant, whose heart is engaged to save souls, and to preach Christ crucified without unscriptural peculiarities, I know not.[31]

In a letter to Lord Dartmouth, Venn said:

> My faithful helper in the Lord's work, after many repeated efforts to continue in the exercise of his duty, is obliged to desist: his behaviour under these afflicting circumstances, glorifies his Saviour and recommends his faith. Invincible patience and the deepest humiliation, justifying God and accepting the strokes of his rod as a punishment for iniquity, joined to steadfast confidence in the Lord Jesus Christ, are the abiding tempers of his heart. It is my prayer that he may be restored to help me; for I may really say of Mr Burnett as Paul of Timothy, I know few like-minded, who preach the hatred and the mortification of sin, whilst they exalt the free grace and righteousness of our God and Saviour; who teach men to live in the denial of every evil temper, and in the exercise of every heavenly grace, and at the same time, sensible of their vileness, to cry, 'God, be merciful to me, a sinner.'[32]

In a letter from Lord Dartmouth to Rawlings (26 June, 1760), the former noted that 'Mr Venn laments exceedingly the loss of Mr Burnett, whose infirm state has I find at last obliged him to seek the benefit of change of air.'[33] Burnett spent about a year in Kent.

During Walker's last illness both Burnett and Haweis were at his side, and he rejoiced and was comforted by their fight of faith, 'not doubting that they should soon meet him in a better world'. Burnett, who was then curate of Slaithwaite in Yorkshire, wrote to Conon and William Rawlings, and passed on Walker's last messages and then the news of his death. In July, 1793, after a successful ministry at Elland, in the parish of Halifax, where he 'spent his large fortune in works of charity, and his exertions in acts of grace',[34] and where he continued the clerical society meetings that Venn had started at Huddersfield, Burnett himself died. He was fifty-eight.

Before his conversion Thomas Haweis, to use his own words, lived in a 'common course of carelessness and dissipation'. He 'never prayed', never felt 'any compunction or fear in the prospect of appearing before God in my sins', and rarely attended church. But one afternoon, probably early in 1754, after the death of a young lady he had been courting, he was constrained to go to St Mary's. Walker was preaching as usual and the effect on Haweis was dramatic.

> Mr Walker was led that day to speak in a very affecting manner on death and its consequences, and the discourse for the first time found such a congeniality in my feelings that though I should probably have heard him as forcibly urge the same truth before, for the first moment of my life, that I can reflect upon, I felt an impression on my conscience which never since has been, and I hope never will be, obliterated...
>
> My convictions were not indeed, as was then the case with many others, terrifying and deeply distressing, but they were attended with a clearness of evidence respecting my state before God that led me to fly for refuge from the danger I apprehended, and that very day I spoke to another young gentleman, Mr Tippett, who sat with me at Church, and I knew frequented Mr Walker's house, to introduce me to him, which with the greatest of pleasure he undertook to do. Mr Walker embraced me tenderly, spoke to me with the affection of a father and the fidelity of a pastor, and from that day commenced that tender friendship, shall I call it, or

rather paternal and filial regard, that was interrupted only by his departure to glory.[35]

Haweis immediately became a member of Walker's religious society. He learned to search the Scriptures and to practise private prayer, and he read many books that Walker recommended. Almost inevitably his mind turned to the ministry. With various obstacles blocking his path on the one hand, and the divine call ever-strengthening on the other, he decided to unburden his troubled heart to Walker. After Conon had been consulted, Haweis was advised to 'remain in his profession until his apprenticeship expired. Meanwhile Walker and Conon undertook to direct and assist him in his studies for the ministry, and to take what steps they could to facilitate his admission to orders.' Skevington Wood remarked that the foundations of his theology were firmly laid 'under the influence of Conon and Walker, and his position scarcely varied to the end of his days'.[36]

Both men assured Haweis 'that if the call was indeed of God, some door would be opened for its fulfilment', but they were not immediately inclined to recommend a university career for their protégé, partly because 'of the strong anti-Evangelical bias of the authorities', which they feared might adversely affect Haweis, and partly because of his limited financial resources. So they turned to Adam and agreed that after further tuition at Truro he should go to Wintringham to be educated privately under Adam's supervision. On the basis of such a course of instruction, and with the help of Adam's friend and neighbour, Archdeacon Bassett of Glentworth, they hoped to secure his ordination.

But just before Haweis went to Wintringham, Joseph Jane intervened and urged him to go to Oxford, where, he thought, 'Any opposition he might meet would serve to strengthen his fidelity to Evangelicalism.' He also promised Haweis 'that if I would follow his advice and come to College, I need not give myself a moment's thought about a provision, as he would undertake to supply all deficiencies. Mr Walker regarded this as an offer so providential that I ought to accept it.'[37] So Haweis travelled to Oxford, where he soon formed a society along the lines of Wesley's 'holy club'. In April, 1757, Walker wrote to Adam about Haweis's Oxford adventure: 'Tom Haweis is at Christ Church, and doing service among a few of the young gentlemen there. He tells me today, he is remarked as a dangerous fellow; and adds, that Romaine has been again in the University pulpit, where he preached imputed righteousness, but it is said will be allowed to preach no more there.'[38] Charles Wesley heard Haweis at Oxford and enthused that he preached 'with amazing success, both townsmen and gownsmen flocking in crowds to hear him'.

After some difficulty Haweis was admitted to deacon's orders at Cuddesdon on 9 October, 1757, and embarked on what was to be a useful, if not trouble free, ministry. Two days before Walker died, Lord Dartmouth, in a letter to William Rawlings (17 July, 1761), wrote: 'I think everything of Mr Haweis that you can wish; he seems to me, to grow in humility, which, as in all, so I take it more particularly in him, is to be looked upon as the only foundation of all other graces. His zeal is lively and I hope prudent, and his success, thank God, proportionable.'[39]

Walker enjoyed an interesting and profitable friendship with Risdon Darracott, an Independent minister at Wellington, Somerset. He had been a theological student of Philip Doddridge at Northampton. 'The hearts of Doddridge and Darracott,' remarked Edwin Sidney, 'were as warm as their gifts and graces were brilliant; and the sound of Zion's trumpet in the church made them exult in a hope that it would rouse multitudes from the sleep of death.'[40] In a letter to Darracott, Walker observed, 'I have not your warm heart; Doddridge was not my tutor.'[41] Doddridge himself, writing to his wife on 18 June, 1742, called Darracott 'absolutely the most successful minister I have known among us for many years. He prayed last night in a manner which came as near inspiration as anything I have heard or expect to hear.'[42] And again: 'Mr Darracott is one of the most devoted and extraordinary men I ever sent out, and a person who has within these few years been highly useful to numbers of his hearers.'[43]

In October, 1743, George Whitefield stayed and preached at Wellington, and seven years later he described Darracott as 'a flaming successful preacher of the gospel, and who, I think, may justly be styled ... the star of the west'. Even godless men acknowledged the power and effect of his ministry. 'A profane gentleman once said to his friend, as they met Mr Darracott going to his meeting house to preach on a week day, "There," said he, "goes a man who serves God as if the devil was in him."'[44] Walker's correspondence with Darracott began in 1754. Their letters were designed to

> ... encourage each other in the true faith, to tell of souls rescued from Satan's bondage, and brought into the liberty of the gospel, or to lament their own deficiencies and the obduracy of their people. Mr Walker congratulated Mr Darracott on the piety of Dissenters at Wellington; and the latter expressed his joy at receiving tidings of good among churchmen at Truro.[45]

Their first recorded meeting took place when Walker visited Wellington on his return from Wintringham in the autumn of 1757, and he was delighted with what he found there. It was then that Darracott pressed both Walker and Adam to appear in print repeatedly as he thought others 'not clear'. When Fawcett preached his funeral sermon at Wellington on 15 April, 1759, a month after his death, he commented:

> In proportion to the number of his stated hearers, I must say, from a long acquaintance with their circumstances, that I never knew any one congregation, which appeared to me to have so many instances of abiding religious impressions;

and I have good reason to believe that it has pleased God to own Mr Darracott's ministry, both occasionally and statedly, to the effectual conversion of many hundreds of souls. As one consequence of this remarkable success, he left behind him, at Wellington, more than two hundred communicants.[46]

William Talbot, vicar of Kineton in Warwickshire from 1745-1768, and then vicar of St Giles, Reading, until his death in 1774, was another friend of Walker. They were probably friends at Oxford. In a letter to Adam dated 25 July, 1759, Walker said that Talbot, 'who was in our college in my days, has been long searching with diligence and simplicity [for salvation]. By what I can gather, he began with the law; then the Moravians came in his way, and a year or two ago, he was settled by Romaine.' He went on to quote from a letter he had received from Thomas Haweis, who had just returned from spending a week with Talbot at Kineton. Haweis gave Talbot 'a most extraordinary character', which Walker could not help transcribing for Adam's comfort and quickening.

July 16, 1759, Oxford... Mr Talbot's ... living is nothing in value, but most laborious in service. He took in merely with a view to do good, having that desire in great simplicity, before he could be at all said to be evangelical, which he has been about a twelve month or more. He had always a doctrinal knowledge of the scheme, but till then, no inward experimental acquaintance with it. He has two churches, mother and daughter church, the value of both together being £28 per annum, two miles distant. His vicarage houses at both places are thatched cottages, which cost him their value in repairs, and his own house almost takes away in rent the whole income of his living. He has also handsomely new-built the church, chiefly at his own expense. His temper being naturally generous, he is abundantly munificent.

He preaches twice a day at the mother church, and once at the daughter, besides an evening exposition of the Scriptures at his own house for as many as will come. Thursday, he preaches in the church. Tuesday, he has a public exposition in his house, two rooms of which are fitted with forms, a desk, mats, and all the other necessaries. Morning and evening, he constantly prays, expounds Scripture, and sings in his family. He is cried out against as a Methodist by most of the clergy, but is quite sound from all leaning that way.

He has an excellent woman for his wife, but no children. His parts are strong, judgement piercing, heart open, zeal great, simplicity most astonishing. His work prospers. I suppose forty or fifty persons seriously concerned about their souls, and a great impression evident upon them. But is he established? Judge yourself what a man must be who determines to ride more than two hundred miles, to get a thorough acquaintance with the work.[47]

Talbot intended to arrive in Truro the first week in September, 1759, after he had been to the assizes at Warwick, and to stay with Walker for three weeks 'that he may take a thorough view, and enter into the spirit of his method'. Haweis continued:

His connections with multitudes of the great, were most intimate and familiar, and the intimacy still continues, though he sees them now but seldom. He will give you hints perhaps of his freedom with them, which will surprise you. He seems most dead to the world respecting its esteem among those who were his former snares, but like others, will be in danger of making the serious world supply their place; but at present he is an astonishing instance of the power of divine grace... When you see him you will be highly pleased.[48]

Talbot arrived at Truro during the last week in August, a few days before expected, and stayed with Walker for a month. After he had returned home Walker wrote to Adam (11 October, 1759) and gave this account of Talbot's character:

I cannot express the esteem I have of him. With all the delicacy of a man of quality, and as much quick and strong sense as I ever met with, he is surprisingly humble, diffident of his own judgement, and teachable; into which he has been led by long and deep distress of mind under the sense of sin, and out of which he is as yet but imperfectly delivered. He is, indeed, much dead to the world in every view of it, and seems possessed by an apostolic zeal for the honour of our Master. His manner in conversation is so happy, that he really says the freest things, without raising the least anger in those he is talking to. I trust he has been blessed to us; for my own part, everything about him confounded my pride, and was some sort of balance to that inbred and contracted conceit of mine, which had too much fuel afforded it by a visit from such a man. O sir, what cause of condemnation have I from that quarter![49]

In the autumn of 1760 he was for a short period Walker's host after the latter had left Truro. He was well respected in many circles and on 2 March, 1774, he died at the age of fifty-three, in the house of his friend William Wilberforce. On 11 March, John Newton, after receiving an account of his death, wrote in his diary that his friend Mr Talbot 'might justly be numbered amongst the first worthies. Considering his character, abilities and situation, the Church of God could hardly have sustained a heavier loss in the removal of one minister.'[50]

Little is known about Walker's best friend at Truro, George Conon, a devout Anglican and 'the first Evangelical [layman] in Cornwall', but the value of his friendship is repeatedly emphasized in Walker's correspondence. Walker even referred to him as 'the father of the regular work of God in these parts' and freely acknowledged that he was instrumental in his own conversion. In answer to Adam's inquiry: 'Is Mr Conon your father?' Walker replied, 'I think I may say yes. I had little knowledge, and less practice of vital Christianity, till known to him. His manner struck me at first sight; and under God, I am more indebted to him than to the whole world beside. He is indeed an excellent Christian, bore with me while I was weak, and now stands by me in all my endeavours.'[51]

According to Davies he not only laid the 'spiritual foundation for Walker's ministry', but his example was one of the main
reasons for the Cornish revival before the arrival of the Wesleys.
'We may conjecture that the Cornish revival owed an incalculable
debt to his life and ministry from Walker's frequent and
emphatic assertions of the power of his example and witness.'[52]
As well as Walker and Haweis, Conon influenced for good men
of the calibre of Thomas Tregenna Biddulph of Bristol and
Thomas Wills, both pupils of his at Truro, who became fellow
labourers in the gospel. Of Wills *The Dictionary of National
Biography* stated: 'As a popular preacher Wills was second only
to George Whitefield, and his preaching in the open air, especially on Tower Hill, attracted great crowds.'[53]

Joseph Jane was another loyal friend of Walker, whom he
met about 1755. He was the son of Joseph Jane senior, Conon's
predecessor at the Grammar School, and the rector of St Mary's
Truro from 1711 to his death in 1745.[54] He was a staunch Evangelical, and his church St Mary Magdalene in the city of Oxford
was 'the great centre of Evangelicalism in this early period'. He
rejoiced at the news of Walker's labours and success in Cornwall, and, whenever necessary, defended him against reproach.
He was at Walker's side during his final illness. In a letter written
by a layman 'of an excellent character', there is a good sketch
of Jane's simplicity and Christian humility:

> Mr Walker has had for this month past a faithful fellow
> labourer in the Lord, the Rev Mr Jane, from Oxford, whose
> heart is much enlarged in love to all God's people. Mr Walker's
> labours and success strike him prodigiously. I trust he will go
> and do likewise. One good symptom I find in him, though he
> is one of the greatest scholars in the university, yet he
> condescends to be taught by Mr Baxter's little plain book,
> *The Call to the Unconverted*. He is a man of great abilities,
> considerable rank and an honest heart, from which excel-
> lent qualifications put together, we may hope for much fruit.

> This is the gentleman, who, having a considerable living in
> the city, permits as many of the young students as are desir-
> ous to seek God by Jesus Christ, to come to a meeting which
> he has erected in his house, where he reads them proper
> lectures about caring for souls.[55]

William Rawlings was also a good friend of Walker and one of
his most attached and pious correspondents. He must not be
confused with his son of the same name, who was the vicar of
Padstow from 1790-1836. Rawlings senior was not a minister,
but a prominent merchant of St Columb. He moved to Padstow
about the year 1770, and 'became the means of considerably
increasing the commerce of that place'. It is likely that his
conversion was due to the ministry of Walker, who was always
ready to advise and encourage his friend, especially when he
was disturbed by the apparent failure of the gospel:

> Dear William,
>   You must learn to stand by a little, and leave the head of
> the church to manage his own matters. It is a mournful sight
> indeed when any fall back, and go no more after Jesus. Yet
> this ought not to make us fret and repine, as if all were over.
> A sad view I have before me every Lord's day; a multitude
> blind, and I fear past feeling. I speak, but they hear not;
> nevertheless I cannot but acquiesce in the justice of the
> divine procedure, yea and be sensible that my unfaithful-
> ness deserves much more, and wonder at the salvation God
> is working. What I mean is, you ought not to murmur against
> the ministrations of the Spirit. With love to all,
>   Yours, S.W.[56]

In another letter Walker reminded Rawlings that

> ... Christ's kingdom is not of this world; and therefore we
> must not expect that it will succeed by worldly influences...
> My friend, Christ is able to support his church; he needs no
> human props to help him out; when we look for them we
> distrust him, and when they have been gained, it has been

soon seen, that the strictness of Christian walking has been quickly relaxed. But while we are eagerly looking for such worldly influences, do not we mean ourselves more than Christ; to screen ourselves from the battering of tongues, and to save our interests which seem to be at stake? I believe this is commonly the case; and then I think we must be upon the brink of denying and renouncing Christ. Let us leave him to manage his own matters. All we have to do is to do our duty without warping; making no compliances with our own hearts. This I am sure we shall do if we be truly in the faith.[57]

Walker went on to transcribe a passage from a sermon he had just been writing in the hope that it would minister comfort and courage to his friend.

When Rawlings was in deep distress concerning the serious illness of his wife, Walker wrote to him with the wisdom and compassion of a pastor, urging him to 'cry hard for that faith' that is 'unquestionably sure that, notwithstanding all second clauses, dear –'s disorder is from God, and that every pang and every respite of it is by his immediate direction'. When this point is obtained by grace

... you will see [the affliction] is a *loving correction*, and say, 'See God shows his kindness to me and his displeasure at my sins;' so you will humble your soul. You will see it is a *special warning*, and say, 'Is my interest in Christ clear? How stands my faith? And is it proved by love?' You will see it is a *gracious preservative*, and say, 'My God saw my comforts to be dangerous, and so dashed this bitter potion into my cup.' You will see it is a *needful purgation*, and say, 'I wanted so severe a discipline to refine my graces and mortify my earthly affections.' Affliction cannot be received as it ought, unless we see God's hand in it, for without that, it can neither humble nor purify.[58]

In this letter he added advice on how to deal with the accusations of conscience that arise at such seasons, with 'the uncertainty of the issue and the delay of its coming', and on what to say to his wife if she was restored. 'To be able to say, not only "as you will, but in what manner and at what time you will", is what I earnestly beg the Lord to bestow upon you... You have a special occasion to honour your master, and to show forth the power of his religion to his glory, by an exemplary exercise of the silent graces of meekness, quietness and submission.' He closed his letter with the words, 'O my dear friend, the Lord will make all work for your good. He is the kindest father and the nearest friend.'[59] It was correspondence such as this that endeared Walker to so many.

William Legge, another good friend and supporter of Walker, succeeded his grandfather as second Earl of Dartmouth on 15 December, 1750. Lord Dartmouth, 'a truly good man', as Benjamin Franklin called him, was 'one of the most enlightened and cultured men of his day, and was constantly consulted by persons interested in science, art, literature and social progress, as well as on Church affairs'.[60] In Seymour's *The Life and Times of Selina Countess of Huntingdon* he is spoken of as one who 'loved the Lord Jesus Christ with sincerity and fervour, and was hearty in the support of his cause'.[61] He held positions of power in the government and, whenever the opportunity arose, advocated the Evangelical cause among the nobility and at Court. It was his habit to invite Evangelical clergymen to preach at the chapel in his country home near Cheltenham and then, with the rector's permission, in the parish church. He was a close friend of the Countess of Huntingdon, through whom he was converted in 1756, and owing to his strong attachments to the Methodists, he acquired the nickname 'The Psalm Singer'. He played a significant role in securing preferment for the early Evangelical clergy – he nominated John Newton to the curacy of Olney and sent Henry Venn to Huddersfield, for instance – and, in the words of Luke Tyerman, was their 'principal patron ... of that period'.[62]

He was certainly a help to Walker. In a letter to Adam dated April, 1757, Walker wished that an addition could be made to his yearly income, so that he could employ an 'occasional assistant' and use 'horse exercise' for the re-establishment of his health. He asked Adam, who had previously suggested applying to Lord Dartmouth, to submit to his lordship's consideration

> ... the state of the work of God here, the narrowness of my circumstances, the weight of labours lying on me, and my inability to provide an occasional assistant, my no very good state of health in comparison of what it was, though now much better than a year ago, and want of exercise to improve and re-establish it. [If you do] you will represent my desires, and I am sure I shall not be disappointed if a favour, to which I have not the least pretence, be not granted.[63]

Immediately on Adam's application, Lord Dartmouth afforded generous assistance to Walker, who, with a heart full of gratitude, informed Adam in a letter (12 May, 1757), that he had received fifty pounds, which will 'sufficiently answer the purpose it is designed for', as well as a 'very obliging Christian letter' from Lord Dartmouth. This act of charity Walker kept secret from all but Adam, partly in accordance with the earl's wishes, and partly 'to disappoint any impertinent curiosity we suspect is sometimes used in prying into our letters at the post office'.[64]

In June, 1757, Adam told Walker that Lord Dartmouth had written to him, saying,

> I am truly thankful to you for making Mr [Walker]'s situation known to me. It happens not to be in my power to assist him so largely as I could wish; what I could spare I have sent him, and shall be very ready at another time to supply him further. He, with all who are of the household of faith, have a more especial claim upon me, who have received the good things of this life. God grant they may not turn to my future condemnation.[65]

On an earlier occasion (7 October, 1756), Walker wrote to Adam, who had asked for his advice on how Lord Dartmouth should divide his time, according to his station. Walker stressed that

> ... the duties of worship, his calling and courtesy must divide his time. His main difficulty lies in the latter, to be in such manner courteous, as not to comply. He must have in aid to preserve him, a large stock of zeal and love; and so his temper being right, he will be obliging without betraying his cause...
>
> He must not encourage in any sort, that vain idle way of squandering time so much in fashion, nor join in such things as are the great instruments of God's dishonour and of total forgetfulness of all seriousness, in the person of his, and indeed of almost every rank. Yet he must be courteous, receive his friends cheerfully, and entertain them with a degree of liberality proportioned to his fortune and station. Yet I suppose he must have especial care that his civility do not run him into an abuse of time, and so the neglect of the more important duties, whether of worship or his calling. And in this view, I should be heartily glad if his Lordship were well rid of those fashionable amusements, which are so nicely contrived to kill time, and souls with it. On the whole, it will be safer for the honour of Christ, and for himself, that he lean to the side of denial rather than of compliance and conformity.[66]

It was advice such as this that no doubt endeared Lord Dartmouth to Walker and moved him, not only to support him financially, but to offer him generous hospitality in his last illness, when he did all in his power to make Walker as comfortable as possible; all of which proved the earl to be 'one of those excellent men, who, in a period of wide-spread error and apathy towards real religion, enjoyed the privilege of a knowledge of divine truth, and manifested a sincere love for preachers of the gospel'.[67] It was with such men that Walker was privileged to be acquainted.

Appendix
1

Directing Persons to Christ

On 22 May, 1754, Samuel Walker wrote to Henry Phillips at Gwennap and included in his letter 'two or three hints about directing persons, who enquire what they must do to be saved'. These hints are particularly relevant today when the answer given by many in the church to the question: 'How do I become a Christian' is so vague. In the three 'cases' below, Walker gives the Biblical response to persons under spiritual impressions.

In general, they must be brought to a sense of their *misery*, as being *guilty* and *corrupted*; and of their *helplessness*, as having no *satisfaction* to make, nor *ability* to resist sin. When thus prepared, Christ must be set before them as *able* and *willing* to help them; and they engaged to quit all other hopes, and *trust* to Him; which *faith*, if real, will produce love of God in the heart, &c. The means to be used (not depended on, for they must be well advised that the work is the Spirit's) are keeping from vain conversation, trifling companions, places of evil resort, which would quench the impressions of grace; and to be instant and constant in prayer, reading God's word, religious conversation, and self-examination; which means must be recommended to all.

More particularly, according to circumstances this work must be conducted; and what I know of it may be found in the following cases.

CASE 1
Of a Person Under Slight Impressions

Party. Sir, I would have your advice about my soul; being desirous of knowing the way of salvation.

Minister. I would you took it deeply to heart, and am glad you are thinking about it. Consider, you are living for eternity. You must have your portion in heaven or hell, and death advances. I pray you consider how careless you have hitherto been, living without God; that He has been witness of all, being ever present with you; and that you must give an account of all at the judgement. You are more guilty than you think; try your past ways by God's commandments; and remember the curse that is declared against those who have broken them. I pray you withal to make much of this impression; it is God's call by His Spirit; and will end in your eternal salvation, if you improve it. To which end be instant and constant in prayer, &c. as in the general above.

CASE 2
Impressions Attended with Fear

Party. Sir, the course I have lived hitherto has been utterly wrong; I must change my life, amend and do better; or otherwise I shall perish.

Minister. You are indeed guilty, and have much cause to fear. Nay, if you look well to the enmity you have borne towards God in your heart, through the dominion of corrupt nature, you shall find yourself a sinful wretch indeed; having disobeyed a righteous God, you are condemned. And I must tell you, it is out of your power to help yourself. Your future obedience will not make God satisfaction for the past; not discharge the old debt; and withal, at best, it will be unworthy of God; nor, such as it shall be, can you attain to it by your own power, though you seem to have done it already in your imagination and purpose. Beware of resolutions about amendment. What you want is a sense of your misery and guilt and helplessness; and, as you see, that God should be reconciled to you. Pray, therefore, that you may find yourself utterly lost, and that irrecoverably, for anything you can do to prevent it.

CASE 3

Impressions Attended with Terror

Party. Sir, what shall I do, I am just sinking into hell? Will God have mercy upon such a monster?

Minister. You deserve his wrath indeed; let me tell you, that you have committed all these sins against a most gracious Father. How good was He to make you at all; how good in preserving you; in the deliverances He has given you; in giving His Son for you; and in inviting you to His own bosom in heaven! Nay, but what patience has He exercised towards you, while you were so filthy in His pure eyes! Indeed you deserve His indignation; and I should wish you to weigh God's goodness, and your sins, one against the other, that you may be more sensible hereof; and withal not remain without hope from your own experience, that He is ready to receive you, if you return to Him by Jesus Christ. Are you willing to do so? Go and pray Him to enable you to cast off everything in your conduct that is contrary to His will. Make this immediate sacrifice; and keep your eye constantly upon Christ, assuring yourself that in Him you may be saved. But do not run to idle company for quiet of mind; betake yourself to prayer and the word.[1]

Appendix
2

An Act of Self-Examination at the close of the day, in order to watchfulness, spiritual improvement, and growth in grace

Self-examination was a discipline that Walker not only encouraged his congregation to exercise, but one in which he daily participated in order to live a life worthy of his calling. The following piece is a typical example of Walker's thoroughness in dealing with spiritual issues and of his desire for all to have a closer communion with God. It is useful in this day when the art of self-examination is all but forgotten.

> May the Searcher of hearts enable me to try my ways, that the devices of my spiritual enemies may be made known to me; and that, through the power of Divine grace, I may come nearer to God from the experience of this day's infirmities and failures! And remember, my soul, that you must, at the awful tribunal, render an account of these hours and of what you have done in them. Consider yourself, then, as you would on a dying bed, or at the bar of God's judgement. How would you, at such a time, approve or condemn your conduct this day?
>
> **First,** have I walked this day in a practical sense of the Divine presence? Have I had through the day a solemn impression on my mind that I have been under the eye of the Almighty, Wise, Good, and Holy God, considering Him as reconciled to penitent sinners through the Redeemer?

Secondly, have I used all means this day of being engaged in this spiritual communion; and what have I done, which might tend thereto? Particularly, have I diligently and gladly improved every opportunity of prayer in private and public, of godly conversation, of meditation, reading, and the like? Did I look up to the throne of Divine grace for a blessing on such exercises; or did I formally rest in the use of them, as so much good done?

Thirdly, have I lost or weakened this spiritual communion; and what have I done which might tend thereto? Did I indulge a slothful frame by lying too late in bed; by hurrying over my morning's devotions; or by neglect of reflecting afterwards on what I had been doing? By not calling back my thoughts to God in frequent ejaculations through the day? By too much lightness, or too long a continuance in unprofitable conversation, by laziness in my worldly calling, and squandering my precious time? Has it been occasioned by any company or recreations I have been in? Have anger, impatience, or evil thoughts been unresisted and indulged, delighted in, and suffered to run on to some length in my mind? Have these, or such like things, distracted my frame of mind, and set me at a distance from God?

Fourthly, has communion with God led me to do whatever good I have done, with a view to God's glory? or, has it not been food for pride and vain glory?

Fifthly, have I watched my corruptions, especially that which most easily besets me? Have I kept clear of yesterday's failings? And, as much as possible, of the temptations which led to them?

Sixthly, have I had compassion towards such as are sinful and miserable? Have I in my own judgement preferred to myself, and also gladly applauded the more striking and shining behaviour of others? And have I used every opportunity of doing good, both to the souls and bodies of my neighbours?

Seventhly, have I made any undue compliances through fear or shame; been afraid to speak what my conscience told me I ought to have said, and hereby neglected opportunities of doing good to souls?

Eighthly, have I been thankful for ordinary blessings, as well as extraordinary providences?

Ninthly, have I walked this day like a penitent sinner, purchased by the blood of Christ, and therefore working out my salvation with fear and trembling; yet frequently delighting myself with the thoughts of God's gracious purposes towards me in Jesus Christ, and expecting the arrival of death and eternity?

Have I made this examination of myself solemnly, as I would on my death bed? And am I, after all, so ashamed of my good works, that even with blushing I look back on the best part of this review? And, if it please God that I never more rise again from my bed, do I this evening, humbly and meekly submitting to His will, commit my spirit into the hands of Christ, to be presented before the throne of His Father and my Father, to be pardoned only for His merits, and completely sanctified by His grace? Or, if it be His blessed will that I see again the light of another day, am I fully desirous, and humbly determined, through Divine grace, to go on in all the ways of holiness?[2]

Appendix
3

Samuel Walker's Published Works

Walker's works reached a wide public, Charles Simeon and William Wilberforce both testifying to their importance, and the many subscribers included those who were of a different theological persuasion. The list below is chronological.

A Sermon on 1 Samuel 20:3, preached at Truro at the funeral of a young man who drowned while bathing on Sunday 3 June, 1753. It is also printed in the 1812 edition of *Practical Christianity*, which was exhibited among the specimens of the local press at the Caxton Exhibition in 1877.

The Christian, Being a Course of [Eleven] Practical Sermons, London, 1755. It is addressed 'To the inhabitants of Truro' and signed 'Samuel Walker, Truro, May 2, 1755'. It passed through a second and third edition in 1756 and 1759. In 1788 a new and corrected edition appeared, with a recommendatory preface by Thomas Adam. An 1825 edition (Glasgow) has an introductory essay by Charles Simeon, and forms part of a series of works called *Select Christian Authors*. *The Christian* reached its twelfth edition in 1879.

The Christian's Mirror or the Features of the Christian Delineated as they are to be seen in his Daily Life and Conversation, 1788. This is an extract from *The Christian*.

Prepare to Meet thy God, two sermons on Amos 4:12 preached at Truro on a day appointed by authority for a general fast, Friday 6 February, 1756. London, 1756.

A Letter from a Clergyman Concerning the First Question in the Office for the Ordaining of Deacons, 1758.

Regulations and Helps Proposed for Promoting Religious Conversation among Christians, 175_.

A Discourse on a Chief Point of Christianity or the Necessity of our being Acquainted with our Fallen State, 1759. It is in three parts.

A Familiar Catechism, or the Operations of the Holy Spirit Illustrated and Proved, Being a Summary of Practical Christianity, 1759.

A Short Instruction and Examination for the Lord's Supper, 175_. Revised and enlarged by Walker in his last illness. It is also found in the 1812 edition of *Practical Christianity*.

A Treatise on Conviction of Sin, 175_.

A Familiar Introduction to the Knowledge of Ourselves, 1762. Chiefly composed by Walker in his last illness. It is in two parts.

A Tract on Helps to Self-Examination.

Fifty-Two Sermons on the Baptismal Covenant, the Creed, the Ten Commandments, and Other Important Subjects of Practical Religion, Being one for each Sunday in the Year, to which is prefixed a preface, containing a full and authentic account of the author's life and ministry by James Stillingfleet (2 vols),

London, 1763. Stillingfleet signed his preface 'Oxford, June 15, 1763'. It was Walker's design, had God spared him, to go through the whole of the Church Catechism in a set of practical and expository lectures and then to publish them. The sermons were corrected and revised by Rev Samuel Burder, of Clare Hall, Cambridge, in 1810 (London), and republished as *Lectures on the Church Catechism*. A new edition, with four additional sermons on the creed by Rev John Lawson and a brief introductory memoir by Edward Bickersteth, was printed in 1836.

Practical Christianity, Illustrated in Nine Tracts on Various Subjects, London, 1765.

Tracts, Sermons, &c... Selected from Different Authors, Edinburgh, 1785. It contains *Three Tracts* by Samuel Walker: The necessity of being acquainted with our fallen state; a familiar introduction to the knowledge of ourselves; helps to self-examination.

Nine Sermons on the Covenant of Grace, to which are added three letters to a candidate for ordination, and a letter on the first question in the office for the ordination of deacons, with a brief memoir of the author, Hull, 1824. The *Nine Sermons* originally appeared in *Theological Miscellany*, 1787.

Ten Sermons Entitled: The Refiner or God's Method of Purifying his People, with a recommendatory preface by Rev Barker, vicar of St Mary's, Kingston upon Hull, Hull, 1790. This is the same work as *Christ the Purifier*, but the sermons are in a different order. The sermons originally appeared in *Theological Miscellany*, 1789.

Christ the Purifier, ten discourses upon the sanctification of believers through the love and grace of Jesus Christ, with a preface by Ambrose Serle, London, 1794.

The Christian Armour, ten sermons on Ephesians 6:11, published from the author's remains, with a preface by Edwin Sidney, London, 1841. An 1878 edition (Chichester), republished by T. Greene has a brief memoir of the author.

Distrust Removed, a sermon on Romans 5:7,8, 1869.

Abbreviations and Bibliography

Abbreviations

ES   Edwin Sidney, *The Life and Ministry of Samuel Walker* (London, R. B. Seeley and W. Burnside, 1838).

GCBD G. C. B. Davies, *The Early Cornish Evangelicals 1735-60* (London, SPCK, 1951).

JS   Samuel Walker, *Fifty-Two Sermons on the Baptismal Covenant, the Creed, the Ten Commandments*, 2 vols (London, J. & W. Oliver, 1763).

Primary Sources

Davies, G. C. B., *The Early Cornish Evangelicals 1735-60*. London, SPCK, 1951.

Sidney, Edwin, *The Life and Ministry of Samuel Walker*. London, R. B. Seeley and W. Burnside, 1838.

Walker, Samuel, *Fifty-Two Sermons on the Baptismal Covenant, the Creed, the Ten Commandments* (2 vols). London, J. & W. Oliver, 1763.

Periodicals

Christian Guardian, London, 1804.

Christian Observer (vol.1), Boston, William Wells & T. B. Wail & Co., 1802.

Christian Observer, London, 1877. Hole, *Biographical Sketches*.

Church Quarterly Review, April-June, 1946. Miles H. Brown, *The Rise of Methodism in Cornwall*.

Church Quarterly Review, Oct-Dec, 1947. G. C. B. Davies, *Truro Clerical Club 1750-60*.

Church of England Magazine (vol.1), London, L. & G. Seeley, 1836.

Cornish Banner, Truro, George Clyma, 1846.

Evangelical Magazine, London, T. Williams, 1800, 1803, 1810 & 1813.

Evangelical Magazine of Wales, Bridgend, 1961. G. C. B. Davies, *Samuel Walker of Truro*.

Evangelical Times, Nov, 1994. Leslie Porter, *Samuel Walker of Truro*.

Evangelical Times, Dec, 1994. George M. Ella, *The Poor Man's Preacher*.

Religious Tract Society, No.984, London. *Rev Samuel Walker of Truro*.

West Briton, July, 1944.

Zion's Trumpet, A Theological Miscellany, London, 1798, 1799 & 1801.

Secondary Sources

Abbey, Charles J. & Overton, John H., *The English Church in the Eighteenth Century*. London, Longmans, Green and Co., 1902.

Balleine, G. R., *A History of the Evangelical Party in the Church of England*. London, Longmans, Green and Co., 1909.

Bennett, James, *The Star of the West*. London, Hamilton, 1813.

Bennett, Richard, *Howell Harris and the Dawn of Revival*. Bridgend, Evangelical Press of Wales, 1987.

Beynon, Tom, *Howell Harris, Reformer and Soldier 1714-1773*. Caernarvon, The Calvinistic Methodist Bookroom, 1958.

Boase, George Clement & Courtney, William Prideaux, *Bibliotheca Cornubiensis*. London, Longmans, Green, Reader & Dyer, 1878.

Boggis, R. J. E., *A History of the Diocese of Exeter*. Exeter, William Pollard & Co. Ltd, 1922.

Bogue, David, & Bennett, James, *History of Dissenters, From the Revolution in 1688 to the Year 1808* (4 vols). London, Printed for the Authors, 1808-12.

Bonar, Andrew R. (editor), *The Last Days of Eminent Christians*. London, Thomas Nelson, 1849.

Bourne, F. W., *Billy Bray: Converted Drunkard*. Stoke-on-Trent, Harvey Christian Publishers, n.d.

Brown, Abner William, *Recollections of the Conversation Parties of the Rev Charles Simeon*. London, Hamilton, Adams & Co., 1863.

Brown, H. Miles, *A Cornish Incumbency 1741-1776*. Published privately, 1945.

Brown, H. Miles, *The Church in Cornwall*. Truro, Oscar Blackford, 1964.

Brown, H. Miles, *Methodism and the Church of England in Cornwall 1738-1838*. Torpoint (Thesis, London University), 1946.

Brown-Lawson, Albert, *John Wesley and the Anglican Evangelicals of the Eighteenth Century*. Edinburgh, Pentland Press, n.d.

Bull, Josiah, *But Now I See: The Life of John Newton*. Edinburgh, Banner of Truth Trust, 1998.

Bullock, Frederick William Bagshawe, *A History of the Parish Church of St Mary, Truro, Cornwall*. Truro, A. W. Jordan, 1948.

Bullock, Frederick William Bagshawe, *Voluntary Religious Societies 1520-1799*. St Leonards on Sea, Budd & Gillatt, 1963.

Cadogan, William Bromley, *The Life of the Rev William Romaine*. London, T. Bensley, 1796.

Carter, C. Sydney, *The English Church in the Eighteenth Century*. London, Longmans, Green and Co., 1910.

Chope, Richard Pearse (editor), *Early Tours in Devon and Cornwall*. Exeter, J. G. Commin, 1918.

Clinnick, A. A., *Notable Events in the History of Truro*. Truro, A. W. Jordan, 1922.

Cook, Faith, *William Grimshaw of Haworth*. Edinburgh, Banner of Truth Trust, 1997.

Coxon, Francis, *Christian Worthies* (vol.2). Ossett, Zoar Publications, n.d.

Cragg, G. R., *The Church in the Age of Reason (1648-1789)*. Harmondsworth, Penguin Books, 1960.

Dallimore, Arnold, *A Heart Set Free: The Life of Charles Wesley*. Darlington, Evangelical Press, 1991.

Dallimore, Arnold, *George Whitefield* (2 vols). Edinburgh, Banner of Truth Trust, 1989.

Davies, Horton, *Worship and Theology in England from Watts and Wesley to Maurice 1690-1850*. London, Oxford University Press, 1961.

Davies, Rupert. George, A. Raymond. Rupp, Gordon (general editors), *A History of the Methodist Church in Great Britain* (4 vols). London, Epworth Press, 1965 & 1978.

Deacon, Malcolm, *Philip Doddridge of Northampton*. Northampton, Northamptonshire Libraries, 1980.

Defoe, Daniel, *Tour Through the Whole Island of Great Britain*. Webb & Bower, 1989.

Dictionary of National Biography (22 vols). London, Oxford University Press, 1960.

Doddridge, Philip, *The Life of Col. James Gardiner*. Halifax, William Milner, 1844.

Doughty, W. L., *John Wesley: His Conferences and his Preachers*. London, Epworth Press, 1944.

Edwards, Jonathan, *Jonathan Edwards on Revival*. Edinburgh, Banner of Truth Trust, 1984.

Edwards, Jonathan, *Sinners in the Hands of an Angry God*. Phillipsburg, P&R Publishing, 1992.

Ella, George M., *James Hervey, Preacher of Righteousness*. Eggleston, Go Publications, 1997.

Ella, George M., *William Cowper: Poet of Paradise*. Darlington, Evangelical Press, 1993.

Elliot-Binns, L. E., *The Early Evangelicals: A Religious and Social Study*. Greenwich, The Seabury Press, 1955.

Evans, Eifion, *Daniel Rowland*. Edinburgh, Banner of Truth Trust, 1985.

Evans, Eifion, *Fire in the Thatch*. Bridgend, Evangelical Press of Wales, 1996.

Fawcett, Arthur, *The Cambuslang Revival*. Edinburgh, Banner of Truth Trust, 1996.

Friend (by a), *Memoirs of the Life of the Rev Thomas Wills*. London, T. Williams, 1804.

Gill, Frederick C., *Charles Wesley, the First Methodist*. London, Lutterworth Press, 1964.

Gillies, John, *Historical Collections Relating to Remarkable Periods of the Success of the Gospel*. Edinburgh, Banner of Truth Trust, 1981.

Gladstone, J. P., *George Whitefield: Supreme Among Preachers*. Belfast, Ambassador, 1998.

Halliday, F. E., *A History of Cornwall*. London, Gerald Duckworth & Co., 1959.

Hanbury, Benjamin, *Extracts from the Diary, Meditations and Letters of Joseph Williams*. London, C. Taylor, 1815.

Haweis, Thomas, *An Impartial ... History of the Rise, Declension and Revival of the Church of Christ* (3 vols). London, 1800.

Hockin, Frederick, *John Wesley and Modern Methodism*. London, Rivingtons, 1887.

Horne, C. Silvester, *A Popular History of the Free Churches*. London, James Clarke & Co., 1903.

Hughes, Hugh J., *Life of Howell Harris*. Stoke-on-Trent, Tentmaker, 1996.

Hylson-Smith, Kenneth, *Evangelicals in the Church of England 1734-1984*. Edinburgh, T&T Clark, 1989.

Isaac, Peter, *A History of Evangelical Christianity in Cornwall*. Published privately, 2000.

Jackson, Thomas, *The Life of Charles Wesley* (2 vols). London, John Mason, 1841.

Jay, William, *Autobiography*. Edinburgh, Banner of Truth Trust, 1974.

Jenkin, A. K. Hamilton, *Cornwall and its People*. Newton Abbot, David & Charles, 1970.

Jenkin, A. K. Hamilton, *The Story of Cornwall*. London, Thomas Nelson and Sons, 1935.

Knight, Helen C., *Lady Huntingdon & her Friends*. Grand Rapids, Baker Book House, 1979.

Lach-Szyrma, W. S., *A Church History of Cornwall and of the Diocese of Truro*. London, Elliot Stock, n.d.

Lawson, A. B., *John Wesley and the Christian Ministry*. London, SPCK, 1963.

Lewis, Donald M. (editor), *The Blackwell Dictionary of Evangelical Biography 1730-1860* (2 vols). Blackwell Reference, n.d.

Lundie, Mary, *History of Revivals of Religion in the British Isles, Especially in Scotland*. Edinburgh, William Oliphant & Son, 1836.

Manning-Sanders, Ruth, *The West of England*. London, B. T. Batsford Ltd, 1949.

Mee, Arthur (editor), *The King's England: Cornwall*. London, Hodder and Stoughton, 1951.

Middleton, Erasmus, *Evangelical Biography* (4 vols). London, W. Baynes, 1816.

Murray, Iain H., *Jonathan Edwards*. Edinburgh, Banner of Truth Trust, 1988.

New, Alfred Henry, *The Coronet and the Cross*. London, Partridge & Co., 1857.

Nuttall, Geoffrey F., *Howel Harris 1714-1773: The Last Enthusiast*. Cardiff, University of Wales Press, 1965.

Nuttall, Geoffrey F., *The Correspondence of Philip Doddridge 1702-1751*. London, Her Majesty's Stationery Office, 1979.

Overton, John Henry, *The Evangelical Revival in the Eighteenth Century*. London, Longmans, Green & Co., 1886.

Overton, John H. & Relton, Frederic, *A History of the English Church 1714-1800*. London, Macmillan and Co., 1906.

Pearce, John, *The Wesleys in Cornwall*. Truro, D. Bradford Barton, 1964.

Penrose, John, *Of Christian Sincerity*. Oxford, 1829.

Pibworth, Nigel R., *The Gospel Pedlar*. Welwyn, Evangelical Press, 1987.

Plummer, Alfred, *The Church of England in the Eighteenth Century*. London, Methuen & Co., 1910.

Polwhele, R., *Biographical Sketches in Cornwall* (3 vols). Truro, Nichols & Son, Longman, Simpkin & Marshall & Whittaker & Co., 1831.

Polwhele, R., *Reminiscences in Prose and Verse* (3 vols). London, J. B. Nichols & Son, 1836.

Probert, John C. C., *The Sociology of Cornish Methodism to the Present Day*. Cornish Methodist Historical Association Occasional Publication, 1971.

Roberts, Richard Owen, *Whitefield in Print*. Wheaton, Richard Owen Roberts, 1988.

Rowe, John, *Cornwall in the Age of the Industrial Revolution*. St Austell, Cornish Hillside Publications, 1993.

Ryle, J. C., *Christian Leaders of the 18th Century*. Edinburgh, Banner of Truth Trust, 1978.

Sargent, John, *The Life of Henry Martyn*. Edinburgh, Banner of Truth Trust, 1985.

Selley, W. T., *England in the Eighteenth Century*. London, A & C Black Ltd, 1934.

Seymour, A. C. H., *The Life and Times of Selina Countess of Huntingdon* (2 vols). Stoke-on-Trent, Tentmaker, 2000.

Shaw, Thomas, *A History of Cornish Methodism*. Truro, D. Bradford Barton, 1967.

Simon, John S., *John Wesley and the Advance of Methodism*. London, Epworth Press, 1925.

Simon, John S., *John Wesley and the Methodist Societies*. London, Epworth Press, 1937.

Simon, John S., *John Wesley the Master Builder*. London, Epworth Press, 1927.

Simon, John S., *The Revival of Religion in England in the Eighteenth Century*. London, Charles H. Kelly, n.d.

Smith, Alan, *The Established Church and Popular Religion 1750-1850*. London, Longman, 1971.

Smith, E., *Life Review'd*. Exeter, B. Thorn, 1780.

Smyth, Charles Hugh Egerton, *Simeon and Church Order*. Cambridge, University Press, 1940.

Southey, Robert, *The Life of John Wesley* (abridged & edited by Arthur Reynolds). London, Hutchinson & Co., 1820.

Stevens, Abel, *The History of the Religious Movement of the Eighteenth Century Called Methodism* (2 vols). London, Wesleyan Conference Office, 1878.

Tregellas, Walter H., *Cornish Worthies* (2 vols). London, Elliot Stock, 1884.

Tyerman, Luke, *The Life of George Whitefield* (2 vols). London, Hodder & Stoughton, 1877.

Tyerman, Luke, *The Life and Times of John Wesley* (3 vols). London, Hodder and Stoughton, 1890.

Tyerman, Luke, *The Oxford Methodists*. London, Hodder & Stoughton, 1873.

Venn, John, *The Life and Letters of Henry Venn*. Edinburgh, Banner of Truth Trust, 1993.

Walker, Samuel, *The Christian*. Glasgow, Chalmers & Collins, 1825.

Walker, Samuel, *Christ the Purifier*. London, J. Mathews, 1794.

Walker, Samuel, *A Familiar Catechism: Or the Operations of the Holy Spirit*. London, J. Oliver, 1759.

Walker, Samuel, *Fifty-Two Lectures on the Church Catechism*. London, Hamilton, Adams & Co., 1836.

Walker, Samuel, *A Letter from a Clergyman Concerning the First Question in the Office for the Ordaining of Deacons*. London, 1758.

Watts, Michael R., *The Dissenters*. Oxford, Clarendon Press, 1999.

Wearmouth, Robert F., *Methodism and the Common People of the Eighteenth Century*. London, Epworth Press, 1945.

Webber, F. R., *A History of Preaching in Britain and America*. Milwaukee, Northwestern Publishing House, 1952.

Wesley, John, *The Journal of* (8 vols). London, Epworth Press, 1938.

Wesley, John, *The Letters of* (8 vols). London, Epworth Press, 1931.

Wesley, John, *The Works of* (14 vols). London, Wesleyan Methodist Bookroom, n.d.

Westoby, A. (editor), *An Exposition of the Four Gospels by the Rev Thomas Adam*. London, J. Hatchard & Son, 1837.

Whitefield, George, *Journals*. Edinburgh, Banner of Truth Trust, 1985.

Whiteley, J. H., *Wesley's England*. London, Epworth Press, 1945.

Wills, Thomas, *The Spiritual Register* (3 vols). London, 1795.

Wood, A. Skevington, *The Burning Heart: John Wesley Evangelist*. Minneapolis, Bethany House, 1978.

Wood, A. Skevington, *The Inextinguishable Blaze*. Exeter, Paternoster Press, 1967.

Wood, A. Skevington, *Thomas Haweis 1734-1820*. London, SPCK, 1957.

Notes

Preface
1. John Rowe's *Cornwall in the Age of the Industrial Revolution* was originally published in 1953. The second edition was published in 1993 and includes two chapters on 'religious and subsequent change', which deal with the impact of John Wesley on the Cornish scene. Both chapters were written for the first edition but omitted for reasons of space.
2. Dr James Whetter's book *Cornish People in the Eighteenth Century* was privately published in November 2000. It contains eleven essays on well-known Cornishmen.
3. J. C. Ryle, *Christian Leaders of the 18th Century* (Edinburgh, Banner of Truth Trust, 1978), p.327.
4. John Henry Overton, *The Evangelical Revival in the Eighteenth Century* (London, Longmans, Green & Co., 1886), pp.82-83.
5. Luke Tyerman, *The Life and Times of John Wesley*, 3 vols (London, Hodder and Stoughton, 1890), vol.2, p.252.
6. Rupert Davies, A. Raymond George, Gordon Rupp (general editors), *A History of the Methodist Church in Great Britain*, 4 vols (London, Epworth Press, 1965-1988), vol.1, pp.xxvii-xxviii.
7. R. J. E. Boggis, *A History of the Diocese of Exeter* (Exeter, William Pollard & Co. Ltd, 1922), p.455.
8. Arnold Dallimore, *George Whitefield*, 2 vols (Edinburgh, Banner of Truth Trust, 1989), vol.2, p.314.

Chapter 1 – 'A County of Lawless Barbarians'?
1. A. K. Hamilton Jenkin, *The Story of Cornwall* (London, Thomas Nelson and Sons, 1935), p.157.
2. A. C. H. Seymour, *The Life and Times of Selina Countess of Huntingdon*, 2 vols (Stoke-on-Trent, Tentmaker, 2000), vol.2, pp.618-619.
3. Ibid., vol.1, p.293.
4. Ibid., vol.2, p.464.
5. A. K. Hamilton Jenkin, *Cornwall and its People* (Newton Abbot, David and Charles, 1970), p.19.

6. J. H. Whiteley, *Wesley's England* (London, Epworth Press, 1945), p.196.

7. Ibid.

8. Hamilton Jenkin, *Cornwall and its People*, p.9.

9. Ibid., p.10.

10. John Rowe, *Cornwall in the Age of the Industrial Revolution* (St Austell, Cornish Hillside Publications, 1993), p.263.

11. Hamilton Jenkin, *Cornwall and its People*, p.14.

12. Ibid., p.12.

13. F. E. Halliday, *A History of Cornwall* (London, Gerald Duckworth & Co., 1959), p.263.

14. Rowe, *Cornwall in the Age of the Industrial Revolution*, p.276.

15. Hamilton Jenkin, *Cornwall and its People*, p.15.

16. Tyerman, *John Wesley*, vol.2, p.618.

17. Hamilton Jenkin, *Cornwall and its People*, p.13.

18. Ibid., p.10.

19. Ibid., p.4.

20. Rowe, *Cornwall in the Age of the Industrial Revolution*, p.34.

21. Ruth Manning-Sanders, *The West of England* (London, B. T. Batsford Ltd, 1949), p.15.

22. Rowe, *Cornwall in the Age of the Industrial Revolution*, p.35.

23. Halliday, *A History of Cornwall*, p.262.

24. Ibid., pp.262-263.

25. Rowe, *Cornwall in the Age of the Industrial Revolution*, p.36, n.2.

26. Hamilton Jenkin, *Cornwall and its People*, p.158.

27. The wages of miners were pitifully small, often close to starvation level. 'By 1730 a good miner was making about 24s a month, but even fifty years later that seems to have been the average reward of a St Just miner... the average in the middle of the century was probably little more than 30s.' Halliday, *A History of Cornwall*, p.259.

28. Ibid., p.260.

29. Ibid., p.261.

30. Rowe, *Cornwall in the Age of the Industrial Revolution*, p.67.10, n.10.

31. 'The bulldog of the present day derives its name from this sport. Its nose being well set back between the eyes allowed the dog to breathe when its teeth were fastened into the flesh of the bull.' Hamilton Jenkin, *The Story of Cornwall*, p.58.

32. John Pearce, *The Wesleys in Cornwall* (Truro, D. Bradford Barton, 1964), p.49, n.35.

33. Rowe, *Cornwall in the Age of the Industrial Revolution*, p.32.

34. Daniel Defoe, *Tour Through the Whole Island of Great Britain* (Exeter, Webb & Bower, 1989), pp.85-86.

35. Manning-Sanders, *The West of England*, p.15.

36. Ibid., p.40.
37. Hamilton Jenkin, *Cornwall and its People*, p.273.
38. Manning-Sanders, *The West of England*, pp.41-42.
39. G. R. Balleine, *A History of the Evangelical Party in the Church of England* (London, Longmans, Green and Co., 1909), p.96.

Chapter 2 – The Church in Eighteenth Century Cornwall

1. L. E. Elliot-Binns, *The Early Evangelicals: A Religious and Social Study* (Greenwich, The Seabury Press, 1955), pp.351-352.
2. W. S. Lach-Szyrma, *A Church History of Cornwall and of the Diocese of Truro* (London, Elliot Stock, n.d.), p.105.
3. H. Miles Brown, *Methodism and the Church of England in Cornwall 1738-1838* (Torpoint, London University Thesis, 1946), p.29.
4. Hamilton Jenkin, *Cornwall and its People*, p.167.
5. John S. Simon, *The Revival of Religion in England in the Eighteenth Century* (London, Charles H. Kelly, n.d.), p.264.
6. Rowe, *Cornwall in the Age of the Industrial Revolution*, p.261.21.
7. Brown, *Methodism and the Church of England in Cornwall*, p.44.
8. Hamilton Jenkin, *The Story of Cornwall*, p.57.
9. John Gillies, *Historical Collections Relating to Remarkable Periods of the Success of the Gospel* (Edinburgh, Banner of Truth Trust, 1981), p.511.
10. Geoffrey F. Nuttall, *Howel Harris 1714-1773: The Last Enthusiast* (Cardiff, University of Wales Press, 1965), p.74.
11. Elliot-Binns, *The Early Evangelicals*, p.343.
12. Tyerman, *John Wesley*, vol.1, p.416.
13. Hamilton Jenkin, *The Story of Cornwall*, p.57.
14. John S. Simon, *John Wesley and the Methodist Societies* (London, Epworth Press, 1937), p.136.
15. Rowe, *Cornwall in the Age of the Industrial Revolution*, p.31.
16. H. Miles Brown, *The Church in Cornwall* (Truro, Oscar Blackford, 1964), pp.65-66.
17. Ibid., p.67.
    There were 205 parishes in Cornwall in 1744.
18. GCBD, p.24.
19. Brown, *Methodism and the Church of England in Cornwall*, p.34.
    The bishops of Exeter were: Nicholas Claggett (1742-1746), George Lavington (1747-1762), Frederick Keppel (1762-1777), John Ross (1778-1792).
20. GCBD, pp.23-24.
21. Other examples are: 'John Penneck, chancellor of Exeter Cathedral (1706-1724), vicar of St Hilary (1699-1724), and rector of St Ewe

(1700-1724). Jonathan Dagge held the livings of Fowey and St Endellion together between the years 1709-1730; and Charles Peters ... held the benefice of Bratton Clovelly in Devonshire in addition to the rectory of St Mabyn in Cornwall.' Brown, *Methodism and the Church of England in Cornwall*, p.51.

22. Rowe, *Cornwall in the Age of the Industrial Revolution*, p.67.5.
23. Ibid., pp.67.6-67.7.
24. GCBD, p.24.
25. Rowe, *Cornwall in the Age of the Industrial Revolution*, p.67.8.
26. Frederick Hockin, *John Wesley and Modern Methodism* (London, Rivingtons, 1887), pp.167-169.
27. Elliot-Binns, *The Early Evangelicals*, p.155.
   At this time the practice of catechizing children in preparation for the occasionally administered rite of confirmation was mostly confined to Lent and the summer months, and was often performed in a slovenly and half-hearted manner. Eventually Sunday Schools replaced catechizing.
28. GCBD, pp.22-23.
29. Pearce, *The Wesleys in Cornwall*, p.23.
30. Rowe, *Cornwall in the Age of the Industrial Revolution*, p.67.40.
31. Defoe, *Tour Through ... Great Britain*, p.81.
32. GCBD, p.25.
33. Ibid., p.26.
34. Brown, *The Church in Cornwall*, p.86.
35. A. Skevington Wood, *The Inextinguishable Blaze* (Exeter, Paternoster Press, 1967), p.141.
36. Seymour, *Selina Countess of Huntingdon*, vol.1, p.181.
37. George M. Ella, *James Hervey, Preacher of Righteousness* (Eggleston, Go Publications, 1997), p.65.
38. Brown, *Methodism and the Church of England in Cornwall*, p.264.
39. Seymour, *Selina Countess of Huntingdon*, vol.1, p.180.
40. Brown, *Methodism and the Church of England in Cornwall*, p.288.
   Whitefield visited Bideford in 1743 and stayed there for two weeks, 'preaching regularly in the neighbourhood. After the services at St Gennys, Whitefield and Thomson always found many weeping, convicted sinners who could not go home until they found peace with God. Thomson went from seat to seat to counsel the penitent and lead them to the Saviour.' Ella, *James Hervey*, p.66.
41. Nuttall, *Howel Harris*, p.31.
42. Seymour, *Selina Countess of Huntingdon*, vol.1, p.182n.
43. Ella, *James Hervey*, pp.65-66.
44. GCBD, pp.37-38.

45. Tyerman, *John Wesley*, vol.1, p.458.
46. Ella, *James Hervey*, p.66.
47. Balleine, *A History of the Evangelical Party*, p.97.

Chapter 3 – Walker's Early Years
 1. ES, p.1.
 2. Iain H. Murray, *Jonathan Edwards* (Edinburgh, Banner of Truth Trust, 1988), p.xv.
 3. Dallimore, *George Whitefield*, vol. 2, inside flap.
 4. Arnold A. Dallimore, *A Heart Set Free: The Life of Charles Wesley* (Darlington, Evangelical Press, 1991), p.101.
 5. Helen C. Knight, *Lady Huntingdon and her Friends* (Grand Rapids, Baker Book House, 1979), p.6.
 6. Ryle, *Christian Leaders*, p.179.
 7. Nigel R. Pibworth, *The Gospel Peddlar* (Welwyn, Evangelical Press, 1987), p.4.
 8. Ryle, *Christian Leaders*, pp.386-387.
 9. Ibid, p.424.
10. William Jay, *Autobiography* (Edinburgh, Banner of Truth Trust, 1974), p.285.
11. Ella, *James Hervey*, p.9.
12. *Dictionary of National Biography*, 22 vols (London, Oxford University Press, 1960), vol.12, p.733.
13. George M. Ella, *William Cowper: Poet of Paradise* (Darlington, Evangelical Press, 1993), p.228.
14. Richard Bennett, *Howell Harris and the Dawn of the Revival* (Bridgend, Evangelical Press of Wales, 1987), p.9.
15. Hugh J. Hughes, *Life of Howell Harris* (Stoke-on-Trent, Tentmaker, 1996), p.ix.
16. Eifion Evans, *Daniel Rowland* (Edinburgh, Banner of Truth Trust, 1985), pp.1,2.
17. Nuttall, *Howel Harris*, p.29.
18. John Sargent, *The Life of Henry Martyn* (Edinburgh, Banner of Truth Trust, 1985), p.407.
19. F. W. Bourne, *Billy Bray: Converted Drunkard* (Stoke-on-Trent, Harvey Christian Publishers, n.d.), p.9.
20. Wood, *The Inextinguishable Blaze*, p138.
21. Elliot-Binns, *The Early Evangelicals*, p.169.
22. GCBD, p.53.
23. Ryle, *Christian Leaders*, p.308.
24. Ibid., p.327.
25. Ibid., p.324.

26. Abner William Brown, *Recollections of the Conversation Parties of the Rev Charles Simeon* (London, Hamilton, Adams & Co., 1863), p.320.

27. JS, p.vii.

28. James Bennett, *The Star of the West* (London, Hamilton, 1813), p.vii.

29. Thomas Wills, *The Spiritual Register*, 3 vols (London, 1795), vol.3, p.37.

30. *Evangelical Magazine of Wales* (Bridgend, 1961), G. C. B. Davies, *Samuel Walker of Truro*, p.25.

31. *Dictionary of National Biography*, vol.8, p.963.

32. Ella, *James Hervey*, pp.102-103.

33. George Whitefield, *Journals* (Edinburgh, Banner of Truth Trust, 1985), p.287.

34. R. Polwhele, *Biographical Sketches in Cornwall*, 3 vols (Truro, Nichols & Son, Longman, Simpkin & Marshall & Whittaker & Co., 1831), vol.1, p.78n.

35. *Dictionary of National Biography*, vol.20, p.530.

36. ES, p.424.

37. Ibid., pp.2-3.

38. *Zion's Trumpet: A Theological Miscellany* (London, 1798), pp.241-242.

39. Ibid., p.242.

40. ES, p.558.

41. Ibid., p.311.

42. JS, pp.xxiii-xxiv.

43. Samuel Walker, *A Letter from a Clergyman Concerning the First Question in the Office for the Ordaining of Deacons* (London, 1758), pp.5-8.

44. GCBD, p.56.

45. Walker's successor at Lanlivery was Thomas Hurrell, who was instituted on 23 September, 1746.

Chapter 4 – A Gradual but Remarkable Change

1. *Jonathan Edwards on Revival* (Edinburgh, Banner of Truth Trust, 1984), pp.80-81.

2. Richard Pearse Chope (editor), *Early Tours in Devon and Cornwall* (Exeter, J. G. Commin, 1918), p.191.

3. Frederick William Bagshawe Bullock, *A History of the Parish of St Mary, Truro, Cornwall* (Truro, A. W. Jordan, 1948), pp.65-66.

4. ES, p.6.

5. JS, p.xxv.

6. ES, p.6.

7. Wills, *The Spiritual Register*, vol.3, p.9.

8. ES, p.324.

9. *Christian Observer* (London, 1877), Hole, *Biographical Sketches*, p.158.

10. JS, p.xix.

There is a story connected with this period of Walker's experience, the authenticity of which is doubtful. 'The first intimation of the change [in Walker] is said to have been given from a window which looked into a court, now the entrance to Bethesda Chapel. One of his intimate friends entered this court, threw something at the window of his study, and said to him, "Squire – begs his compliments to you, and would be glad of your company to supper tonight on a roasted pig, to celebrate the erection of a set of bells in Kenwyn Church."

'He replied, "Give my compliments to the Squire, and say that I am better employed."

'The party met, the message was delivered, and wonder and surprise filled the circle and gave much room to conjecture. But the circumstance was soon explained in the new strain of his ministry, and the altered character of his life.' *The Cornish Banner* (Truro, George Clyma, 1846), p.84.

Commenting on this incident, Polwhele remarked, 'Walker, a member of the Ringing Club at Kenwyn, was too urbane a man to treat them with incivility. He was too well-bred to break off thus abruptly.' R. Polwhele, *Reminiscences in Prose and Verse*, 3 vols (London, J. B. Nichols & Son, 1836), vol.2, p.94.

This story is omitted from the second edition of Sidney's biography of Walker.

11. Bullock, *A History of the Parish Church of St Mary*, p.66.

12. A. Skevington Wood, *Thomas Haweis 1734-1820* (London, SPCK, 1957), pp.28-29.

13. By a Friend, *Memoirs of the Life of the Rev Thomas Wills* (London, T. Williams, 1804), p.10.

14. *Christian Observer*, 1877, p.229.

15. ES, p.10.

16. Thomas Biddulph, vicar of Padstow (1770-1790), married one of Walker's converts, Martha Tregenna. He was a great friend of James Hervey and corresponded with George Whitefield.

17. Wills, *The Spiritual Register*, vol.3, p.30.

18. ES, p.11.

19. Ryle, *Christian Leaders*, pp.311-312.

20. Wood, *Thomas Haweis*, p.27.

21. Wills, *The Spiritual Register*, vol.3, pp.34-35.

22. Ibid., pp.36-37.

23. JS, pp.xix-xx.

24. Ibid., pp.xxiv-xxv.

25. Ibid., pp.xxi-xxii.

26. Ibid., pp.lxxiv-lxxv.
27. Wills, *The Spiritual Register*, vol.3, pp.12-13.
28. Ibid., pp.18,19.
29. Bennett, *The Star of the West*, pp.90-91.
30. Wills, *The Spiritual Register*, vol.3, p.13.
31. JS, p.xxii.
32. Ibid., pp.xxii-xxiii.
33. ES, pp.14-15.
34. Ibid., pp.15-16.
35. Ibid., p.16.
36. Ryle, *Christian Leaders*, p.312.
37. ES, p.13.
38. JS, pp.xxv-xxvi.
39. Ibid., pp.li-lii.
40. ES, p.17.
41. JS, p.xxvi.
42. Gillies, *Historical Collections*, p.510.

Chapter 5 – Two Schemes of Private Instruction

1. Wills, *The Spiritual Register*, vol.3, p.7.
2. Ibid., p.14.
3. Ibid., p.17.
4. Gillies, *Historical Collections*, p.510.
5. JS, pp.xxvi-xxvii.
6. ES, p.22.
7. Ibid., p.26.
8. Ibid., p.28.
9. Ibid., p.29.
10. For Walker's complete 'Scheme of Private Instruction in the Christian Religion' see ES, pp.22-41.
11. Ibid., pp.41-43.
   For Walker's complete second 'Scheme' see ES, pp.41-46.
12. Ibid., pp.47-48.

Chapter 6 – The Clerical Club

1. Wood, *Thomas Haweis*, p.19.
2. *Christian Observer*, 1877, p.153.
3. JS, p.xxviii.
4. Ibid., pp.lxxiii-lxxiv.
5. Gillies, *Historical Collections*, p.511.
6. GCBD, p.75.
7. Ibid.

8. Gillies, *Historical Collections*, p.513.

9. JS, pp.xlviii-xlix.

10. ES, p.76.

11. JS, pp.xlix-l.

12. ES, p.79.

13. JS, pp.l-li.

14. Ibid., p.lxxix.

15. Wills, *The Spiritual Register*, vol.3, pp.16-17.

16. ES, pp.78-79.

17. GCBD, pp.172,173.

18. Gillies, *Historical Collections*, p.515.

19. Wood, *Thomas Haweis*, p.175.

20. Ibid., p.54.

21. GCBD, pp.77-78.

22. Ibid., p.79.

23. H. Miles Brown, *A Cornish Incumbency 1741-1776* (privately published, 1945), p.1.

   Over the remains of John Penrose his friends and relations erected a tablet, on which his friend Hannah More wrote the following lines:

   > 'If social manners, if the gentlest mind
   > If zeal for God, and love for human kind –
   > If all the charities that life endear
   > Can claim affection or demand a tear,
   > Then PENROSE, o'er thy venerable urn
   > Domestic love may weep and friendship mourn,
   > The path of duty still untired he trod –
   > He walked with safety, for he walked with God,
   > When passed the power of precept and of pray'r
   > Yet still the flock remained the shepherd's care;
   > Their wants still nobly watchful to supply,
   > He taught his last best lesson, how to die.'

   Ibid., p.8.

24. GCBD, p.86.

25. ES, p.451.

26. Pearce, *The Wesleys in Cornwall*, p.126.

27. John Wesley, *The Journal of*, 8 vols (London, Epworth Press, 1938), vol.4, pp.529-530.

28. Gillies, *Historical Collections*, p.529.

29. Ibid., p.532.

30. Ibid.

31. Pearce, *The Wesleys in Cornwall*, pp.133-134.

32. Ibid., p.140.

33. GCBD, p.82.
34. *Zion's Trumpet*, 1799, p.392.
35. GCBD, p.83.
36. Polwhele, *Biographical Sketches*, vol.1, p.78.
37. *Christian Observer*, 1877, p.236.
38. Elliot-Binns, *The Early Evangelicals*, p.134.
39. GCBD, p.84.

Chapter 7 – Times of Testing and Self-Denial

1. *The Holy Bible – New King James Version* (Nashville, Thomas Nelson, 1991), p.1165.
2. Ibid., p.1006.
3. General Editors, *A History of the Methodist Church*, vol.1, pp.95-96.
4. Seymour, *Selina Countess of Huntingdon*, vol.1, p.147.
5. Simon, *John Wesley the Master Builder*, p.119.
6. Rowe, *Cornwall in the Age of the Industrial Revolution*, p.67.14.
7. Tyerman, *John Wesley*, vol.2, pp.91-92.
8. Ibid., p.150.
9. Ibid., p.151.
10. Wood, *Thomas Haweis*, p.54.
11. Ibid., p.55.
12. Bullock, *A History of the Parish Church of St Mary*, p.66.
13. Brown, *Methodism and the Church of England in Cornwall*, p.298.
14. ES, p.49.
15. Ibid., pp.49-50.
16. Gillies, *Historical Collections*, p.532.
17. Ryle, *Christian Leaders*, p.314.
18. Benjamin Hanbury, *Extracts from the Diary, Meditations and Letters of Joseph Williams* (London, C. Taylor, 1815), pp.459-460.
19. ES, p.311.
20. Ibid., p.448.
21. JS, p.lvii.
22. Ibid., p.lviii.
23. ES, p.318.
24. GCBD, p.173.
25. ES, pp.51-52.
26. Ibid., pp.308-309.
27. Ibid., pp.52-53.
28. Ibid., pp.53-54.
29. Ibid., pp.54-55.
30. JS, pp.lxx-lxxii.
31. Ibid., pp.lxxii-lxxiii.

32. Ibid., p.lxxiv.
33. Wills, *The Spiritual Register*, vol.3, p.8.
34. Ibid., p.12.
35. Ibid., p.15.
36. Ibid., p.19.
37. Ibid., pp.9,11-12.
38. Ibid., p.14.

Chapter 8 – Religious Societies at Truro

1. *Evangelical Magazine of Wales*, p.27.
2. JS, p.xlii.
3. Ibid., pp.xxvii-xxviii.
4. Walker carefully studied Woodward's *Account*. 'A comparison of Walker's "orders" 3, 4, 5, 6, 9 and 11 with Woodward's "orders" 1, 2, 3, 7, 13 and 14 respectively will show a close verbal indebtedness; in addition, there is some correspondence between Walker's "orders" 7, 8 and 10 and Woodward's "orders" 8, 9 and 10. It is clear that Walker was using one of Woodward's later editions, probably the fourth of 1712 (possibly the third of 1701), because he follows word for word Woodward's language in its later form, wherever it differs from that of the earliest editions, for example in Walker's "order" 3, which is derived from Woodward's "order" 1.' Frederick William Bagshawe Bullock, *Voluntary Religious Societies 1520-1799* (St Leonards on Sea, Budd & Gillatt, 1963), p.209.
5. JS, p.xxix.
6. Michael R. Watts, *The Dissenters* (Oxford, Clarendon Press, 1999), p.423.
7. Simon, *John Wesley the Master Builder*, p.147.
8. Tyerman, *John Wesley*, vol.1, p.254.
9. Alfred Plummer, *The Church of Englnad in the Eighteenth Century* (London, Methuen & Co., 1910), p.21.
10. Dallimore, *George Whitefield*, vol.1, p.29.
11. Wernos was a farmhouse, situated 'seven or eight miles below Builth, near the main road which leads down the Wye valley'. Bennett, *Howell Harris*, pp.86-87.
12. Ibid., p.79.
13. Hughes, *Howell Harris*, p.31.
14. Tyerman, *John Wesley*, vol.1, p.278.
15. ES, p.57.
16. Ibid., p.58.
17. Ibid., pp.63-64.
18. Ibid., pp.65-66.

19. JS, pp.xxxix-xlii.
20. GCBD, p.172.
21. Gillies, *Historical Collections*, pp.510-511.
22. Ryle, *Christian Leaders*, pp.318-319.
23. A. Westoby (editor), *An Exposition of the Four Gospels by the Rev Thomas Adam* (London, J. Hatchard & Son, 1837), p.35.
24. ES, pp.69-70.
25. JS, p.xlv.
26. Ibid., pp.xlvi-xlvii.
27. For Walker's complete 'Hints for Prayer' see ES, pp.72-75.
28. ES, p.75.
29. Bullock, *Religious Societies*, p.212.
30. Wood, *Thomas Haweis*, p.49.
31. John Wesley, *Journal*, vol.4, p.238.
32. Ella, *James Hervey*, pp.162-163.

Chapter 9 – Teaching a Growing Church

1. Samuel Walker, *Fifty-Two Lectures on the Church Catechism* (London, Hamilton, Adams & Co., 1836), pp.2-3.
2. Gillies, *Historical Collections*, p.511.
3. Ibid., p.532.
4. Ibid.
5. Ibid., p.511.
6. Ibid.
7. Ibid., p.510.
8. ES, p.81n.
9. Ibid., p.83.
10. Ibid., pp.82-83.
11. Gillies, *Historical Collections*, p.511.
12. GCBD, p.172.
13. ES, p.86.
14. GCBD, p.172.
15. JS, p.lvi.
16. See ES, pp.90-123.
17. See ES, pp.125-136.
18. ES, pp.89-90.
19. Ibid., pp.90,97.
20. Ibid., p.98.
21. Ibid., pp.110,119.
22. Ibid., pp.122-123.
23. Ibid., p.126.
24. Ibid., p.135.

25. Ibid., pp.135-136.
26. Ibid., p.138.
27. GCBD, p.162.
28. ES, p.141.
29. Wills, *The Spiritual Register*, vol.3, pp.10-11.
30. ES, pp.144-145.
31. Ibid., p.146.
32. Ibid., pp.147-148.

Chapter 10 – Methodism in Cornwall: The Beginning

1. Pearce, *The Wesleys in Cornwall*, p.10.
2. Miles Brown wrote that we can imagine John Penrose, who was particularly sensitive to any savour of Dissent, 'hearing with dismay of the erection sometime before 1755 of a Methodist Society Room at the back of Penryn main street, and being but partially reassured by the attendance at Church of the local Society members in accordance with the then usual custom'. Brown, *A Cornish Incumbency*, p.5.
3. John C. C. Probert, *The Sociology of Cornish Methodism to the Present Day* (Cornish Methodist Historical Association Occasional Publication, 1971), p.10.

    Anglican clergymen could point to Thomas Williams, a convert of Charles Wesley, who was excluded from the Methodist societies for licentiousness; or to the ups and downs of James Roberts, a tinner from St Ives, 'who had been one of the first Methodists there before he relapsed into his old drunken ways'. Later he was again restored. Brown, *Methodism and the Church of England in Cornwall*, p.96.
4. Ibid., p.40.
5. Simon, *John Wesley and the Methodist Societies*, p.139.
6. Thomas Shaw, *A History of Cornish Methodism* (Truro, D. Bradford Barton, 1967), pp.14-15.
7. Hamilton Jenkin, *Cornwall and its People*, p.162.
8. Pearce, *The Wesleys in Cornwall*, p.67.
9. Tyerman, *John Wesley*, vol.1, p.453.
10. Pearce, *The Wesleys in Cornwall*, p.10.
11. Simon, *John Wesley the Master Builder*, p.35.
12. Brown, *Methodism and the Church of England in Cornwall*, p.224.
13. Pearce, *The Wesleys in Cornwall*, p.13.
14. Dallimore, *George Whitefield*, vol.2, p.216.
15. Rowe, *Cornwall in the Age of the Industrial Revolution*, p.67.13.
16. Lord Falmouth was one of the men who spread the rumour that John Wesley was in league with the Young Pretender.

    Seymour summed up the accusations against Wesley: 'It was

commonly reported that Mr Wesley was a Papist, if not a Jesuit; that he kept Popish priests in his house; nay it was beyond dispute that he received large remittances from Spain, in order to make a party among the poor, and when the Spaniards landed, he was to join them with twenty thousand men. Sometimes it was reported that he was in prison upon a charge of high treason; and there were people who confidently affirmed that they had seen him, with the Pretender, in France. Reports to this effect were so prevalent, that when a proclamation was issued requiring all Papists to leave London, he thought it prudent to remain a week there, that he might cut off all occasion of reproach; but this did not prevent the Surrey magistrates from summoning him, and making him take the oath of allegiance, and sign the declaration against Popery.' Seymour, *Selina Countess of Huntingdon*, vol.1, pp.111-112.

17. Brown, *Methodism and the Church of England in Cornwall*, p.225.
18. Seymour, *Selina Countess of Huntingdon*, vol.1, pp.113-114.
19. John Wesley, *Journal*, vol.2, p.431.
20. Ibid., vol.3, p.73.

On 7 November, 1745, a Mr Baron, having travelled in Cornwall late in that year, wrote to the Duke of Newcastle, warning him of the 'subversive activities of the Methodists'. In his letter he said, 'I can look on these [Methodists] in no other light than emissionaries of the Pretender, the King of France, employed to prepare the people to join the threatened invasion, if made in that part of the kingdom, or also to begin a new insurrection whenever any favourable opportunity may offer.' Brown, *Methodism and the Church of England in Cornwall*, pp.241-242.

21. Brown described Symonds as a 'zealous churchman of a somewhat Pharisaic spirit and worldly outlook', who was 'in the habit of attending the local inn on Sundays'. Ibid., pp.228-229.
22. Pearce, *The Wesleys in Cornwall*, p.33.
23. Ibid., pp.34-35.
24. Ibid., p.41.
25. Ibid., p.70.
26. Hamilton Jenkin, *Cornwall and its People*, p.163.
27. Pearce, *The Wesleys in Cornwall*, p.77.
28. Ibid., p.43.
29. Ibid., p.48.
30. Ibid., p.49.
31. Ibid., p.84.
32. Ibid., pp.91-92.
33. Ibid., p.53.

34. Ibid., p.60.

35. Ibid., p.101.

36. Ibid., p.102.

37. Tyerman, *John Wesley*, vol.1, pp.554-555.

38. John Wesley, *The Letters of*, 8 vols (London, Epworth Press, 1931), vol.2, p.107.

39. Probert, *Cornish Methodism*, p.6.

40. The reason why Wesley visited Cornwall on so many occasions was that 'The mining areas of the western half were then among the most densely populated parts of England, St Just [was] almost as big as Manchester, St Ives considerably larger than Liverpool, and the rough and godless Celtic miners were the sort of men whom Wesley set out to save.' Halliday, *A History of Cornwall*, p.266.

Chapter 11 – Walker Disagrees with Some of the Practices and Beliefs of the Methodists

1. Hockin, *John Wesley*, p.166.

2. ES, p.322.

3. Shaw, *Cornish Methodism*, p.16.

4. ES, p.152.

5. Tyerman, *John Wesley*, vol.1, p.555.

6. ES, p.153.

7. Ibid., p.155.

8. GCBD, p.83.

9. ES, p.563.

10. Ibid., p.154.

11. Ibid., p.156.

12. Ibid., p.493.

13. Ibid., p.214.

14. Ibid., pp.157-158.

15. John Wesley, *Journal*, vol.4, p.529.

16. Walker, *Fifty-Two Lectures*, p.121.

   There was also friction between the Calvinistic clergy and the Arminian Methodists, although that theological dispute did not erupt until later. The clergy stood aloof of John Wesley almost to a man, alarmed at the developing tendencies in Methodism's life and doctrine. Little was written by Walker about Wesley's Arminianism, but it was another area of disagreement.

17. Charles J. Abbey & John H. Overton, *The English Church in the Eighteenth Century* (London, Longmans, Green and Co., 1902), p.378.

18. John Wesley, *Letters*, vol.4, p.143.

19. Brown, *Methodism and the Church of England in Cornwall*, p.311.

20. Seymour, *Selina Countess of Huntingdon*, vol.1, pp.105,106.
21. John Wesley, *Journal*, vol.4, p.115.
22. John S. Simon, *John Wesley and the Advance of Methodism* (London, Epworth Press, 1925), p.297.
23. John Wesley, *Journal*, vol.4, p.130.
24. ES, pp.167-168.
25. Ibid., pp.170-172.
26. John Wesley, *The Works of*, 14 vols (London, Wesleyan Methodist Bookroom, n.d.), vol.13, pp.194-196.
27. ES, p.179.
28. Ibid., pp.179-180.
29. Ibid., pp.180-181.
30. Ibid., pp.181-182.
31. Ibid., p.182.
32. Ibid., p.207.
33. For Wesley's letter of 31 October, 1755, to Thomas Adam, see John Wesley, *Letters*, vol.3, pp.149-152.
34. John Wesley, *Letters*, vol.3, pp.152-153.

Chapter 12 – Walker Opposes Separation from the Church of England (part 1)

1. ES, pp.309-310.
2. *Christian Observer*, 1877, p.154.
3. Gillies, *Historical Collections*, p.512.
4. ES, p.191.
5. *Evangelical Magazine* (London, T. Williams, 1810), pp.347-348.
In the same letter Walker wrote: 'The churches here are poor, though we live in, perhaps, the wealthiest county of the kingdom. Not many rich are called. Not more than two or three in this place are able to do anything in the way of liberality and it is worse everywhere else. Yet I know not of any but ourselves through whom useful books are likely to be dispersed. The most useful tract I know is the *Compassionate Address*, a number of which I had some time since from your society, through Mr Cruttenden. It was particularly well received, seems peculiarly calculated to awaken and instruct, and, from the great desire of very many to have it, I could wish it in the number of those you have been publishing.' The addressee of the letter is missing.
6. ES, pp.189-190.
7. Ibid., pp.190-191.
8. *Evangelical Magazine*, 1810, p.348.
9. ES, pp.192-193.
10. JS, p.lxxv.

11. ES, pp.195-196.
12. Ibid., p.199.
13. John Wesley also fell critically ill in the winter of 1753/54. Rumours circulated that he had died.
14. Tyerman, *John Wesley*, vol.2, p.269.
15. ES, p.186.
16. Faith Cook, *William Grimshaw of Haworth* (Edinburgh, Banner of Truth Trust, 1997), p.220.
17. ES, pp.201-202.
18. Ibid., pp.202-203.
19. Ibid., p.205.
20. Ibid., pp.205-206.
21. Ibid., pp.208-209.
22. Ibid., pp.210-211.
23. Ibid., pp.215-216.
24. Ibid., pp.217-218.
25. Ibid., p.218.
26. Ibid., p.220.

Chapter 13 – Walker Opposes Separation from the Church of England (part 2)

1. John Wesley, *Letters*, vol.3, p.152.
2. John Wesley, *Journal*, vol.4, p.407.
3. JS, pp.lxxv-lxxx.
4. Wills, *The Spiritual Register*, vol.3, pp.7-8.
5. Ibid., p.9.
6. Ibid., p.14.
7. JS, p.lxxx.
8. ES, p.221.
9. Ibid., pp.224-225.
10. Ibid., pp.225-226.
11. John Wesley, *Works*, vol.13, p.197.
12. This is an extraordinary statement for Wesley to make. If he had stayed a year in one place, would his preaching have become so lifeless that he and his congregation would have fallen asleep? Is he resting on his own ability, or in the Spirit of God to inspire and anoint? And what of other preachers, without Wesley's gifts or power, what hope for them? Does Wesley mean there should be no settled ministry anywhere and that all preachers should be itinerants?
13. Can souls for whom Christ died perish? The argument he adopted shows his Arminian bias.
14. John Wesley, *Works*, vol.13, pp.199-200.

15. Charles Wesley attended the 1756 Bristol conference, although he had vowed never to attend another. In a shorthand note, he declared 'that for the rest of his life he would follow the [lay] preachers with buckets of water to quench the flame of strife and division which they had kindled or might kindle'. Frederick C. Gill, *Charles Wesley, the First Methodist* (London, Lutterworth Press, 1964), p.172.
16. ES, pp.228-229.
17. Dallimore, *Charles Wesley*, pp.202-203.
18. Gill, *Charles Wesley*, p.172.
19. GCBD, p.124.
20. John Wesley, *Works*, vol.13, pp.202-203.
21. The place and date of Helstone, 16 September, 1757, given in John Wesley's *Works*, vol.13, p.201, is incorrect. The correct place and date of Penryn, 19 September, 1757, is found in John Wesley's *Letters*, vol.3, p.221.
22. Pearce, *The Wesleys in Cornwall*, p.126.
23. John Wesley, *Works*, vol.13, pp.202-203.
24. Ibid., p.204.
25. Ibid., pp.204-205.
26. GCBD, p.128.
27. Ibid., p.129.
28. Gillies, *Historical Collections*, p.512.
29. GCBD, p.129.
30. As late as 1786 John Wesley said, 'I am now, and have been from my youth a member and minister of the Church of England. I have no desire to separate from it till my soul separates from my body.' Eifion Evans, *Fire in the Thatch* (Bridgend, Evangelical Press of Wales, 1996), p.129.
31. By 'binding themselves to no peculiar discipline' Wesley meant that some preachers should remain regular while others should remain irregular.
32. John Wesley, *Journal*, vol.5, p.185.

Chapter 14 – Ill Health, *The Christian* and a Regiment of Soldiers
1. ES, pp.561-562.
2. Elliot-Binns, *The Early Evangelicals*, p.401.
3. Gillies, *Historical Collections*, p.512.
4. ES, pp.270-271.
5. Ibid., p.271.
6. Ibid., p.310.
7. Ibid., p.323.
8. Ibid., p.561.

9. Ibid., p.274.

10. Westoby (editor), *The Four Gospels*, p.50.

11. ES, p.275.

12. Ryle, *Christian Leaders*, p.324.

13. Samuel Walker, *Christ the Purifier* (London, J. Mathews, 1794), p.iv.

14. Samuel Walker, *The Christian* (Glasgow, Chalmers & Collins, 1825), pp.xvii-xviii.

15. There are three almost identical letters written by Walker that mention the soldiers' arrival in Truro and all have different dates. The first, written to John Gillies, is dated Truro 14 January, 1755. In the letter Walker referred to the soldiers arriving at 'the beginning of November', presumably the previous year, 1754. Gillies, *Historical Collections*, pp.513-514. The second letter is dated 6 January, 1756, and is addressed to Mr S. Sheape of London. It is Walker's receipt of some books he had received from 'The Society of Promoting Religious Knowledge Among the Poor'. If the date of this letter is correct, the soldiers arrived late in 1755. *Evangelical Magazine*, 1803, pp.242-244. The third letter is found in JS, pp.lviii-lxi and ES, pp.277-279. Both authors date the arrival of the soldiers as November, 1756. Stillingfleet said the letter was written to 'his friend', and Sidney, who had the original MS in his possession, said it was to 'his good friend at Wintringham', that is, Thomas Adam. In *The Spiritual Register*, vol.3, p.8, where Walker's diary for 29 March, 1757, is quoted, Walker wrote that he had been labouring for the [soldiers'] souls since their arrival on 4 November, 1756.

   The best solution to this problem is to say that Gillies's date is wrong – it should be 14 January, 1757; the date in the *Evangelical Magazine* is also wrong – it should be 6 January, 1757; and that Walker wrote the same letter three times in January, 1757, with slight alterations, to Sheape, Gillies and Adam. In the letter to Gillies, Walker said, 'It is my way in writing my friends to speak what is most nearly on my heart; and especially, if it be any thing which I may hope will excite their praises, and engage their intercessions in my behalf.' Walker's own 'praises' were so excited by what was happening among the soldiers, that at the beginning of 1757 he told everyone to whom he wrote about the progress of the gospel among them.

16. JS, pp.lix-lxi.

17. Gillies, *Historical Collections*, pp.513-514.

18. *Evangelical Magazine*, 1803, p.242.

19. Wills, *The Spiritual Register*, vol.3, p.16.

20. ES, p.280.

21. Ibid., pp.281-282.

22. For the complete letter see ES, pp.283-286.

23. Wills, *The Spiritual Register*, vol.3, p.11.

24. ES, pp.319-320.

25. Wills, *The Spiritual Register*, vol.3, pp.8-9,13-14.
    There is some confusion as to when the second detachment of soldiers left Truro. The first detachment arrived on 4 November, 1756 and left nine weeks later, about 6 January, 1757. The second detachment arrived on the same day the first detachment left and supposedly stayed for about twelve weeks. This would mean they returned to Plymouth about 30 March. In his diary Walker said that the soldiers left on the 28 March, 1757. Then on the 3 April he remarked, 'I have laboured with the soldiers this evening,' which implies that some of the men were still with him. On 12 April he was thankful for the news that his soldiers were still standing their ground at Plymouth Dock. He was probably referring to men from both detachments, who had by then left Truro. Six days later he asked himself: 'How have I bore the insult this day put upon my office by the captain of the soldiers, forbidding his men publicly to come to my house for instruction?' Walker must have been thinking back to the day of the 'insult', which still upset him. Wills, *The Spiritual Register*, vol.3, pp.8,11,13-14,16. See the narrative for how I have solved this problem.

26. JS, pp.lxii-lxiii.

Chapter 15 – To Wintringham and Back

1. Westoby (editor), *The Four Gospels*, pp.75-76.

2. ES, p.331.

3. Ibid., p.334.

4. Gillies, *Historical Collections*, p.529.

5. Bennett, *The Star of the West*, p.90.

6. Polwhele, *Reminiscences*, vol.2, p.158.

7. ES, pp.400-401.

8. Ibid., p.327.

9. Ibid., pp.327-328.

10. Ibid., p.402.

11. Ibid., p.425.

12. Ibid., p.436.

13. Ibid., p.405.

14. Ibid., p.406.

15. Ella, *James Hervey*, p.162.

16. Westoby (editor), *The Four Gospels*, pp.59-60.

17. ES, pp.345-346.

18. Ibid., pp.410-411.

19. Ibid., p.409.
20. Ibid.
21. Bennett, *The Star of the West*, pp.89,91.
22. ES, p.409.
23. Ibid.
24. Ibid., p.411.
25. Ibid., pp.420-421.
26. Ibid., pp.425-426.
27. Ibid., p.428.
28. Ibid., p.462.

Chapter 16 – Walker Corresponds with his Best Friend

1. ES, pp.303-304.
2. Ibid., p.424.
3. Ibid., p.425.
4. Ibid.
5. Ibid., pp.426-427.
6. Ibid., pp.427-428.
7. Ibid., p.432.
8. Ibid., pp.436-437.
9. Ibid., p.438.
10. Ibid., pp.445-446.
11. Ibid., pp.449-451.
12. Ibid., pp.456-457.
13. Ibid., pp.453-454.
14. Ibid., pp.454-455.
15. Ibid., p.455.
16. Ibid., p.458.
17. Ibid., p.460.
18. Ibid., pp.468-469.
19. Ibid., pp.469-471.
20. Ibid., p.474.
21. Ibid., p.475.
22. Ibid., p.476.
23. Ibid., p.483.
24. *Christian Observer* (Boston, William Wells & T. B. Wail & Co., 1802), vol.1, p.163.
25. ES, p.437.

Chapter 17 – A Wise Counsellor

1. ES, pp.367-368.
2. Ibid., p.368.

3. Thomas Jackson, *The Life of Charles Wesley*, 2 vols (London, John Mason, 1841), vol.2, p.84.

4. Gillies, *Historical Collections*, p.511.

5. ES, pp.296,298.

6. Ibid., pp.363-364.

7. Ibid., p.369.

8. Ibid., p.370.

9. Ibid., p.379.

10. Ibid., p.380.

11. Ibid., p.364.

12. Ibid., p.365.

13. Ibid., p.394-395.

14. Ibid., p.375.

15. Ibid., p.366.

16. Bennett, *The Star of the West*, pp.122-123.

17. Pibworth, *The Gospel Pedlar*, pp.36-37.

18. ES, p.490.

19. Ryle, *Christian Leaders*, p.157.

20. ES, pp.488-489.

21. Ibid., p.497.

22. GCBD, p.178.

23. ES, pp.493-494.

24. Ibid., p.494.

25. Ibid., pp.495-496.

26. Ibid., p.499.

Chapter 18 – Heading to the Journey's End

1. Walker, *Fifty-Two Lectures*, pp.238-239.

2. ES, p.502.

3. JS, p.lxviii.

4. Walker, *Fifty-Two Lectures*, pp.235-236.

5. Ibid., pp.239-240.

6. ES, pp.508-509.

7. Ibid., p.509.

8. Westoby (editor), *The Four Gospels*, p.66.

9. ES, pp.513-515.

10. Ibid., p.517.

11. *Zion's Trumpet*, 1801, p.101.

12. Ibid., pp.101-102.

13. Ibid., p.102.

14. John Wesley, *Letters*, vol.4, p.108.

15. John Wesley, *Journal*, vol.4, p.418.

16. ES, p.523.

17. Ibid., p.524.
18. Ibid., p.525.
19. Ibid., p.528.
20. John Venn, *The Life and Letters of Henry Venn* (Edinburgh, Banner of Truth Trust, 1993), pp.84-85.
21. ES, p.530.
22. Ibid., pp.532-533.

Chapter 19 – 'God is Love, all Live to Him'

1. ES, p.486.
2. Ibid., p.511.
3. Ibid., p.534.
4. Ibid., p.535.
5. Ibid., p.539.
6. JS, p.lxxxiv.
7. Ibid., pp.lxxxv-lxxxvi.
8. Ibid., p.lxxxvi.
9. Ibid., p.lxxxvii.
10. ES, pp.541-542.
11. JS, pp.lxxxviii-lxxxix.
12. ES, pp.545-546.
13. Wills, *The Spiritual Register*, vol.3, pp.2-3.
14. Ibid., p.4.
15. JS, pp.lxxxix-xc.
16. Ibid., p.xc.
17. Ibid., pp.xc-xci.
18. ES, pp.547-548.
19. Ibid., p.549.
20. JS, p.xci.
21. John Wesley, *Letters*, vol.4, p.143.
22. Ibid., p.160.
23. JS, pp.xci-xcii.
24. ES, pp.551-553.
25. JS, p.xcii.
26. Nuttall, *Howel Harris*, p.31.
27. ES, p.553.
28. Ibid., p.554.
    James Browne, formerly of Bristol, wrote an elegy on the death of Samuel Walker, a few verses of which are given below:
    The Almighty call'd, the fatal arrow's fled,
    And pious WALKER's number'd with the dead;
    His full fledg'd soul releas'd from cumberous clay
    Soars to the regions of eternal day.

But from his lips what heavenly counsels flow'd!
How well he knew to point the soul to God,
How with incessant toils he fill'd the day,
Let his lamenting flock at TRURO stay.

O Truro! wail th' invaluable friend,
The shepherd true who lov'd you to the end.
His foes (if foes he had) must surely own
His fervent zeal for their salvation shown.

Let hundreds now in bliss, with raptures, tell
How they escap'd the gloomy depths of hell.
And of his grateful flock who yet survive,
How thro' his labours blessed, by Christ you live.

But Walker, pious saint, shall he depart,
Without some warmer beams around his heart?
Will not the sun of righteousness arise
And place his heaven before his closing eyes?
Yes, the bright glory breaks upon his sight
A blessed antepast of endless light.
Wills, *The Spiritual Register*, vol.3, pp.21-23.

29. Westoby (editor), *The Four Gospels*, p.75.
30. ES, p.556.
31. Ibid.
32. *Cornish Banner*, 1846, p.85.
33. Polwhele also said, 'With all his failings, Pye was a very charitable man. Many were the halt, and the blind – many were the poor destitutes whom he relieved by money and by clothes, as their necessities required, expending much more than the whole income of his living.' Bullock, *A History of the Parish Church of St Mary*, p.81.
34. Polwhele, *Biographical Sketches*, vol.1, p.91.
35. Seymour, *Selina Countess of Huntingdon*, vol.2, p.465.
36. Even in 1766 the Independent congregation in Truro did not regard itself as definitely separated from the Established Church. The Methodists, however, were inclined to claim that the Walkerites were really members of their body.
37. Jackson, *Charles Wesley*, vol.2, p.419.
38. The last known disciple of Walker, Gabriel Davey, died in June, 1827, aged 91.
39. Walker, *Fifty-Two Lectures*, pp.185-186.

Chapter 20 – 'That Excellent Man, Mr Walker'

1. GCBD, pp.171-173.
2. Venn, *Henry Venn*, p.277.
3. C. Sydney Carter, *The English Church in the Eighteenth Century* (London, Longmans, Green and Co., 1910), p.92.
4. Boggis, *The Diocese of Exeter*, p.456.
5. Westoby (editor), *The Four Gospels*, p.150.
6. E. Smith, *Life Review'd* (Exeter, B. Thorn, 1780), p.17n.
7. JS, p.xii.
8. Ibid., p.lxiv.
9. *Christian Observer*, 1877, p.153.
10. ES, p.526.
11. Ibid., pp.343-344.
12. Ibid., pp.341-342.
13. Ibid., p.342.
14. Ibid., pp.448-449.
15. Wills, *The Spiritual Register*, vol.3, pp.8,11,13,14,18.
16. ES, p.376.
17. JS, pp.xliii-xliv.
18. Gillies, *Historical Collections*, p.512.
19. *Religious Tract Society*, No.984 (London), *Rev Samuel Walker of Truro*, p.18.
20. ES, p.333.
21. Wills, *The Spiritual Register*, vol.3, p.12.
    There is an anecdote that Polwhele remembered. 'Walker, adverting to the deference too exclusively paid to men of consequence, agreed with [Polwhele's father] that, in one instance in particular, they might well take shame to themselves. And quoting St James: "If there comes a *great man* with a gold ring ..." and observing that, to a person of little consideration who was just dismissed they had scarcely offered a seat, Walker had no sooner uttered the words than Lemon made his appearance. They both rose, and bowed with all humility to the *great man*, as if overawed by his presence...
    'In his explanation of the Church Catechism to the children in the church, Walker, illustrating the fear of God and man, proceeded thus: "Suppose a great man were present – Mr Lemon, for instance – would you swear? No, but you swear before a greater one than he!" This was repeated to Lemon, and he was angry. Possibly he did not like to be meddled with, possibly he felt himself degraded from his divinityship.' Polwhele, *Reminiscences*, vol.1, pp.9-10.
22. ES, p.344.
23. Ibid., pp.344-345.

24. GCBD, p.172.
25. ES, p.346.
26. Wills, *The Spiritual Register*, vol.3, p.11.
27. Ibid., p.10.
28. Ibid., p.20.
29. JS, pp.lxxii-lxxiii.
30. Ibid., p.lxxiii.
31. ES, p.465.
32. Ibid., p.367.
33. Ibid., pp.353-354.
34. Ibid., p.354.
35. Ibid., p.357.
36. Ibid., pp.360-361.
37. Elliot-Binns, *The Early Evangelicals*, p.401.
38. JS, pp.liii-liv.390.
39. *Cornish Banner*, 1846, p.84.
40. Ryle, *Christian Leaders*, p.317.
41. ES, p.559.
42. Gillies, *Historical Collections*, p.514.

Chapter 21 – 'My Dear Friends'

1. ES, p.306.
2. Ibid., pp.443-444.
3. Carter, *The English Church*, p.92.
4. Wood, *Thomas Haweis*, p.17.
5. ES, pp.336-337.
6. Westoby (editor), *The Four Gospels*, p.13.
7. Ibid., pp.19-20.
8. Elliot-Binns, *The Early Evangelicals*, pp.159-160.
9. Gillies, *Historical Collections*, p.512.
10. Venn, *Henry Venn*, p.387.
11. Ibid., p.85.
12. ES, pp.437-438.
13. Ibid., p.426.
14. Ibid., p.465.
15. Gillies, *Historical Collections*, p.429.
   In a letter dated 14 January, 1755, Adam wrote, 'The advice for one
in your circumstances, and which is offered with brotherly freedom at
your request, is humility and strict watchfulness over your spirit, that
you be not puffed up with anything that God has done by you, not
grounding yourself upon it for your own salvation, but sinking low in
a deep sense of your own instrumentality; and then, that you consider

your past success as a loud call to you, if need be, to double your diligence.' Ibid., p.513.

16. ES, pp.330-331.
17. Ibid., pp.335,337.
18. Westoby (editor), *The Four Gospels*, p.153.
19. *Dictionary of National Biography*, vol.1, p.89.
20. Elliot-Binns, *The Early Evangelicals*, p.402.
21. Westoby (editor), *The Four Gospels*, p.155.
22. Ibid., p.151.
23. Wood, *Thomas Haweis*, p.42.
24. Ibid.
25. ES, pp.275-276.
26. Ibid., p.325.
27. Ibid., pp.328-329.
28. Ibid., pp.452-453.
29. Ibid., p.493.
30. Ibid., pp.276-277.
31. Venn, *Henry Venn*, p.82.
32. ES, p.512.
33. Ibid., p.511.
34. Seymour, *Selina Countess of Huntingdon*, vol.1, p.357.
35. Wood, *Thomas Haweis*, p.33.
36. Ibid., p.125.
37. Ibid., pp.43,44.
38. ES, p.329.
39. Ibid., p.552.
40. Ibid., p.412.
41. Ibid., p.413.
42. Geoffrey F. Nuttall, *The Correspondence of Philip Doddridge 1702-1751* (London, Her Majesty's Stationery Office, 1979), p.151.
43. GCBD, p.171.
44. Gillies, *Historical Collections*, p.533.
45. ES, p.413.
46. Gillies, *Historical Collections*, p.533.
47. ES, pp.479-480.
48. Ibid., p.481.
49. Ibid., p.487.
50. Josiah Bull, *But Now I See: The Life of John Newton* (Edinburgh, Banner of Truth Trust, 1998), p.200.

Seymour called Talbot 'an extraordinary man, both for piety and generosity... Being a ready and pathetic speaker, he was everywhere heard with attention.' James Hervey, writing to John Ryland, then minister at Warwick, said of him: 'I had, not long ago, the favour of a visit from your worthy neighbour, Mr Talbot. He came, accompanied by Mr Madan; and both were like men baptized with the Holy Ghost and with fire – fervent in spirit, and setting their faces as flint.' Seymour, *Selina Countess of Huntingdon*, vol.2, p.442.

51. ES, p.223.
52. GCBD, p.218.
53. *Dictionary of National Biography*, vol.21, p.518.
54. Joseph Jane was instituted as rector of Truro on 29 May, 1711. He was master of Truro School from 1714 to 1728, and vicar of Gwinear from 1710-1711. He was the last of the rectors of Truro who was also master of the School.
55. Gillies, *Historical Collections*, p.512.
56. ES, pp.294-295.
57. Ibid., p.371.
58. Ibid., p.374.
59. Ibid., p.375.
60. John H. Overton & Frederic Relton, *A History of the English Church 1714-1800* (London, Macmillan and Co., 1906), p.202.
61. Seymour, *Selina Countess of Huntingdon*, vol.2, p.305.
62. Tyerman, *John Wesley*, vol.2, p.511.
63. ES, p.328.
64. Ibid., p.330.
65. Ibid., p.338.
66. Ibid., pp.307-308.
67. Ibid., p.529.

Appendices
1. *Zion's Trumpet*, 1799, pp.393-395.
2. Ibid., 1798, pp.30-32.

Index

By the same author

D. M. Lloyd-Jones speaks of 'the great Christmas Evans, who, some would say, was the greatest preacher that the Baptists have ever had in Great Britain – certainly he and Spurgeon would be the two greatest'.

Yet many Christians today ask 'Christmas who?' Few are aware of the great influence he had on the Baptist denomination during the late eighteenth and early nineteenth centuries. Tim Shenton has sought to correct this imbalance whilst also providing sketches of the lives and ministries of other Welsh preachers, who either influenced or were associated with Christmas Evans.

ISBN 0 85234 483 X

'This book truly warms the heart and is a timely reminder of what the Lord can do through the simple preaching of the gospel.' *Evangelical Presbyterian Magazine*

'Tim Shenton has done Baptists and the Church of Jesus Christ a great favour in producing this new and definitive biography.' *The Baptist Page*

'Tim Shenton has certainly done us all a great service in his fine biography of this great servant of Christ.' *Grace Magazine*

'... a well-researched and excellent biography ... a spiritually uplifting work.' *Peace and Truth*

'Tim Shenton's extensive, thorough and well-documented research has produced the most accurate work on Christmas Evans that has ever appeared; it is certainly going to be the standard work for many years to come. It is written in a style that everyone can enjoy, and with a spiritual insight that makes every page worthwhile.' *Stuart Olyott, The Evangelical Theological College of Wales, Bryntirion*